Jean
Aitchison

The Articulate Mammal

An introduction to psycholinguistics

With a foreword by the author

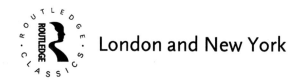 London and New York

First published 1976 by the Academic Division of Unwin Hyman Ltd

First published by Routledge 2008

First published in Routledge Classics 2011
by Routledge
2 Park Square, Milton Park, Abingdon, Oxon OX14 4RN

Simultaneously published in the USA and Canada
by Routledge
711 Third Avenue, New York, NY 10017

Routledge is an imprint of the Taylor & Francis Group, an informa business

© Jean Aitchison 1976, 1983, 1989, 1998, 2008

Foreword © 2011 Jean Aitchison

British Library Cataloguing in Publication Data
A catalogue record for this book is available from the British Library

Library of Congress Cataloging in Publication Data
Aitchison, Jean, 1938–
    The articulate mammal : an introduction to psycholinguistics / Jean, Aitchison ; with a foreword by the author.—Routledge classic ed.
      p. cm.—(Routledge Classics)
      Includes bibliographical references and index.
      ISBN 978–0–415–61018–6 (pbk. : alk. paper)—ISBN: 978–0–203–82824–3 (e-book)   1. Psycholinguistics.   I. Title.
P37.A37 2011
401'.9—dc22
2011003600

ISBN: 978–0–415–61018–6 (pbk)
ISBN: 978–0–203–82824–3 (ebk)

Typeset in Joanna
by RefineCatch Limited, Bungay, Suffolk

The Articulate Mammal

'An excellent and very welcome guide to psycholinguistics
. . . highly recommended.'

The Washington Post

'The reader's curiosity about the complexities of the mother
tongue is kept right to the end.'

The Times Educational Supplement

'This is an excellent text which would give the undergraduate
student as fine an introduction to the field of psycholinguistics
as is available today.'

Choice

Routledge Classics contains the very best of Routledge publishing over the past century or so, books that have, by popular consent, become established as classics in their field. Drawing on a fantastic heritage of innovative writing published by Routledge and its associated imprints, this series makes available in attractive, affordable form some of the most important works of modern times.

For a complete list of titles visit
www.routledge.com/classics

Contents

FOREWORD TO THE ROUTLEDGE CLASSICS EDITION

Psychology and linguistics are sometimes claimed to have been first connected in the writings of Wilhelm Wundt (1831–1920), a 19th century psychology pioneer. His linking of the topics predated the label *psycholinguistics*, which came later. It was still in its early days in the 1960s, when it became an increasingly popular topic in psychology textbooks.

The Articulate Mammal, when it was first published (1976), was possibly the first introduction to psycholinguistics written from the point of view of a linguist, that is, a professional scholar of linguistics, the science of language. Its aim was threefold: first, to spread information about the biological nature of language, and to outline current work on how children acquire language; second, to explain the ideas of Noam Chomsky to non-linguists; and third, to summarize recent ideas on speech comprehension and production. The book received a batch of encouraging reviews, especially in the USA, where an American library journal selected it as one of its outstanding academic books of the year.

The information about the biological nature of language was based on the pioneering work of the biologist Eric Lenneberg, who had written a lucid and inspirational account in his groundbreaking book *Biological Foundations of Language* (1967). Lenneberg was possibly the first person to explain that language, much like walking or sexual behaviour, was biologically triggered. It was scheduled to emerge at a particular time in an individual's life, provided that the surrounding environment was normal, in that the child must hear language spoken around him/her. Lenneberg died unexpectedly in 1975, and I was pleased to be able to spread news of his work to a wider audience. (My book was already in press when Lenneberg's death was announced). *The Articulate Mammal* therefore not only made Lenneberg's ideas more widely known, but also (hopefully) kept his name and findings in the minds of future generations.

Lenneberg was prescient in ways he could never have imagined. In the years since his death, the biological aspects of language and the brain have come to the forefront in research, as outlined in the latest (5th) edition of *The Articulate Mammal* (2008). First, and most importantly, brain scans have become the norm. These can not only provide new information about language and the brain, but can also support (or disprove) linguistic hypotheses.

In the earliest brain scans, the data obtained were fairly general. Scans could, for example, show up the density of brain tissue, which might aid in identifying a tumour. Later scans (summarized in chapter 3) provide a three-dimensional image of blood flow in the brain, which can reveal brain activity. Early scans were invasive, in that they required radioactive water to be injected into a vein in the arm. The subjects were asked to perform progressively more complicated tasks. For example, researchers might ask subjects to listen to words at one time, at another time to read them, and the brain areas activated were recorded and compared. Then subjects were asked to supply a verb for any nouns they heard or saw: the noun *hammer* might elicit the verb *hit*, or the noun *apple* the verb *eat*. This research suggested again that linguistic and neurological studies could usefully support one another.

But the study that caused the greatest interest was one which investigated verbs, comparing brain activation for regular past tense formations (e.g. *jumped*) with irregular ones (e.g. *sang*). The researchers found that irregular past tenses elicited a significantly greater amount of brain activity than the regular past tenses. This finding was no surprise to linguists, who had long ago concluded that past tenses of regular verbs are formed by the application of rules, but that irregular past tenses involve lexical memory. The importance of this finding was that it showed yet again that linguistic assumptions could now be checked by neurologists.

These days, brain scans are non-invasive and have become increasingly sophisticated. Functional magnetic resonance imaging (fMRI) is now widespread. The patient is placed in a scanner, and a painless (though noisy) procedure produces 3-D images of blood and oxygen in the brain. The main drawback (at the present time) is that these scans provide almost too much data, and researchers are still struggling to isolate the most relevant.

As these studies show, Lenneberg's work inspired huge steps forward, and neurolinguistics (language and the brain) is expected to take further leaps ahead in the future.

The work of Noam Chomsky provided another vital springboard for psycholinguistics, arising initially from his review of a book *Verbal Behaviour* (1957), whose author B.F. Skinner was a leading behavioural psychologist. Skinner had argued that, just as rats and pigeons could be trained to do a series of complex tasks by means of 'operant conditioning' (trial-and-error learning), so human language learning could be explained in a similar way. Chomsky wrote a witty and devastating review of this book, pointing out that the behaviour of trained rats is irrelevant to human language. Anyone who made ambitious assertions about language needed to know more about its basic nature, he argued. The Articulate Mammal begins (chapter 1) by summarizing the key points of Chomsky's review, and agreeing that he was essentially right when he said that anyone who made strong claims about language needed to understand it. The Articulate Mammal tries to do this by explaining both its biological nature (as explained above), and also by summarizing some of Chomsky's basic ideas.

In the influential 'classic' version of his work (1965), Chomsky put forward a new conception of a 'grammar'. In the past, he observed, linguists had written descriptive grammars, which had tried to describe an accumulation of already uttered sentences. But a person who has acquired a language has not simply memorized past sentences. Instead, he or she has internalized a set of 'rules' that allow him/her to produce and understand an indefinite number of novel utterances. Chomsky was interested in the workings of this internalized rule structure. In short, he hoped to encapsulate a speaker's knowledge of his/her language, rather than just their usage. This knowledge, he suggested (1965), might be captured best by a type of grammar he labelled a 'transformational' grammar', which had two levels of structure, deep and surface.

Chomsky's ground-breaking transformational grammar began (at that time) with a set of basic phrase structure rules. These outlined the essential underlying sentence structure. Then so-called transformations changed this 'deep' structure into the surface structure of a sentence.

Chomsky had promoted a new way of approaching the study of language. Yet some students found his writing difficult to understand. This student reaction to Chomsky prompted a chapter in The Articulate Mammal called 'Celestial unintelligibility: Why do linguists propose such bizarre grammars?' (chapter 8). This chapter, much enjoyed by students, was written as a fairy tale, about a mythical Emperor of Jupiter who became intrigued by the ability of a space-ship full of English speakers to communicate with one another. He arrested their captain, a man called Noam, who clarified how language worked. Noam explained by recounting in a simplified way how he had reached his idea of a transformational grammar. This chapter is still included in the latest edition of The Articulate Mammal, though with minor updating, including some extra comments about why transformational grammar has appeared to be abandoned by Chomsky in his latest work.

Chomsky himself has always denied that transformational grammar was related to sentence production. In his view, it encapsulated sentence relatedness, not sentence processing procedures.

Yet to psychologists, this type of grammar appeared (at first) to follow a sequence of steps which, they argued, (wrongly) might be viewed as the way in which speakers prepared a sentence for utterance. The rise and fall of transformations in the minds of psychologists is described in chapter 10, 'The white elephant problem'.

In spite of Chomsky's warnings that transformational grammar was primarily about sentence relatedness, George Miller, a prominent psychologist and a professor at Harvard University, conducted a series of experiments in the 1960s to test the relevance of transformations to speech processing. He explored whether the sequence of rules used in the grammatical derivation of a sentence corresponded to the psychological steps that are executed when a person processed that sentence.

Miller reasoned that if transformations affected processing time, this could be measured. He therefore checked how long it took to match a simple active declarative sentence such as *Joe warned the old woman* with its passive *The old woman was warned by Joe*, or its negative *Joe didn't warn the old woman*, or, lastly, passive and negative together. Just as he had hoped, he found (initially), that it took twice as long to match a simple sentence such as *Joe warned the old woman* to one which differed by two translations (passive and negative) such as *The old woman wasn't warned by Joe*, as it did to match a sentence with either a negative or passive alone. He and his fellow psychologists were jubilant, and the so-called 'correspondence hypothesis' – the idea that a transformational grammar corresponded to a person's processing of language was (briefly) enthusiastically embraced.

But then disillusion crept in. Numerous transformations were found which certainly did not take up processing time. In some cases, the version closest to the deep structure took longer to process. For example, a sentence *John runs faster than Bill* took less time to process than a similar meaning sentence which was nearer to the deep structure, *John runs faster than Bill runs*. Eventually, the correspondence hypothesis was abandoned. Reluctantly, psychologists accepted that transformational grammar was not relevant to speech production

Chomsky has changed his mind repeatedly over the way in which linguists should handle language, and in the last two decades of the twentieth century proposed several new versions of transformational grammar, each one more abstract than the last, and (to the average student), harder and harder to understand. His latest version even abandoned just about all transformations! He claimed that he was no longer interested in looking at individual constructions, instead he was trying to find basic laws of nature, the linguistic equivalent of the law of gravity. *The Articulate Mammal* in its latest edition (chapter 5) has tried to explain (in outline) Chomsky's newer views.

But just because Chomsky's ideas have become more wide-ranging and abstract, this is not necessarily true of the views of all linguists. Others have argued that language is a complex interweaving of linguistics with other cognitive abilities. The origin of language has become a trendy topic and multiple books are beginning to be published, showing how the various human cognitive abilities are interwoven.

Meanwhile, language processing has not been forgotten, and psycholinguists have continued to explore speech comprehension, as well as speech production. These topics are outlined in chapter 10 and 11 of *The Articulate Mammal*. And a key to much of this is turning out to be the lexicon, the human word store. Humans, it seems, rarely acquire words as single packages, apart from a few names of people and objects. Instead, they often learn them alongside words frequently found with them. *The Articulate Mammal* refers to some of this work, but also refers readers to my own book on the topic: *Words in the Mind: An Introduction to the Mental Lexicon* (3rd edition 2003, 4th edition in preparation), Oxford: Blackwell.

Overall, psycholinguistics is in a healthy state. Study of the biological basis of language is still in a vigorous state of development, both via studies of the brain, and the origin of language. Chomsky is no longer the key force he once was, though it is still important to understand his contribution to linguistics, as it broadened the topic out into a general study of human linguistic ability, and how much of it might be preprogrammed. These days, researchers are moving into even wider questions, trying to understand how our various cognitive abilities link together. The next century will be an exciting one, as all these various strands (hopefully) come together.

PREFACE TO THE FIRST EDITION

Some years ago, I gave an evening course entitled 'Psycholinguistics'. I was quite amazed at the response. A large, eager and intelligent group of people arrived, many of them with a serious reason for wanting to know about the subject. There were speech therapists, infant school teachers, an advertising executive, a librarian, an educational psychologist – to name just a few of those whose jobs I noted. There were also parents interested in understanding how children acquire language, and one student who wanted to know how she might help a relative who had lost her language as a result of a stroke. In addition, there were a number of men and women who said they 'just wanted to find out more about language'.

The Articulate Mammal was written for the members of that class, and for others like them: people like me who would like to know why we talk, how we acquire language, and what happens when we produce or comprehend sentences. The book is also intended for students at universities, polytechnics and colleges of education who need an introduction to the subject. It cannot, of course, provide all the answers. But I have tried to set out clearly and briefly what seem to me to have been the major topics of interest in psycholinguistics in recent years, together with an assessment of the 'state of play' in the field at the moment. I hope it will be useful.

I am extremely grateful to a number of scholars who made helpful comments on the manuscript. In particular, and in alphabetical order, Michael Banks of the London School of Economics, David Bennett of the School of Oriental and African Studies, Paul Fletcher of Reading University, Jerry Fodor of the Massachusetts Institute of Technology, Phil Johnson-Laird of the University of Sussex, Geoffrey Sampson of Lancaster University, and Deirdre Wilson of University College, London.

The book would probably have been better if I had taken more notice of their comments – but as the suggested improvements were often contradictory, it was difficult to decide whose opinion to accept. In cases of doubt, I preferred my own, so I am wholly responsible for any errors or oversimplifications that the text may still contain.

My thanks also go to Irene Fekete, the evening-course student (and Hutchinson's executive) who persuaded me to write this book.

Let me add a brief note on style. In English, the so-called 'unmarked' or 'neutral between sexes' pronoun is *he*. Had I used this all the way through *The Articulate Mammal*, it might have given the misleading impression that only male mammals are articulate. I have therefore tried to use an equal number of *hes* and *shes* in passages where a 'neutral between sexes' pronoun is required.

Jean Aitchison
London, 1975

PREFACE TO THE FIFTH EDITION

In the thirty plus years since this book was first published, psycholinguistics has increased considerably, both in popularity and in the amount written about it. It has expanded like a young cuckoo, and is in danger of pushing some more traditional interests out of the nest. Or, to take another metaphor, it has behaved like an active volcano, belching out an increasing lava-flow of important findings which have poured out over almost all areas of linguistics and psychology, and have – to some extent – changed the shape of the landscape.

Luckily, many of the questions asked remain the same, though many more answers have been proposed. It is clearly impossible to include all the new developments in this revised edition. I have, however, attempted to outline those which seem most relevant to the issues discussed in this book. No chapter remains unaltered, and some have undergone substantial additions and/or changes. For example, human 'mind-reading', the ability to understand the intentions of others, is turning out to be a key property underlying language (Chapters 2–3). Huge steps forward have been taken in understanding the brain, largely due to the increased sophistication of modern brain scans (Chapter 3). Chomsky's ideas are still recognized as playing a foundational role in modern psycholinguistics, but are these days being pushed out of the limelight by the work of a younger generation of scholars (Chapter 5). Verbs have continued to take centre stage in children's acquisition of language (Chapter 7) and in speech comprehension (Chapter 10). And so on, and so on. In addition, numerous new references have been added. I hope this new edition will enable readers to keep up with what is happening in the field at the moment.

As before, I am grateful for the skill and help of those at Routledge, especially (for this edition) Nadia Seemungal.

Jean Aitchison
London, 2007

I find my position as an articulate mammal bewildering and awesome
Would to God I were a tender apple blawssom

Ogden Nash

INTRODUCTION

Psycholinguistics is sometimes defined as the study of language and the mind. As the name suggests, it is a subject which links psychology and linguistics. The common aim of all who call themselves psycholinguists is to find out about the structures and processes which underlie a human's ability to speak and understand language.

Both psychologists and linguists are involved in studying psycholinguistics. As one group of researchers has noted:

> The name says it all ... it is simultaneously psychology and linguistics. At the heart of the discipline, therefore, is the relationship between these two fields, each of which can boast centuries of research tradition ... By contrast, psycholinguistics itself is relatively young ... psycholinguistics as we understand it today and as a discipline with its own name has only been in existence since the mid-twentieth century.
>
> (Cutler *et al.* 2005: 1)

(A complete list of references quoted in the text is contained in the References on pp. 246–69.)

Both psychologists and linguists can be classified as social scientists, so in one way their approach has long been similar. All social scientists work by forming and testing hypotheses. For example, a psycholinguist might hypothesize that the speech of someone who is suffering from a progressive disease of the nervous system will disintegrate in a certain order, perhaps suggesting that the constructions the patient learned most recently will be the first to disappear. This hypothesis will then be tested against data collected from the speech of someone who is brain-damaged. This is where psychologists and linguists sometimes differ. Psychologists test their hypotheses mainly by means of carefully controlled experiments. Linguists, on the other hand, test their hypotheses mainly by checking them against spontaneous utterances. They feel that the rigidity of experimental situations sometimes falsifies the results. Neither way is right or wrong. Provided that each side is sympathetic to and interested in the work of the other, it can be a great advantage to have two approaches to the subject. And when the results of linguists and psychologists coincide, this is a sure sign of progress.

Most introductory books published so far have been written by psychologists. A few have even argued that the name 'psycholinguistics' should be restricted to psychological experiments on language. This book is an attempt to provide an introduction to the subject from the linguist's point of view – although inevitably and rightly, it includes accounts of work done by psychologists. It also covers some of the work done by both linguists and psychologists under the broad umbrella label 'language and mind', or (more recently) 'cognitive linguistics'. This book does not presuppose any knowledge of linguistics – though for those who become interested in the subject, a number of elementary books are suggested on pp. 240–5.

Psycholinguistics is in many ways like the proverbial hydra – a monster with an endless number of heads: there seems no limit to the aspects of the subject which could be explored. This is a rather unsatisfactory state of affairs. As one researcher expressed it: 'When faced with the inevitable question, "What do psycholinguists do?" it is somehow quite unsatisfactory to have to reply, "Everything" ' (Maclay 1973: 574). Or, as another psychologist put it:

> Trying to write a coherent view of psycholinguistics is a bit like trying to assemble a face out of a police identikit. You can't use all of the pieces, and no matter which ones you choose it doesn't look quite right.
>
> (Tanenhaus 1988: 1)

In this situation, it is necessary to specialize fairly rigidly. And amidst the vast array of possible topics, three seem to be of particular interest:

1   *The acquisition problem* Do humans acquire language because they are born equipped with some special linguistic ability? Or are they able to learn language because they are highly intelligent animals who are skilled at solving problems of various types? Or could it be a mixture of these two possibilities?

2   *The link between language knowledge and language usage* Linguists often claim to be describing a person's representation of language (language *knowledge*), rather than how that knowledge is actually *used*. How then does usage

link up with knowledge? If we put this another way, we can say that anybody who has learned a language can do three things:

1	Understand sentences.	LANGUAGE
2	Produce sentences.	USAGE
3	Store linguistic knowledge.	LANGUAGE KNOWLEDGE

Many pure linguists claim to be interested in (3) rather than (1) or (2). What psycholinguists need to know is this: do the types of grammar proposed by linguists really reflect a person's internalized knowledge of their language? And how do people make use of that knowledge in everyday speech?

3 *Producing and comprehending speech* What actually happens when a person produces or comprehends a chunk of speech?

These are the three questions which this book examines. It does so by considering four types of evidence:

1 animal communication;
2 child language;
3 the language of normal adults;
4 the speech of aphasics (people with speech disturbances).

As the diagram below shows, these are not watertight compartments. Each type of evidence is connected to the next by an intermediate link. Animal communication is linked to child language by the 'talking chimps' – apes who have been taught a language-like system. The link between child and adult language is seen in the speech of 8- to 14-year-olds. The language of normal adults is linked to those with speech disturbances by 'speech errors', which occur in the speech of all normal people, yet show certain similarities with the speech of aphasics.

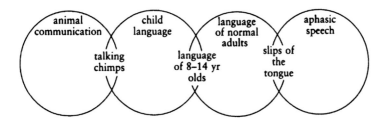

Before moving on to the first topic, the acquisition problem and the question of linguistic knowledge, we must make a few comments about the use of the word *grammar*.

We assume that, in order to speak, every person who knows a language has the grammar of that language internalized in their head. The linguist who writes a grammar is making a hypothesis about this internalized system, and is in effect saying, 'My guess as to the knowledge stored in the head of someone who knows a language is as follows. . . .' For this reason, the word *grammar* is used interchangeably to mean both the internal representation of language within a person's head, and a linguist's 'model' or guess of that representation.

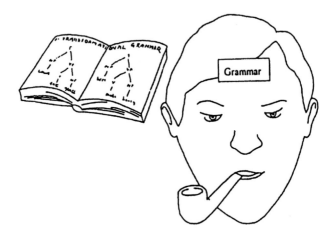

Furthermore, when we talk about a person's internalized grammar the word *grammar* is being used in a much wider sense than that found in some old textbooks. It refers to a person's total knowledge of their language. That is, it includes not just a knowledge of *syntax* (word patterns) but also *phonology* (sound patterns), *semantics* (meaning patterns), as well as the *lexicon* (the mental dictionary) which ties everything together.

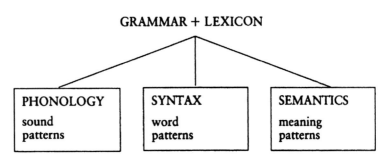

Increasingly, linguists are finding that syntax and semantics are intrinsically linked together, and cannot easily be separated. It is far easier to split off phonology. Syntax and semantics together form the essence of any language. They, alongside the lexicon, will therefore be the basic concern of this book. Phonology will mostly be omitted, and only referred to where it illuminates syntactic and semantic problems.

Perhaps here we need to mention also a vast and woolly subject which is *not* the concern of this book – the relationship of language to thought. Although it is clear that thought is *possible* without language, it seems that people *normally* think in terms of their language. That is, a person's thoughts are 'pre-packaged' into words and grammatical categories. This means that when we are discussing production and comprehension, we shall not spend time discussing an abstract layer of 'concepts' which some people have assumed to exist at a level 'above' language. When discussing, say, producing speech, we shall take it for granted that the first thing a person tells herself to do is, 'Select the relevant words and syntax' rather than 'Package together concepts and see if they can be translated into language'. In other words, if it is necessary to take sides in the controversy as to which came first, language or thought, we are more on the side of the nineteenth-century poet Shelley, who said 'He gave men speech, and speech created thought' than that of the eighteenth-century lexicographer Samuel Johnson, who claimed that 'Language is the dress of thought.' Consequently, the vast and fascinating area known as 'cognitive linguistics', which links language with thought, will only intermittently be mentioned – though reading suggestions will be added in the Suggestions for Further Reading on pp. 240–5.

Another voluminous topic which is not discussed in this book is that of 'communicative competence'. In recent years, a number of psychologists have made the rather obvious point that children do not merely acquire the structural patterns of their language, they also learn to use them appropriately within various social settings. Therefore, it is argued, psycholinguists should pay as much attention to social context as to language structure itself, particularly as children in the early stages of speech are heavily dependent on their surroundings. This work is interesting and important, and most people nowadays agree wholeheartedly that it is useless to consider child utterances in a vacuum. However, humans, if they so wish, are able to rely on structure alone when they communicate. They often manage to comprehend and produce quite unexpected and inappropriate utterances. In fact, it might even be claimed that the ultimate goal of language acquisition is to lie effectively, since 'real lying . . . is the deliberate use of language as a tool . . . with the content of the message unsupported by context to mislead the listener' (De Villiers and De Villiers 1978: 165). This book, therefore, takes more interest in the steps by which this mastery of structure is attained, than in the ways in which utterances fit into the surrounding context.

Finally, I have tried not to repeat material from other books I have written, though occasional references and outline notes are inevitable, particularly from *Words in the Mind: An Introduction to the Mental Lexicon* and *The Seeds of Speech: Language Origin and Evolution*.

1

THE GREAT AUTOMATIC GRAMMATIZATOR
Need anything be innate?

> He reached up and pulled a switch on the panel. Immediately the room was filled with a loud humming noise, and a crackling of electric sparks . . . sheets of quarto paper began sliding out from a slot to the right of the control panel . . . They grabbed the sheets and began to read. The first one they picked up started as follows: 'Aifkjmbsaoegweztpplnvo qudskigt, fuhpekanvbertyuiolkjhgfdsazxcvbnm, peruitrehdjkgmvnb, wmsuy. . . .' They looked at the others. The style was roughly similar in all of them. Mr Bohlen began to shout. The younger man tried to calm him down.
>
> 'It's all right, sir, Really it is. We've got a connection wrong somewhere, that's all. You must remember, Mr Bohlen, there's over a million feet of wiring in this room.'
>
> 'It'll never work,' Mr Bohlen said.
>
> Roald Dahl, *The Great Automatic Grammatizator*

Every normal human being can talk. So the average person tends to think that there is little or nothing mysterious about language. As the linguist Noam Chomsky has pointed out:

> We lose sight of the need for explanation when phenomena are too familiar and 'obvious'. We tend too easily to assume that explanations must be transparent and close to the surface . . . As native speakers, we have a vast amount of data available to us. For just this reason it is easy to fall into the

trap of believing that there is nothing to be explained. Nothing could be
further from the truth . . .

(Chomsky 1972a: 25–6)

But the mysterious nature of human language becomes more apparent
when one realizes that no one has yet managed to simulate the language
ability of a human being. Computers can play chess, sort bank statements, and
even talk about limited topics such as cubes, squares and cones. But we are far
from producing a 'great automatic grammatizator' which could unaided hold
conversations on any topic. Why is this? Perhaps we should think about
language more carefully.

NATURE OR NURTURE?

When people start thinking about language, the first question which often
occurs to them is this: is language *natural* to humans? – in the same way that
grunting is natural to pigs, and barking comes naturally to dogs. Or is it just
something we happen to have *learned*? – in the same way that dogs may learn
to beg, or elephants may learn to waltz, or humans may learn to play the
guitar.

Clearly, in one sense, children 'learn' whatever language they are exposed
to, be it Chinese, Nootka or English. So no one would deny that 'learning' is
very important. But the crucial question is whether children are born with
'blank sheets' in their head as far as language is concerned – or whether
humans are 'programmed' with an outline knowledge of the structure of
languages in general.

This question of whether language is partly due to *nature* or wholly due to
learning or *nurture* is often referred to as the *nature–nurture* controversy, and has
been discussed for centuries. For example, it was the topic of one of Plato's
dialogues, the *Cratylus*. Controversies which have been going on for literally
ages tend to behave in a characteristic fashion. They lie dormant for a while,
then break out fiercely. This particular issue resurfaced in linguistics in 1959
when the linguist Noam Chomsky wrote a devastating and witty review of
Verbal Behavior, a book by the Harvard psychologist B.F. Skinner (Skinner 1957;
Chomsky 1959). This book claimed to 'explain' language as a set of habits
gradually built up over the years. According to Skinner, no complicated innate
or mental mechanisms are needed. All that is necessary is the systematic
observation of the events in the external world which prompt the speaker to
utter sounds.

Skinner's claim to understand language was based on his work with rats
and pigeons. He had proved that, given time, rats and pigeons could be trained
to perform an amazing variety of seemingly complex tasks, provided two

basic principles were followed. First, the tasks must be broken down into a number of carefully graduated steps. Second, the animals must be repeatedly rewarded.

In a typical experiment, a rat was put in a box containing a bar. If it pressed the bar, it was rewarded with a pellet of food. Nothing forced it to press the bar. The first time it possibly did so accidentally. When the rat found that food arrived, it pressed the bar again. Eventually it learned that if it was hungry, it could obtain food by pressing the bar. Then the task was made more difficult. The rat only got rewarded if it pressed the bar while a light was flashing. At first the rat was puzzled. Eventually it learned the trick. Then the task was made more difficult again. This time the rat only received food if it pressed the bar a certain number of times. After initial confusion, it learned to do this also. And so on, and so on.

This type of 'trial-and-error' learning was called *operant conditioning* by Skinner, which can be translated as 'training by means of voluntary responses' (the word 'operant' means a voluntary response rather than an automatic one). Skinner suggested that it is by means of this mechanism that the vast majority of human learning takes place, including language learning:

> The basic processes and relations which give verbal behaviour its special characteristics are now fairly well understood. Much of the experimental work responsible for this advance has been carried out on other species, but the results have proved to be surprisingly free of species restrictions. Recent work has shown that the methods can be extended to human behaviour without serious modification.
>
> (Skinner 1957: 3)

All one needed to do in order to understand language, he said, was to identify the 'controlling variables', which would enable us to predict specific utterances. For example, in the same way as it was possible to say that a rat's bar-pressing behaviour was partly 'under the control' of a flashing light, so a feeling of hunger might 'control' or predict a human utterance such as 'Please pass the bread and butter.' Or the presence of a beautiful painting might call forth the exclamation, 'Oh how beautiful.' Or a bad smell might cause one to exclaim 'Oh what a terrible smell.' A French notice, such as 'Ne touchez pas', might result in one saying, 'That means "Don't touch".' And if a child said 'Hickory dickory dock', you are likely to continue 'The mouse ran up the clock.' In theory, Skinner saw no difficulty in linking up any particular set of words which a human might wish to produce with an identifiable external happening.

In practice, the matter is far from simple, as Chomsky pointed out. Chomsky made two major criticisms of Skinner's work. First, the behaviour of rats in boxes is irrelevant to human language. Second, Skinner fundamentally misunderstood the nature of language.

THE IRRELEVANCE OF RATS

Chomsky pointed out that the simple and well-defined sequence of events observed in the boxes of rats is just not applicable to language. And the terminology used in the rat experiments cannot be re-applied to human language without becoming hopelessly vague.

For example, how do you know that someone is likely to say 'Oh what a beautiful picture' when looking at a beautiful painting? They might say instead, 'It clashes with the wallpaper', 'It's hanging too low', 'It's hideous.' Skinner would say that instead of the utterance being 'controlled' by the beauty of the picture, it was 'controlled' by its clash with the wallpaper, its hanging too low, its hideousness. But this reduces the idea of 'control' to being meaningless, because you have to wait until you hear the utterance before you know what controlled it. This is quite unlike the predictable behaviour of rats which could be relied upon to respond to certain stimuli such as a flashing light with a fixed response.

Another problem was that the rats were repeatedly rewarded. It is quite clear that children do not receive pellets of food when they make a correct utterance. However, the idea of reward or reinforcement (since it reinforces the behaviour that is being learned) can in humans be naturally extended to approval or disapproval. One might suppose that a parent smiles and says 'Yes dear, that's right' when a child makes a correct utterance. Even if this were so, what happens to this idea of approval when there is nobody around, since children are frequently observed to talk to themselves? Skinner suggested that in these cases children automatically 'reinforce' themselves because they know they are producing sounds which they have heard in the speech of others. Similarly, Skinner assumed that someone like a poet who is uttering words aloud in an empty room will be 'reinforced' by the knowledge that others will be influenced by the poetry in the future. So reinforcement seems a very woolly notion, since an actual reward need not exist, it need only be imagined or hoped for. Such a notion is certainly not comparable to the food pellets given to rats when they make a correct response.

Studies by Roger Brown and his associates provided even more problems for Skinner's notion of reinforcement. After observing mother–child interactions they pointed out that parents tend to approve statements which are true rather than those which are grammatically correct. So a boy who said 'Teddy sock on' and showed his mother a teddy bear wearing a sock would probably meet with approval. But if the child said the grammatically correct utterance

'Look, Teddy is wearing a sock', and showed his mother a bear without a sock, he would meet with disapproval. In other words, if approval and disapproval worked in the way Skinner suggested, you would expect children to grow up telling the truth, but speaking ungrammatically. In fact the opposite seems to happen (Brown *et al.* 1968).

Another example of a problem which crops up in trying to match rat and human behaviour is that of defining the notion of *response strength*. When a rat has learned to respond to a particular external happening, the extent to which it has learned the lesson can be measured in terms of the speed, force and frequency of the bar-pressing. Skinner suggested that similar measures of response strength might be found in some human responses. For example, a person who was shown a prized work of art might, much to the gratification of the owner, instantly exclaim 'Beautiful!' in a loud voice. Chomsky pointed out:

> It does not appear totally obvious that in this case the way to impress the owner is to shriek 'Beautiful' in a loud, high-pitched voice, repeatedly, and with no delay (high response strength). It may be equally effective to look at the picture silently (long delay), and then to murmur 'Beautiful' in a soft low-pitched voice (by definition, very low response strength).
>
> (Chomsky 1959: 35)

Chomsky used these and similar arguments to show the irrelevance of Skinner's experiments to the problem of understanding language. Perhaps 'irrelevance' is too strong a word, since there are areas of language where habit forming works. For example, some people invariably say 'Damn' if they drop a raw egg, or 'Good night' when they are going to bed, or 'London transport gets worse every day' when standing at a bus-stop. And there is one sad character in a Beatles' song who only ever says 'Good morning':

> I've got nothing to say but it's OK
> Good morning, good morning, good morning.

But apart from trivial exceptions such as these, language is infinitely more complex and less predictable than Skinner's theory would suggest.

Of course, just because Skinner's ideas were over-simple does not automatically mean that Chomsky's ideas were right. Maybe both Skinner's and Chomsky's views are outdated. Now, in the twenty-first century, we know a lot more about language and its special qualities, partly because Chomsky in particular inspired so many to take language seriously as a key to understanding the human mind, and to work on it further.

THE NATURE OF LANGUAGES

What is there about language that makes it so special? There are a large number of human activities such as learning to drive or learning to knit which seem to be learnt in the same way as bar pressing by rats. Why not language also?

Chomsky pointed out some of the special properties of language in his review of Skinner's book, where he suggested that Skinner was not in a position to talk about the causation of verbal behaviour, since he knew little about the character of such behaviour:

> There is little point in speculating about the process of acquisition without a much better understanding of what is acquired.
>
> (Chomsky 1959: 55)

Chomsky has since discussed the nature of language in a number of places (e.g. Chomsky 1972a, 1986, 1995b 2000, 2002). One point which he stressed is that language makes use of *structure-dependent operations*. By this he means that the composition and production of utterances is not merely a question of stringing together sequences of words. Every sentence has an inaudible internal structure which must be understood by the hearer.

In order to see more clearly what is meant by a *structure-dependent* operation, it is useful to look at *structure-independent* operations.

Suppose a Martian had landed on earth, and was trying to learn English. She might hear the sentence:

AUNT JEMIMA HAS DROPPED HER FALSE TEETH DOWN THE DRAIN

as well as the related question:

HAS AUNT JEMIMA DROPPED HER FALSE TEETH DOWN THE DRAIN?

If she was an intelligent Martian, she would immediately start trying to guess the rules for the formation of questions in English. Her first guess might be that English has a rule which says, 'In order to form a question, scan the sentence for the word *has* and bring it to the front.' Superficially, this strategy might occasionally work. For example, a sentence such as:

PETRONELLA HAS HURT HERSELF

would quite correctly become:

HAS PETRONELLA HURT HERSELF?

But it is clearly a wrong strategy, because it would also mean that the Martian would turn a statement such as:

THE MAN WHO HAS RUN AWAY SHOUTING WAS ATTACKED BY A WASP

Into:

*HAS THE MAN WHO RUN AWAY SHOUTING WAS ATTACKED BY A WASP?

which is not English. (An asterisk denotes an impossible sentence.)

Looking at the Aunt Jemima sentence again, the Martian might make a second guess, 'In order to form a question, bring the third word to the front.' Once again, this might superficially appear to work because a sentence such as:

THE ALLIGATOR HAS ESCAPED

would correctly become:

HAS THE ALLIGATOR ESCAPED?

But it is obviously accidental that this type of rule gets the right result, because it also produces a number of non-sentences:

SLUGS ARE SLIMY

would become:

*SLIMY SLUGS ARE?

And:

MARY HAS SWALLOWED A SAFETY PIN

turns into:

*SWALLOWED MARY HAS A SAFETY PIN?

The Martian went wrong in her guesses because she was trying out structure-independent operations – manoeuvres which relied solely on mechanical counting or simple recognition procedures without looking at the internal structure of the sentences concerned. In order to grasp the principles of question formation, the Martian must first realize that:

AUNT JEMIMA, THE MAN WHO HAS RUN AWAY SHOUTING, SLUGS, MARY

each behaves as a unit of structure. The number of words within each unit is irrelevant, so no amount of counting will produce the right result for question formation. In these sentences (though not in all English sentences) the solution is to take the word which follows the first unit and bring it to the front:

AUNT JEMIMA	HAS	DROPPED HER FALSE TEETH DOWN THE DRAIN
THE MAN WHO HAS RUN AWAY SHOUTING	WAS	ATTACKED BY A WASP
SLUGS	ARE	SLIMY
MARY	HAS	SWALLOWED A SAFETY PIN

This may seem an obvious solution to people who already know English – but it is not at all clear why language should behave in this way. As Chomsky pointed out:

> The result is ... surprising from a certain point of view. Notice that the structure-dependent operation has no advantages from the point of view of communicative efficiency or 'simplicity'. If we were, let us say, designing a language for formal manipulations by a computer, we would certainly prefer structure-independent operations. These are far simpler to carry out, since it is only necessary to scan the words of the sentence, paying no attention to the structures which they enter, structures that are not marked physically in the sentence at all.
>
> (Chomsky 1972b: 30)

Yet, amazingly, all children learning language seem to know automatically that language involves structure-dependent operations. On the face of it, one might expect them to go through a prolonged phase of testing out Martian-like solutions – but they do not. This leads Chomsky to suggest that humans may have an innate knowledge of this phenomenon:

> Given such facts, it is natural to postulate that the idea of 'structure-dependent operations' is part of the innate schematism applied by the mind to the data of experience.
>
> (Chomsky 1972b: 30)

This knowledge, he argued (somewhat controversially), 'is part of the child's biological endowment, part of the structure of the language faculty' (Chomsky 1988: 45).

The structure-dependent nature of the operations used in language is all the more remarkable because there are often no overt clues to the structure. Experiments carried out by psycholinguists have made it clear that listeners do not have to rely on auditory clues for interpreting the main structural divisions. For example, Garrett *et al.* (1966) constructed two sentences which each contained the words:

GEORGE DROVE FURIOUSLY TO THE STATION:

1   IN ORDER TO CATCH HIS TRAIN GEORGE DROVE FURIOUSLY TO THE STATION.
2   THE REPORTERS ASSIGNED TO GEORGE DROVE FURIOUSLY TO THE STATION.

In the first sentence, it is GEORGE who is driving furiously. In the second, it is the REPORTERS. In order to understand the sentence, the listener must (mentally) put the structural break in the correct place:

| IN ORDER TO CATCH HIS TRAIN | GEORGE DROVE FURIOUSLY TO THE STATION. |
| THE REPORTERS ASSIGNED TO GEORGE | DROVE FURIOUSLY TO THE STATION. |

Just to check that the listeners were *not* using auditory clues, the experimenters recorded both these sentences on to tapes. Then they cut the words GEORGE DROVE FURIOUSLY TO THE STATION off each tape, and spliced them to the *other* sentence:

| IN ORDER TO CATCH HIS TRAIN | GEORGE DROVE FURIOUSLY TO THE STATION. |
| THE REPORTERS ASSIGNED TO | GEORGE DROVE FURIOUSLY TO THE STATION. |

They then played the newly spliced tapes to students – but into one ear only. In the other ear the students heard a click, which was placed in the middle of a word, for example, GEORGE. The students were then asked whereabouts in the sentence the click had occurred. The interesting result was that in their reports students tended to move the location of the click in the direction of the structural break:

←

IN ORDER TO CATCH HIS TRAIN GEORGE DROVE FURIOUSLY TO
THE STATION

→

THE REPORTERS ASSIGNED TO GEORGE DROVE FURIOUSLY TO
THE STATION.

This indicates clearly that listeners impose a structure on what they hear for which there is often *no* physical evidence.

Another point made by Chomsky (1959) and others is that simple slot-filling operations are inadequate as explanations of language. It has sometimes been suggested that anyone learning language allocates to each sentence a number of 'slots' and then fits units of structure into each hole, for example:

1	2	3
BEES	LOVE	HONEY
I	WANT	MY TEA
MY BROTHER	HAS HIT	ME

No one would deny the existence of such substitutions and their value in language learning. But the problem is that there is a lot more going on besides, which cannot be accounted for by the 'slot' idea: 'It is evident that more is involved in sentence structure than insertion of lexical items in grammatical frames' (Chomsky 1959: 54). For example, look at the following sentences:

PERFORMING FLEAS	CAN BE	AMUSING
PLAYING TIDDLYWINKS	CAN BE	AMUSING

As soon as we try to find other words to fit into the slot occupied by *can be*, we run into problems. *Are* fits in with the first sentence but not the second, whereas *is* fits in with the second but not the first:

PERFORMING FLEAS	ARE	AMUSING
*PERFORMING FLEAS	IS	AMUSING
*PLAYING TIDDLYWINKS	ARE	AMUSING
PLAYING TIDDLYWINKS	IS	AMUSING

If slot-filling was the sole principle on which language worked, one would not expect this result. In fact, slot-filling makes it quite impossible to explain how the listener knows, in the sentences where the centre slot is filled by *can be*, that it is the fleas who are performing, but that it is not the tiddlywinks who are playing. But examples of 'constructional homonymity' (as Chomsky calls such superficially similar utterances) are by no means rare.

Even more inexplicable from a slot-filling point of view are sentences which can be interpreted in two different ways:

CLEANING LADIES CAN BE DELIGHTFUL:

1   LADIES WHO CLEAN CAN BE DELIGHTFUL.
2   TO CLEAN LADIES CAN BE DELIGHTFUL.

THE MISSIONARY WAS READY TO EAT:

1   THE MISSIONARY WAS ABOUT TO EAT.
2   THE MISSIONARY WAS ABOUT TO BE EATEN.

Sentences such as these indicate that merely filling a grammatical frame may be only part of what is happening when we speak. Such examples led Chomsky in the 1960s to suggest that language might be organized on two levels: a *surface* level, in which words are in the place where they actually occur, and a *deep* level, in which words are located in their 'proper' place in the slot structure.

Chomsky's arguments that a 'deeper' level of syntax underlay the surface level were interesting, but not necessarily right. Other explanations are possible, as he himself later stressed (Chomsky 1995b). The important point is that the differing interpretations of the ambiguous sentences described above can *not* be explained by means of the bar-pressing antics of rats, nor by means of simple slot-filling operations. Some more complex procedure is involved.

So far, then, language can be said to be structure-dependent – and the types of structure-dependent operations involved seem to be complex.

Creativity is another fundamental aspect of language which is stressed repeatedly by Chomsky. By this, he seems to mean two things. First, and primarily he means the fact that humans have the ability to understand and produce novel utterances. Even quite strange sentences, which are unlikely to have been uttered before, cause no problems for speakers and hearers:

THE ELEPHANT DRANK SEVENTEEN BOTTLES OF SHAMPOO, THEN
SKIPPED DRUNKENLY ROUND THE ROOM.

THE AARDVARK CLEANED ITS TEETH WITH A PURPLE
TOOTHBRUSH.

This means that it is quite impossible to assume that a person gradually accumulates strings of utterances throughout their life and stores them ready for use on an appropriate occasion. And as well as producing new grammatical sequences, anyone who has mastered a language is automatically able to discard deviant utterances which they may never have met before. Sequences such as:

*HE WILL HAD BEEN SINGING

or:

*GIRAFFE UNDER IN WALKS GORILLA THE

will be rejected instantaneously by any normal speaker of English.

Chomsky also used 'creativity' in a second, subsidiary sense to mean that utterances are not controlled by external happenings. The appearance of a daffodil does not force humans to shriek 'Daffodil'. They can say whatever they like: 'What a lovely colour', 'It's spring, I must remember to clean my car', or 'Why do flowers always give me hay fever?'

Most humans are so used to these properties of language that they no longer seem odd – but they have not yet been fully explained. Chomsky spoke of 'this still mysterious ability' when referring to the creative nature of human speech:

> Having mastered a language, one is able to understand an indefinite number of expressions that are new to one's experience, that bear no simple physical resemblance and are in no simple way analogous to the expressions that constitute one's linguistic experience; and one is able with greater or less facility to produce such expressions on an appropriate occasion, despite their novelty and independently of detachable stimulus configurations, and to be understood by others who share this still mysterious ability. The normal use of language is, in this sense, a creative activity. This creative aspect of normal language is one fundamental factor that distinguishes human language from any known system of animal communication.
>
> (Chomsky 1972a: 100)

Chomsky stressed that the creative aspect of language is *normal*. Humans produce novel utterances all the time, and anybody who does not is likely to be brain damaged:

> It is important to bear in mind that the creation of linguistic expressions that are novel but appropriate is the normal mode of language use. If some indi-

vidual were to restrict himself largely to a definite set of linguistic patterns, to a set of habitual responses to stimulus configurations . . . we would regard him as mentally defective, as being less human than animal. He would immediately be set apart from normal humans by his inability to understand normal discourse, or to take part in it in the normal way – the normal way being innovative, free from control by external stimuli, and appropriate to a new and ever-changing situation.

(Chomsky 1972a: 100)

It becomes clear that there is much more to language than merely stringing together words. In order to speak, a human possesses a highly complex internalized set of instructions or 'rules' which enables him or her to utter any of the permissible sequences of English – though they are unlikely to have any conscious knowledge of these 'rules'. The rules are both complex and stringent, as Mr Knipe discovered (a character in *The Great Automatic Grammatizator* by Roald Dahl):

Then suddenly he was struck by a powerful but simple little truth, and it was this: that English grammar is governed by rules that are almost mathematical in their strictness! . . . Therefore, it stands to reason that an engine built along the lines of the electric computer could be adjusted to arrange words in their right order according to the rules of grammar . . . There was no stopping Knipe now. He went to work immediately. After fifteen days of continuous labour, Knipe had finished building his 'Great Automatic Grammatizator'.

But Mr Knipe is a character in a science-fiction story. As already noted, in real life no linguist, no computer expert has yet managed to build an 'automatic grammatizator' – a device which will account for all and only the permissible sequences of English.

Yet children do it all the time: in a remarkable short period, they acquire a complex set of internalized rules. And children have considerably less data to work from than the linguists who have failed to produce 'automatic grammatizators'. They are often restricted to hearing their parents and relatives talking – and, according to Chomsky, this speech is likely to be full of unfinished sentences, mistakes and slips of the tongue. We must therefore 'explain how we know so much, given that the evidence available to us is so sparse' (Chomsky 1986: xxvii). Furthermore, according to him, the acquisition of one's native language seems to be largely independent of intelligence. The language ability of dim children is not noticeably inferior to that of bright children – yet in most other areas of human activity – such as roller-skating or playing the piano – the gap between different children is enormous.

Although Chomsky is now generally thought to exaggerate the rapidity of acquisition, the substandard nature of the data, and the uniformity of ability, the great mystery remains: how do children construct 'automatic grammatizators' for themselves?

At the moment, the issue is still argued about. Two (main) possibilities exist:

Possibility 1 Human infants 'know' in advance what languages are like. This is the possibility preferred by Chomsky:

> Given the richness and complexity of the system of grammar for a human language and the uniformity of its acquisition on the basis of limited and often degenerate evidence, there can be little doubt that highly restrictive universal principles must exist determining the general framework of each human language and perhaps much of its specific structure as well.
>
> (Chomsky 1980: 232)

Possibility 2 No special advance knowledge is needed, because children are highly efficient puzzle-solvers in all areas of human behaviour. Language is just one type of puzzle which their high level of general intelligence enables them to solve fast and well. In the words of the linguist Geoffrey Sampson:

> Individual humans inherit no 'knowledge of language' . . . they succeed in mastering the language spoken in their environment only by applying the same general intelligence which they use to grapple with all the other diverse and unpredictable problems that come their way.
>
> (Sampson 1980: 178)

It may not be necessary to choose between these possibilities. As this book will suggest, the answer may well lie somewhere between these two extremes. In this controversy, it is important to keep an open mind, and not be swayed by the fashion of the moment. In the 1960s, it was fashionable to follow Chomsky. In the 1970s it was equally fashionable to hold the view of his opponents. Both views were found in the 1990s, and are still found in the twenty-first century.

Chomsky's claim that children are pre-programmed to speak requires serious attention. As the nineteenth-century American philosopher C.S. Peirce pointed out: 'If men had not come . . . with special aptitudes for guessing right, it may well be doubted whether . . . the greatest mind would have attained the amount of knowledge which is actually possessed by the lowest idiot' (Peirce 1932: 476). And as the psychologist Steven Pinker noted in his book *The Language Instinct*:

Some kinds of bats home in on flying insects using Doppler sonar. Some kinds of migratory birds navigate thousands of miles by calibrating the positions of the constellations against the time of day and year. In nature's talent show we are simply a species of primate with our own act, a knack for communicating information about who did what to whom by modulating the sounds we make when we exhale.

(Pinker 1994: 19)

Chomsky's belief that humans are genetically imprinted with knowledge about language is often referred to as 'the innateness hypothesis'. Unfortunately, the word 'innate' has given rise to a considerable amount of confusion. Misunderstandings have arisen in two ways. First, to call Chomsky an 'innatist' wrongly implies that those who disagree with him are 'non-innatists'. Yet his opponents have never asserted that *nothing* is innate. All human skills, even apparently unnatural ones, make use of innate predispositions. For example, driving a car is an 'unnatural' acquired skill, yet it makes use of innate propensities, such as the ability to see, and to co-ordinate arm and leg movements. The issue under discussion is whether an inbuilt language acquisition skill exists independently of other innate inabilities. The point is expressed well by two philosophers:

It is beyond dispute that some innate equipment figures in the acquisition of language (otherwise the baby's rattle would learn language as well as the baby, since they have comparable linguistic environments). The only question at issue is whether this innate structure has significant components that subserve the development of no other faculty than language.

(Osherson and Wasow 1976: 208)

Chomsky claims that the mind is 'constituted of "mental organs" just as specialized and differentiated as those of the body' (1979: 83), and that 'Language is a system . . . easy to isolate among the various mental faculties' (1979: 46). This is the claim which we are trying to evaluate.

The second misunderstanding involves a mistaken belief by some people that 'innate' means 'ready-made for use'. By innate, Chomsky simply means 'genetically programmed'. He does not literally think that children are born with language in their heads ready to be spoken. He merely claims that a 'blueprint' is there, which is brought into use when the child reaches a certain point in her general development. With the help of this blueprint, she analyses the language she hears around her more readily than she would if she were totally unprepared for the strange gabbling sounds which emerge from human mouths.

Or perhaps a better metaphor would be that of a seed, which contains within itself the intrinsic ability to become a dahlia or rose, provided it is planted and tended. Chomsky argues that 'language grows in the mind/brain' (Chomsky 1988: 55). He explains the situation by quoting the eighteenth-century thinker James Harris: 'The growth of knowledge ... [rather resembles] ... the growth of Fruit; however external causes may in some degree cooperate, it is the internal vigour, and virtue of the tree, that must ripen the juices to their maturity' (Chomsky 1986: 2).

In this book, the suggestion that language is a special, pre-programmed activity will be explored further. As Chomsky noted (1979: 84):

> No one finds it outlandish to ask the question: what genetic information accounts for the growth of arms instead of wings?
> Why should it be shocking to raise similar questions with regard to the brain and mental facilities?

Or, as a more recent researcher pointed out (Anderson 2004: 307):

> Language as we know it is a uniquely human capacity, determined by our biological nature, just as the ability to detect prey on the basis of radiated heat is a biological property of (some) snakes.

But we will also be looking at the alternative viewpoint, that humans are intelligent animals, endowed with talented analytic abilities, which enable them to sort out the puzzle of language via their general intelligence.

In the next few chapters, the evidence in favour of each of these viewpoints will be assessed. The next chapter will look at the ability – or non-ability – of animals to communicate with one another in language-like ways.

2

ANIMALS THAT TRY TO TALK
Is language restricted to humans?

An ant who can speak
French, Javanese and Greek
Doesn't exist.
Why ever not?
> Robert Desnos

Judging by newspapers and popular books, there appear to be a vast number of animals which 'talk' – talking budgerigars, talking dolphins – even a talking fish:

Anne, Anne, come quick as you can
There's a fish that talks in the frying pan.
> Walter de la Mare

Clearly, the word 'talk' can be used in two totally different senses. On the one hand, it can mean simply 'to utter words', as in 'Archibald's got a talking parrot which says *Damn* if you poke it.' On the other hand, it can mean 'to use language in a meaningful way'. We already know that animals such as budgerigars can 'talk' in the first sense of the word. Psycholinguists would like to find out whether animals can 'talk' in the second sense also. They are interested in this problem because they want to know the answer to the following question: are we the only species which possesses language? If so, are we the only species capable of acquiring it?

These are the topics examined in this chapter. First, animal communication systems are compared with human language to see if animals can be said to 'talk' in any real sense. Second, various attempts to teach language to animals are considered. The overall purpose behind such inquiries is to find out whether humans alone have the power of speech. Are we biologically singled out as 'articulate mammals' or not?

Of course, if we discover that animals do talk, then we shall not have learned anything useful, just as the fact that we can do the breast stroke does not tell us anything about a frog's innate swimming ability. Or, as three prominent psychologists acidly noted, 'The fact that a dog can be trained to walk on its hind legs does not prejudice the claim that bipedal gait is genetically coded in humans. The fact that we can learn to whistle like a lark does not prejudice the species-specificity of birdsong' (Fodor et al. 1974: 451). If on the other hand, we find that animals do not talk, this will provide some support for the claim that language is restricted to the human race. We are not merely indulging in a neurotic desire to verify that humans are still superior to other species, as has sometimes been suggested. The purpose of this chapter is a more serious one. Some animals, such as dolphins and chimpanzees, have a high level of intelligence. If, in spite of this, we find that language is beyond their capability, then we may have found some indication that language is a genetically programmed activity which is largely separate from general intelligence.

DO ANIMALS TALK NATURALLY?

A first task is to find out whether any animals naturally have a true 'language'. In order to answer this question, we must compare human language with animal communication. But such a comparison presents a number of perhaps unsolvable problems. Two in particular need to be discussed before we can give a coherent reply to the query, 'Do animals talk naturally?'

The first problem is this: are we comparing systems which differ quantitatively or qualitatively? On the one hand, human language may have gradually evolved from a more primitive animal means of communication in a continuous line of growth – a viewpoint sometimes known as a 'continuity' theory. On the other hand, human language may be something quite different from our basic animal heritage, and superimposed on it. This is a 'discontinuity' theory.

Supporters of continuity theories suggest that language grew out of a primate call system, like the ones used by apes today. They assume that humans started out with a simple set of cries in which each one meant something different, such as, 'Danger!' or 'Follow me!' or 'Don't touch that female, she's mine!' These cries gradually became more elaborate, and eventually evolved into language. A possible intermediate stage is seen in the cries of the vervet monkey. This monkey has several alarm calls which distinguish between different types of danger (Struhsaker 1967). The *chutter* announces that a puff adder or cobra is around. The *rraup* gives warning of an eagle. A *chirp* is used for lions and leopards. A less panic-stricken utterance, the *uh!*, signals the presence of a spotted hyena or Masai tribesman. According to some, it is a very short step from an alarm call warning of a poisonous snake to using the *chutter* as a 'word' symbolizing a poisonous snake.

Another interpretation of these signals is possible. The monkeys could merely be distinguishing between the *intensity* of different types of danger. They may be more frightened of puff adders than eagles – or vice versa. This plausible explanation has been ruled out by an experiment in which a concealed loudspeaker played recordings of the various alarm calls. When they heard a *chutter*, the vervets stood on their hind legs and looked around for a snake. At the sound of a *rraup* they dived into the vegetation as if hiding from an eagle. And at the lion–leopard *chirp*, they hastily climbed up a tree (Seyfarth *et al.* 1980a, 1980b; Cheney and Seyfarth 1990). So the monkeys clearly have a special signal for each type of enemy.

Yet the danger cries of monkeys are still far from human language. They are a mix of a shriek of fear and a warning to others, and are only partly a symbol. The huge gulf between these calls and 'real' speech has led many people to argue for a discontinuity theory. Proponents of discontinuity theories claim that humans still retain their basic set of animal cries, which exist alongside language. Yelps of pain, shrieks of fear, and the different types of crying observed in babies may be closely related to the call systems of monkeys. If this view is correct then it is fairly difficult to compare human and animal means of communication. It may be like comparing two things as different as the Chinese language and a set of traffic lights. But a continuity versus discontinuity divide may be over-simple. Language is a complex mosaic in which some features are continuous, and some discontinuous with animal communication. Exactly which is which is still under discussion.

The second major problem we face is that it is not always easy to decide what counts as communication in animals. As one researcher notes:

> Students of animal behaviour have often noted the extreme difficulty of restricting the notion of communication to anything less than every potential interaction between an organism and its environment.
>
> (Marshall 1970: 231)

So that, at the very least, sticklebacks mating, cats spitting and rabbits thumping their back legs must be taken into consideration – and it isn't at all clear where to stop. It is sometimes suggested that this problem could be solved by concentrating on examples where the animal is *intentionally* trying to convey information. But such distinctions are difficult to draw, both in humans and animals. If a man smoothes down his hair when an attractive woman walks into the room, is this an unconscious response? Or is he doing it intentionally in the hope of catching her attention? In the sea, so-called 'snapping shrimps' can produce loud cracks by closing their claws sharply. Since the cracks can upset naval sonar devices, marine biologists have attempted to discover the circumstances which lead the shrimps to produce them. But no one has yet discovered the significance of the snaps. They may be informative – but they may not. There is no way in which we can be sure about making the right decision when it comes to interpreting such a phenomenon.

Having outlined these fundamental problems – which show that any conclusions we draw are only tentative – we can now return to our main theme: a comparison of human language and animal communication. How should we set about this?

A useful first step might be to attempt to define 'language'. This is not as easy as it sounds. Many definitions found in elementary textbooks are too wide. For example: 'A language is a system of arbitrary vocal symbols by means of which a social group cooperates' (Bloch and Trager 1942: 5). This definition might equally well apply to a pack of wolves howling in chorus.

A superficially promising approach was that suggested by the linguist Charles Hockett in the 1960s. In a series of articles stretching over ten years he attempted to itemize the various 'design features' which characterize language. For example: 'Interchangeability: Adult members of any speech community are interchangeably transmitters and receivers of linguistic signals'; 'Complete Feedback: The transmitter of a linguistic signal himself receives the message' (Hockett 1963: 9). Of course, such an approach is not perfect. A list of features may even be misleading, since it represents a random set of observations which do not cohere in any obvious way. To use this list to define language is like trying to define a man by noting that he has two arms, two legs, a head, a belly button, he bleeds if you scratch him and shrieks if you tread on his toe. Or, as a more recent researcher noted: 'Any checklist . . . is almost certain to be superficial. Consider the definition of humans as "featherless bipeds". Who would be content with that as an expression of the nature of humanness . . .?' (Anderson 2004: 57). A major problem is that such a list does not indicate which features are the most important, or how they might be linked to one another. But in spite of this, a definition of language based on design features or 'essential characteristics' may be a useful first step.

But how many characteristics should be considered? Two? Ten? A hundred? The number of design features Hockett considered important changed over the years. His longest list contained sixteen (Hockett and Altmann 1968). Perhaps most people would consider that maybe eleven features capture the essential nature of language, not all of which are mentioned by Hockett.

These are: *use of the vocal–auditory channel, arbitrariness, semanticity, cultural transmission, spontaneous usage, turn-taking, duality, displacement, structure-dependence, creativity, ability to read intentions.* Some of these features are fairly general and occur widely in the animal world. Others are more specialized.

Let us discuss each of these features in turn, and see whether it is present in animal communication. If any animal naturally possesses *all* the design features of human language, then clearly that animal can talk.

The use of the *vocal–auditory channel* is perhaps the most obvious characteristic of language. Sounds are made with the vocal organs, and a hearing mechanism receives them – a phenomenon which is neither rare nor particularly surprising. The use of sound is widespread as a means of animal communication. One obvious advantage is that messages can be sent or received in the dark or in a dense forest. Not all sound signals are vocal– woodpeckers tap on wood, and rattlesnakes have a rattle apparatus on their tail. But vocal–auditory signals are common and are used by birds, cows, apes and foxes, to name just a few. The advantages of this method of producing the sound are that it leaves the body free to carry on other activities at the same time, and also requires relatively little physical energy. But this design feature is clearly neither unique to humans, nor all-important, since language can be transferred without loss to visual symbols (as in sign language, or writing) and to tactile symbols (as in Braille). Patients who have had their vocal cords removed, and communicate mainly by writing, have not lost their language ability. It follows that this characteristic is of little use in an attempt to distinguish animal from human communication. So let us proceed to the second feature, arbitrariness.

Arbitrariness means that human languages use neutral symbols. There is no connection between the word DOG and the four-legged animal it symbolizes. It can equally be called UN CHIEN (French), EIN HUND (German), or CANIS (Latin). GÜL (Turkish) and RHODON (Greek) are equally satisfactory names for a 'rose'. As Juliet famously noted:

What's in a name? that which we call a rose
By any other name would smell as sweet.
(Shakespeare)

Onomatopoeic words such as CUCKOO, POP, BANG, SLURP and SQUISH are exceptions to this. But there are relatively few of these in any language. On the other hand, it is normal for animals to have a strong link between the message they are sending and the signal they use to convey it. A crab that wishes to convey extreme aggression will extend a large claw. A less angry crab will merely raise a leg: 'Extending a major chaliped is more effective than raising a single ambulatory leg in causing the second crab to retreat or duck back into its shell' (Marshall 1970: 231). However, arbitrary symbols are not unique to humans. Gulls, for example, sometimes indicate aggression by turning away from their opponent and uprooting beakfuls of grass. So we conclude that arbitrariness cannot be regarded as a critical distinction between human and animal communication.

Semanticity, the third suggested test for language ability, is the use of symbols to 'mean' or refer to objects and actions. To a human, a CHAIR 'means' a four-legged contraption you can sit on. Humans can generalize by applying this name to all types of chairs, not just one in particular. Furthermore, semanticity applies to actions as well as objects. For example, to JUMP 'means' the act of leaping in the air. Some writers have claimed that semanticity is exclusively human. Animals may be able to communicate only about a total situation. A hen who utters 'danger' cries when a fox is nearby is possibly conveying the message 'Beware! Beware! There is terrible danger about!' rather than using the sound to 'mean' FOX. But, as was shown by the call of the vervet monkey who might mean 'snake' when it chutters, it is difficult to be certain. We must remain agnostic about whether this feature is present in animal communication.

Cultural transmission or tradition indicates that human beings hand their languages down from one generation to another. The role played by teaching in animal communication is unclear and varies from animal to animal – and even with species. Among birds, it is claimed that the song thrush's song is largely innate, but can be slightly modified by learning, whereas the skylark's song is almost wholly learned. Birds such as the chaffinch are particularly interesting: the basic pattern of the song seems to be innate, but all the finer detail and much of the pitch and rhythm have to be acquired by learning (Thorpe 1961, 1963). However, although the distinction between humans and animals is not clear-cut as regards this feature, it seems that a far greater proportion of communication is genetically inbuilt in animals than in humans. A child brought up in isolation away from human beings, does not acquire language. In contrast, birds reared in isolation sing songs that are sometimes recognizable, though almost always abnormal.

The fifth and sixth features are social ones, in that they relate to the way in which language is used. Spontaneous usage indicates that humans initiate speech freely. Speaking is not something which they do under duress, like a dog that will stand on its hind legs only when a biscuit is held above its nose. This feature is certainly not restricted to humans, and many animals use their natural communication systems freely. The other social feature, turn-taking, means exactly what it says: we take it in turns to speak. In the majority of conversations, we do not talk while other people are talking, nor do we compete with them. Instead, we politely wait our turn, as shown in a brief conversation between two characters in P.G. Wodehouse's Carry on Jeeves:

'What ho!' I said.
'What ho!' said Motty.
'What ho! What ho!'
'What ho! What ho! What ho!'

As we can see, Motty and the narrator have no idea what to say to one another. Nevertheless, they know that they have to take it in turns to talk. Such turn-taking begins at a very early age. Even mothers and babies alternate as they mouth nonsense syllables at each other. Once again, this is not an exclusively human characteristic, since birds sometimes sing duets together. One bird sings a few phrases, then pauses while the other has its turn, a phenomenon known as antiphonal singing.

The seventh property, *duality* or *double-articulation*, means that language is organized into two 'layers': the basic sound units of speech, such as P, I, G, are normally meaningless by themselves. They only become meaningful when combined into sequences such as P-I-G PIG. This property is sometimes claimed to be unique to humans. But this is not so. Duality is also present in birdsong, where each individual note is itself meaningless − it is the combinations of notes which convey meaningful messages. So once again we have not found a critical difference between animals and humans in their use of this feature.

A more important characteristic of language is *displacement*, the ability to refer to things far removed in time and place. Humans frequently say things such as 'My Aunt Matilda, who lives in Australia, cracked her knee-cap last week.' It may be impossible for an animal to convey a similar item of information. However, as in the case of other design features, it is sometimes difficult to decide whether displacement is present in an animal's communication system. A bird frequently continues to give alarm cries long after the disappearance of a cat which was stalking it. Is this displacement or not? The answer is unclear. Definite examples of displacement are hard to find. But it is undoubtedly found in bee communication (von Frisch 1950, 1954, 1967). When a worker bee finds a source of nectar it returns to the hive to perform a complex dance which informs the other bees of its location. It does a 'round dance', which involves turning round in circles if the nectar is close to the hive, and a 'waggle dance' in which it wiggles its tail from side to side if it is far away. The other bees work out the distance by noting the tempo of its waggles, and discover what kind of flower to look for by smelling the scent on its body. Bees, incidentally, are not deaf, as was once assumed. As a forager bee dances, it beats its wings. The bees in a dark hive can hear and interpret the wing-beats even when they cannot see the dance (Kirchner and Towne 1994).

This is an unusual ability − but even this degree of displacement is considerably less than that found in human speech. The bee cannot inform other bees about anything further removed than the nectar patch it has just visited. It cannot say 'The day before yesterday we visited a lovely clump of flowers, let's go and see if they are still there' – it can only say, 'Come to the nectar I have just visited.' Nor can it communicate about anything further away in place. It could not say 'I wonder whether there's good nectar in Siberia.' So displacement in bee communication is strictly limited to the number of miles a bee can easily fly, and the time it takes to do this. At last, it seems we may have found a feature which seems to be of importance in human language, and is only partially present in non-human communication.

The ninth feature, *structure-dependence*, was discussed in Chapter 1. Humans do not just apply simple recognition or counting techniques when they speak to one another. They automatically recognize the patterned nature of language, and manipulate 'structured chunks'. For example, they understand that a group of words can sometimes be the structural equivalent of one:

SHE THE OLD LADY WHO WAS WEARING A WHITE BONNET	GAVE THE DONKEY A CARROT

And they can re-arrange these chunks according to conventional 'rules':

A CARROT	WAS GIVEN TO THE DONKEY	BY THE OLD LADY WHO WAS WEARING A WHITE BONNET

As far as we know, animals do not use structure-dependent operations. We do not know enough about the communication of all animals to be sure, but no definite example has yet been found.

The next feature, one that seems to be of overwhelming importance, and possibly unique to humans, is the ability to produce and understand an indefinite number of novel utterances. This property of language has several different names. Chomsky calls it *creativity* (Chapter 1), others call it *openness* or *productivity*. Humans can talk about anything they like – even a platypus falling backwards downstairs – without causing any linguistic problems to themselves or the hearers. They can say *what* they want *when* they want. If it thunders, they do not automatically utter a set phrase, such as 'It's thundering, run for cover.' They can say 'Isn't the lightning pretty' or 'Better get the dog in' or 'Thunder is two dragons colliding in tin tubs, according to a Chinese legend.'

In contrast, most animals have a fixed number of signals which convey a set number of messages, sent in clearly definable circumstances. A North American cicada can give four signals only. It emits a 'disturbance squawk' when it is seized, picked up or eaten. A 'congregation call' seems to mean 'Let's all get together and sing in chorus!' A preliminary courtship call (an invitation?) is uttered when a female is several inches away. An advanced courtship call (a buzz of triumph?) occurs when the female is almost within grasp (McNeill 1970). Even the impressive vervet monkey has only thirty-six distinct vocal sounds in its repertoire. And as this includes sneezing and vomiting, the actual number used for communication is several fewer. Within this range, choice is limited, since circumstances generally dictate which call to use. An infant separated from its mother gives the lost *rrah* cry. A female who wishes to deter an amorous male gives the 'anti-copulatory squeal-scream' (Struhsaker 1967). But perhaps it is unfair to concentrate on cicadas and monkeys. Compared with these, bees, dolphins and birds have extremely sophisticated communication systems. Yet researchers have reluctantly concluded that even they seem unable to say anything new. The bees were investigated by the famous 'bee-man', Karl von Frisch. He noted that worker bees normally give information about the *horizontal* distance and direction of a source of nectar. If bee communication is in any sense 'open', then a worker bee should be able to inform the other bees about *vertical* distance and direction if necessary. He tested this idea by placing a hive of bees at the foot of a radio beacon, and a supply of sugar water at the top. But the bees who were shown the sugar water were unable to tell the other bees where to find it. They duly performed a 'round dance', indicating that a source of nectar was in the vicinity of the hive – and then for several hours their comrades flew in all directions *except* upwards looking for the honey source. Eventually, they gave up the search. As von Frisch noted, 'The bees have no words for "up" in their language. There are no flowers in the clouds' (von Frisch 1954: 139). Failure to communicate this extra item of information means that bee communication cannot be regarded as 'open-ended' in the same way that human language is open-ended.

The dolphin experiments carried out by Jarvis Bastian were considerably more exciting – though in the long run equally disappointing. Bastian tried to teach a male dolphin, Buzz, and a female, Doris, to communicate across an opaque barrier.

First of all, while they were still together, Bastian taught the dolphins to press paddles when they saw a light. If the light was kept steady, they had to press the right-hand paddle first. If it flashed, the left-hand one. When they did this correctly they were rewarded with fish.

As soon as they had learned this manoeuvre, he separated them. They could now hear one another, but they could not see one another. The paddles and light were set up in the same way, except that the light that indicated which paddle to press first was seen only by Doris. But in order to get fish both dolphins had to press the levers in the correct order. Doris had to *tell* Buzz which this was, as only she could see the light. Amazingly, the dolphins 'demonstrated essentially perfect success over thousands of trials at this task' (Evans and Bastian 1969: 432). It seemed that dolphins could *talk*! Doris was conveying novel information through an opaque barrier!

But it later became clear that the achievement was considerably less clever. Even while the dolphins were together Doris had become accustomed to making certain sounds when the light was flashing and different sounds when it was continuous. When the dolphins were separated she continued the habit. And Buzz had, of course, already learnt which sounds of Doris's to associate with which light. Doris was therefore not 'talking creatively'.

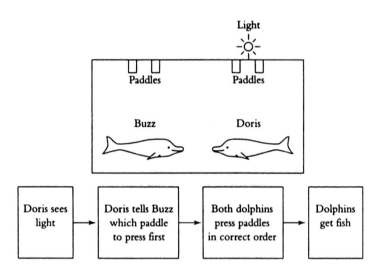

So not even dolphins have a 'creative' communication system in the human sense – even though they make underwater 'clicks' which are astonishingly sophisticated (Au 1993). Their so-called clicks are intermittent bursts of sound, each of which lasts less than a thousandth of a second, in frequencies beyond the range of human hearing. By listening for their echoes, a dolphin can locate a tiny eel in a bed of mud, or a fish the size of a ping-pong ball 70 metres away. The dolphin first sends out a very general click, then progressively modifies it as it gets echoes back, so allowing it to get more and more accurate information. As far as we know, this is restricted to the size and location of shapes – though one interesting recent proposal is that each individual dolphin might have its own 'signature whistle' which could be regarded as its 'name'.

Finally, we come to birds. They also have failed to give any evidence of creativity. We might expect them to communicate about a multiplicity of situations, since the individual notes of a bird's song can be combined in an indefinite number of ways. But as far as researchers can judge, birdsong deals above all with just two aspects of life: courting a mate, and the marking of territory (Nottebohm 1975; Marler 1991). A bird who appears to humans to be indulging in an operatic aria on the pleasures of life is more likely to be warning other birds not to encroach on its own particular area of woodland.

It seems, then, that animals cannot send truly novel messages, and that Ogden Nash encapsulates a modicum of truth in his comment:

The song of canaries
never varies.

And so does Alice in her complaint about kittens:

It is a very inconvenient habit of kittens that, whatever you say to them, they always purr. If they would only purr for 'yes' and mew for 'no', or any rule of that sort, so that one could keep up a conversation! But how *can* you talk with a person if they *always* say the same thing?

(Lewis Carroll)

A final, crucial feature of language has come to the forefront in recent years. This is intention-reading (Tomasello 2003), or mind-reading (Baron-Cohen 1999). Normal humans are able to understand the intentions of other humans. If one saw a child shivering, one might realize it was cold, and try to lend it a warm jersey. This ability to empathize with another, to put oneself into another person's shoes, as it were, may be the key to language, and is not found fully in the (non-human) animal world. Some limited awareness of it has been detected among apes, especially chimps. But humans are the best at this skill: 'Human beings are the world's experts at mind reading. As compared with other species, humans are much more skillful at discerning what others are perceiving, intending, desiring, knowing, and believing. Although the pinnacle of mind-reading is understanding beliefs – as beliefs are indisputably mental and normative – the foundational skill is understanding intentions.' (Tomasello *et al.* 2005).

Animal researchers have suggested that mind-reading is revealed by an ability to deceive one another (Byrne and Whiten 1992; Aitchison 1996/2000), since true deceit requires one to think about another person's mind-set. An infant chimp was observed to scream in order to persuade its mother to comfort it. An older chimp led other chimps away from a hidden store of bananas, then doubled back in order to scoff his bananas alone. The possible brain adaptations which underlie mind-reading will be discussed in Chapter 3, though a basic problem is that intention reading is not an all or nothing skill, it can be partial both in some humans (usually very young or sometimes mentally handicapped people) and perhaps in some apes.

It is now possible to answer the question, can animals talk? If, in order to qualify as 'talkers' they have to utilize all the design characteristics of human language 'naturally', the answer is clearly 'no'. Some animals possess some of the features. Birdsong has duality, and bee dancing has some degree of displacement. But, as far as we know, no animal communication system has duality *and* displacement. No animal system can be proved to have semanticity or to use structure-dependent operations. Above all, no animal can communicate creatively with another animal, and no animal can mind-read with the ease and efficiency of humans.

But although animals do not 'naturally' talk, this does not mean that they are *incapable* of talking. Perhaps they have just never had the chance to learn language. The next section examines the results obtained with animals which have had this opportunity.

In discussing attempts to teach language to animals, mimicry must be distinguished from 'true' language. Mynah birds can imitate humans with uncanny accuracy, but like most talking birds, they are merely 'parroting' back what they hear. A budgerigar I knew heard a puppy being trained with words such as 'Sit!' 'Naughty boy!' and used to shriek 'Sit!' 'Naughty boy!' whenever anyone went near its cage, whether or not the dog was present.

Yet some parrots might be capable of more. Nearly half a century ago, a grey parrot could apparently say 'Good morning' and 'Good evening' at the right times, and 'Goodbye' when guests left (Brown 1958). More recently, Alex, another grey parrot, has gone much further. Alex was bought from a pet store in the Chicago area of America in 1977 when he was 13 months old. After careful training, he could label more than thirty objects, such as grape, chair, key, carrot; seven colours such as blue, yellow, purple; and five shapes such as triangle, square. He could also respond to questions asking whether colours and shapes were the same or different (Pepperberg 2000). This is far more than 'bird-brains' were assumed to be capable of. But even Alex's achievements are low compared with those of apes, as will be outlined below.

TEACHING SIGN LANGUAGE TO APES: WASHOE AND NIM

Over the past 50 or so years, several attempts have been made to teach human language to chimpanzees. The first experiment was a failure. An animal named Gua was acquired by Luella and Winthrop Kellogg in 1931, when she was 7 months old (Brown 1958; Kellogg and Kellogg 1933). She was brought up as if she was a human baby, and was fed with a spoon, bathed, pinned up in nappies, and continuously exposed to speech. Although she eventually managed to understand the meaning of over seventy single words, she never spoke. Gua showed clearly that it was *not* just lack of opportunity which prevents a chimp from learning language. The Kelloggs' son Donald, who was brought up alongside Gua, and was approximately the same age, grew up speaking normally.

A second chimp acquired by Keith and Cathy Hayes in 1947 also proved disappointing (Brown 1958; Hayes 1951). Viki was given intensive coaching in English. She eventually learnt four words: PAPA, MAMA, CUP, UP. But these were very unclearly articulated, and remained the sum total of Viki's utterances after three years of hard training.

It is now clear why these attempts failed. Chimps are not physiologically capable of uttering human sounds. More recent experiments have avoided this trap and used other media. Let us consider some of this later research.

From the mid 1960s, teaching language to apes became a popular pastime among American psychologists. A minor population explosion of 'talking chimps' followed. Broadly, they can be divided into signers, who were taught sign language, and pointers, who pressed symbols on a keyboard. Our discussion will begin with two signers, Washoe and Nim, then move on to two pointers, Lana and Kanzi.

Washoe's exact age is unknown, but she is estimated to now be over 40 years old. She is a female chimp acquired by Allen and Beatrix Gardner in 1966, when she was thought to be approximately a year old. She was taught to use modified American sign language (ASL). In this system signs stand for words. For example, Washoe's word for 'sweet' was made by putting her finger on the top of her tongue, while wagging the tongue. Her word for 'funny' was signalled by pressing the tip of her finger on to her nose, and uttering a snort.

Washoe acquired her language in a fairly 'natural' way. The Gardners kept her continuously surrounded by humans who communicated with her and each other by signs. They hoped that some of this would 'rub off' on her. Sometimes they asked her to imitate them, or tried to correct her. But there were no rigorous training schedules.

Even so, teaching a wild chimpanzee was quite a problem: 'Washoe can become completely diverted from her original object, she may ask for something entirely different, run away, go into a tantrum, or even bite her tutor' (Gardner and Gardner 1969: 666). But her progress was impressive and, at least in the early stages, her language development was not unlike that of a human child.

First, she acquired a number of single words, for example COME, GIMME, HURRY, SWEET, TICKLE – which amounted to thirty-four after 21 months, but later crept up to well over one hundred. The number is accurate because a rota of students and researchers made sure that Washoe, who lived in a caravan in the Gardners' garden, was never alone when she was awake. And a sign was assumed to be acquired only after Washoe had used it spontaneously and appropriately on consecutive days.

Washoe's speech clearly had 'semanticity'. She had no difficulty in understanding that a sign 'meant' a certain object or action, as was shown by her acquisition of the word for 'toothbrush' (index finger rubbed against teeth). She was forced, at first against her will, to have her teeth brushed after every meal. Consequently, she had seen the sign for 'toothbrush' on numerous occasions, though she had never used it herself. One day, when she was visiting the Gardners' home she found a mug of toothbrushes in the bathroom. Spontaneously, she made the sign for 'toothbrush'. She was not asking for a toothbrush, as they were within reach. Nor was she asking to have her teeth brushed, a procedure she hated. She appeared simply to be 'naming' the object. Similarly, Washoe made the sign for 'flower' (holding the fingertips of one hand together and touching the nostrils with them) when she was walking towards a flower garden, and another time when she was shown a picture of flowers.

Washoe could also generalize from one situation to another, as was clear from her use of the sign meaning 'more'. Like all chimps, she loved being tickled, and she would pester any companion to continue tickling her by using the 'more' sign. At first the sign was specific to the tickling situation. Later she used it to request continuation of another favourite activity, being pushed across the floor in a laundry basket. Eventually, she extended the 'more' sign to feeding and other activities. Similarly, the word for 'key' referred originally only to the key used to unlock the doors and cupboards in her caravan. Later, she used the sign spontaneously to refer to a wide variety of keys, including car ignition keys. Her 'speech' also incorporated a limited amount of displacement, since she could ask for absent objects and people.

But most impressive of all was Washoe's creativity – her apparently spontaneous use of combinations of signs. She produced two- and three-word sequences of her own invention, such as GIMME TICKLE 'Come and tickle me', GO SWEET 'Take me to the raspberry bushes', OPEN FOOD DRINK 'Open the fridge', LISTEN EAT 'Listen to the dinner gong', HURRY GIMME TOOTHBRUSH, and ROGER WASHOE TICKLE. Washoe's signs were not just accidental juxtapositions. During a sequence of signs Washoe kept her hands up in the 'signing area'. After each sequence she let them drop. This is comparable to the use of intonation by humans to signal that words are meant to be joined together in a construction. Does this mean that Washoe could actually 'talk'? At least superficially, her sequences seem parallel to the utterances of a human child. Washoe's requests for MORE SWEET, MORE TICKLE seem similar to requests for MORE MILK or MORE SWING recorded from children. But there is one important difference. Children normally preserve a fixed word order. English children put the subject or agent of a sentence before the action word, as in MUMMY COME, EVE READ, ADAM PUT, CAR GONE. But Washoe did not always seem to care in what order she gave her signs. She was as likely to say SWEET GO as GO SWEET to mean 'Take me to the raspberry bushes'.

There are a number of possible explanations. First, the overeagerness of the researchers who worked with Washoe may have been to blame. They were so anxious to encourage her that they rushed to gratify every whim. Since SWEET GO and GO SWEET have only one possible interpretation – Washoe wanted some raspberries – they immediately understood and took her there. The idea that word ordering was necessary may never have occurred to her. Perhaps if she had ever experienced difficulty in making herself understood she might have been more careful about structuring her sequences.

Another possibility is that it may be easier to utter vocal sounds in sequence than it is to maintain a fixed order with signs. Some studies have suggested that deaf adults are inconsistent in their ordering of sign language.

A third possibility is that the fluctuating order in Washoe's signing was merely a temporary intermediate stage which occurred before Washoe eventually learnt to keep to a fixed sequence. This is the point of view supported by the Gardners. They claim that Washoe eventually settled down to a standard sign order which was based on the order of adult English (since, of course, Washoe's companions had used an English word order when they used sign language with her).

Yet another possible explanation of Washoe's unreliable sign order is that she did not, and could not, understand the essentially patterned nature of language. In this case, she certainly did not understand or use structure-dependent operations, one of the key tests for determining whether she can 'talk'. But it is difficult to be sure. And we may never know for certain as she is no longer in the situation where she is continually surrounded by humans whose main task is to hold conversations with her. She grew so large and potentially dangerous that the Gardners were obliged to send her to live at a primate sanctuary. But even when her period of intensive exposure to sign language was over, research assistants still came to talk to her (Fouts 1997). After leaving the Gardners, she continued to use signs creatively, as when she spontaneously signed WATERBIRD to mean 'swan'. However, since she was beside a river when she produced this combination, it is possible that she made two separate signs, one referring to the water, the other to the swan.

In her new home, Washoe was given an infant chimp, Loulis, to adopt, and tried to teach him some signs. On one occasion, Washoe put a chair in front of Loulis, and then demonstrated the CHAIRSIT sign to him five times. And, both through imitating Washoe and other signing chimps, Loulis developed his own repertoire of signs (Fouts et al 1982; Fouts 1983). These days, Washoe, Loulis and two other chimps, Tatu and Dar all live together. They interact with humans and each other by means of signs, though of course also use spontaneous chimp gestures and vocalizations.

Now the fact that Washoe spontaneously transmitted signs to another chimp is interesting and important, but it does not magically turn these signs into 'language'. In brief, we have to conclude that although Washoe's speech is sometimes creative, and showed semanticity and displacement, it has not been shown to be structure-dependent. We cannot be sure, because Washoe's 'speech' was only ever partly analysed – recording it all was impossible, and any repeated signs were usually ignored by the Gardners.

But Nim Chimpsky, a male chimpanzee, who was taught a sign system some years later, was attended by a fleet of graduate students who recorded his every sign. He was for several years under the care of Herbert Terrace at Columbia University, New York. Somewhat ironically, Nim's achievements began to interest psycholinguists mainly after the project ran out of money, and Nim was returned to a chimpanzee colony in Oklahoma. Without Nim around, Terrace found that he had much more time to analyse the material he had collected so far. The data from Project Nim, therefore, have been examined much more carefully than those from any of the other animals. With Nim out of the way, Herbert Terrace was able to sort out and classify the data he had accumulated over the previous 4 years.

At first sight, Nim's sign sequences were impressive. Of the 20,000 recorded, approximately half were two-sign combinations, and 1,378 were different. A superficial look at the signs suggested to Terrace that they were structured (Terrace 1979a: 72). For example, of the two-sign utterances which included the word MORE, 78 per cent had MORE at the beginning as in MORE TICKLE, MORE DRINK, and of the two-sign utterances involving a transitive verb (a verb which takes an object), 83 per cent had the verb before the object, as in TICKLE NIM, HUG NIM. But a closer analysis showed that the appearance of structure was an illusion. Nim simply had a statistical preference for putting certain words in certain places, while other words showed no such preference. He preferred to put the word MORE at the beginning of a sequence, the word NIM at the end, and any foods he was requesting at the beginning also. But many other words had a random distribution. Take the word EAT, a high frequency item in his vocabulary. It occurred in the two-, three- and four-sign sequences set out in the tables below.

Two-sign sequences	
EAT NIM	302
MORE EAT	287
ME EAT	237
NIM EAT	209
EAT DRINK	98
GUM EAT	79
GRAPE EAT	74

Three-sign sequences

EAT ME NIM	48	YOGHURT NIM EAT	20
EAT NIM EAT	46	ME MORE EAT	19
GRAPE EAT NIM	37	MORE EAT NIM	19
BANANA NIM EAT	33	BANANA ME EAT	17
NIM ME EAT	27	NIM EAT NIM	17
BANANA EAT NIM	26	APPLE ME EAT	15
EAT ME EAT	22	EAT NIM ME	15
ME NIM EAT	21	GIVE ME EAT	15

Four-sign sequences

EAT DRINK EAT DRINK	15	DRINK EAT ME NIM	3
EAT NIM EAT NIM	7	EAT GRAPE EAT NIM	3
BANANA EAT ME NIM	4	EAT ME NIM DRINK	3
BANANA ME EAT BANANA	4	ME EAT DRINK MORE	3
GRAPE EAT NIM EAT	4	ME EAT ME EAT	3
DRINK EAT DRINK EAT	4	ME NIM EAT ME	3
NIM EAT NIM EAT	4		

It would require a considerable amount of imagination and wishful thinking to detect a coherent structure in such a collection. Looking at the two-sign sequences, we note that EAT NIM, NIM EAT and ME EAT are all very common, making it impossible to claim that there is a firm subject–verb, or verb–subject order. A similar pattern occurs in the three-sign sequences, with EAT ME NIM, NIM ME EAT, ME NIM EAT and EAT NIM ME all occurring a significant number of times. It is particularly noticeable that Nim's longer utterances were not in any way more interesting and sophisticated than his shorter ones – they were simply more repetitive. Of the thirteen four-sign sequences noted above, ten of them involved repeated items, and five of them were simply a doubling up of two-sign utterances: EAT DRINK EAT DRINK, EAT NIM EAT NIM, DRINK EAT DRINK EAT, NIM EAT NIM EAT, ME EAT ME EAT. Nim's longest recorded utterance was a sixteen-sign sequence which involved only five different signs: GIVE ORANGE ME GIVE EAT ORANGE ME EAT ORANGE GIVE ME EAT ORANGE GIVE ME YOU. On this evidence, it seems incontestable that 'Repetitive, inconsistently structured strings are in fact characteristic of ape signing' (Petitto and Seidenberg 1979: 186).

Terrace found a number of other differences between Nim's signing and true language. For example, when Nim was just over 2 years old, 38 per cent of his utterances were full or partial imitations. Almost 2 years later, the number of imitations had gone up to 54 per cent. Nim was producing more imitations as he got older, the reverse of what happens with human children. Nim was also unable to grasp the give-and-take of conversation, and his signing showed no evidence of turn-taking. Furthermore, he rarely initiated conversations. Only 12 per cent of his utterances were truly spontaneous, and the remaining 88 per cent were in response to his teachers. We may conclude, therefore, that Nim did not use his signs in the structured, creative, social way that is characteristic of human children. It seems reasonable to agree with Terrace that 'It would be premature to conclude that a chimpanzee's combinations show the same structure evident in the sentences of a child' (1979a: 221) and that 'Nim's signing with his teachers bore only a superficial resemblance to a child's conversations with his or her parents' (Terrace 1983: 57).

Somewhat surprisingly, this conclusion has been fiercely challenged. Terrace's critics point out that Nim was a highly disturbed young chimp. Due to frequent changes in those who taught him, Nim was insecure and maladjusted. They claim that his achievements are considerably lower than one might expect from a 'normal' animal. Others have argued that a computer analysis of chimp utterances that takes no account of the actual situation is bound to give an odd result. Negative results are to be expected if one chooses to simply:

> lump together four years' worth of recorded utterances, remove all verbal and nonverbal context and grind the result through a computer to look for statistical regularities.
>
> (Gardner and Gardner 1980: 357)

The dispute is still unsettled, and perhaps will remain so, because signing chimps are enormously labour-intensive: every sign has to be observed or video-recorded. So alternative language-systems may be easier to analyse, as will be discussed in the next section.

CONQUERORS OF THE KEYBOARD: LANA AND KANZI

Lana, a female chimp, was the first animal to use a keyboard with visual symbols. She underwent rigorous training in a sophisticated environment — as perhaps befits an animal whose project was partly funded by the Coca-Cola company. Lana's 'cage' at the Yerkes Regional Primate Research Centre in Atlanta, Georgia, was a room of which one side was a huge keyboard linked up to a computer. Beginning in 1971, she was taught to communicate by pressing the keys, each one of which was marked with a symbol standing for a word. A vending device was attached to the keyboard, so that if Lana correctly requested some item of food or drink, she was able to obtain it immediately (Rumbaugh 1977; Savage-Rumbaugh 1986).

Lana acquired over 100 symbols in her repertoire, which mainly involved items and actions around her, such as 'give', 'banana', 'Coke', and so on. She could cope well with arbitrary symbols, since the symbols on her keyboard were formed by combinations of geometric figures on different coloured backgrounds. For example, a small solid circle inside a larger diamond on a purple background was the symbol for 'Lana', the animal's name. A diamond superimposed on a circle inside a rectangle on a blue background was the symbol for 'eat'.

LANA

EAT

Moreover, Lana's ability to generalize showed that her system had semanticity, that is, she understood that a symbol referred to a certain *type* of object, or colour, not just one particular thing. For example, she was taught the word MORE in connection with an extra ration of fruitjuice. Within a few days, she was reliably attaching the symbol for MORE to other types of food and drink whenever she wanted an additional helping, as in MORE BREAD, MORE MILK. Lana also showed some evidence of creativity. For example, she was taught the words PUT and IN in connection with putting a ball into a bowl or box. Soon after, Tim, one of her trainers, was late with her morning drink of milk. Lana spontaneously made the request TIM PUT MILK IN MACHINE. This shows not only creativity, but also displacement – the ability to talk about absent objects and events. In addition, Lana coined the descriptive phrases APPLE WHICH-IS ORANGE for 'orange', and BANANA WHICH-IS GREEN for cucumber.

So far, then, Lana's language ability seems similar to that of Washoe in that she showed semanticity, displacement and creativity. Let us now look at the way in which she combined symbols. Was she able to cope with structure-dependent operations? Clearly, Lana realized that symbols could not be jumbled together randomly. She learned to follow a set sequence in accordance with her trainer's instructions. She could carry out simple slot-filling exercises, helped by the fact that in her symbol system, each type of word had a different background colour.

Yellow	Purple	Blue	Purple	Red
QUERY	TIM	GIVE	LANA	COFFEE
QUERY	TIM	GIVE	LANA	JUICE
PLEASE	MACHINE	GIVE		COKE
PLEASE	MACHINE	GIVE		MILK

It is possible, though unlikely, that she understood the notion of hierar-chical structure: the idea that a group of symbols could be substituted for a single one without altering the basic sentence pattern. Her colour-coding system probably hindered her from drawing such conclusions, since in a phrase such as THIS BOWL each word would be a different colour. Furthermore, there is no concrete evidence that she manipulated slots in the way humans do.

To be fair to Lana, however, we perhaps need to consider a conversation which she had with her trainer Tim one Christmas Day. On that day, she produced two similar strings of symbols (Stahlke 1980):

QUERY YOU GIVE COKE TO LANA IN CUP.
QUERY YOU GIVE COKE IN CUP TO LANA.

This looks remarkably like the kind of structure-dependent operation performed by humans, in which they manipulate groups of words to produce different effects. But a closer look at Lana's behaviour on that Christmas Day suggests that she was not as clever as one might at first suspect. She had begun by demanding Coke, using the first of the sentences listed above: QUERY YOU GIVE COKE TO LANA IN CUP. She repeated this demand seven times, with no success. Then in desperation, and once only, she tried another variant: QUERY YOU GIVE COKE IN CUP TO LANA. It seems, then, that such struc-tural manipulations were not characteristic of Lana's output, and this one probably occurred by chance. Normally, she adhered rigidly to the sequence she had been taught in order to get her reward, so she had little scope for stylistic modifications. On the basis of this one example, then, it would be premature to conclude that she could cope with structure-dependent operations, which are a crucial characteristic of human language.

Lana's trainers, incidentally, confidently claim that she had 'language', but they define 'language' in a much broader way than we have done. To them, a language is any communication system which refers consistently to the outside world by means of a set of arbitrary symbols which are combined together in accordance with conventional rules (Rumbaugh 1977: 66), a definition which might bring even a set of traffic lights within its scope!

Austin and Sherman also deserve a mention. These two young male chimpanzees have been taught the same system as Lana (Savage-Rumbaugh 1986). They have surpassed her in one way, in that they are able to communicate with one another. If Austin presses a symbol for a banana, then Sherman can go into the next room, select the banana from a tray of food, and take it back to Austin. This impressive piece of cooperation does not, however, make the whole system any more language-like.

Let us now move on to Kanzi. Kanzi is a bonobo, a separate ape species, and one discovered only in the twentieth century. Bonobos or 'pygmy chimps' are not very different in height from ordinary chimps, but they have longer legs, narrower shoulders, a smaller head and long black hair parted in the middle. Some of their gestures look human-like: they beg by stretching out an open hand, for example. According to some, they are a 'living link' between humans and ordinary chimpanzees. Their most noteworthy features are the female-dominated nature of their society, and the high level of sexual activity they indulge in, apparently their preferred method of avoiding conflict. They are also highly intelligent (de Waal 1996, 2006).

Kanzi, a male bonobo, was born in 1980, and taken to the same research centre as Lana. By chance, Matata, an older female bonobo who had already been selected for language training, took a strong liking to him, and became his adopted 'mother'. Kanzi became used to seeing Matata's keyboard, which was somewhat like Lana's. Eventually, Kanzi started to use the keyboard himself.

In the first 18 months of training, Kanzi learned around fifty symbols, and also started to combine them spontaneously, as in MATATA GROUPROOM TICKLE – apparently a request that Matata should be allowed to join in a game of tickle in the room where bonobos met together (Savage-Rumbaugh and Lewin 1994).

Kanzi's language was monitored continuously, but was analysed in detail for a 5-month period when he was 5½. Over 13,000 'utterances' were recorded, of which just over 10 per cent comprised two or more elements. Of these multiword sequences, 723 were spontaneous, in that they were not produced in response to a caregiver, or in imitation.

During the first month of those 5, Kanzi showed no particular symbol ordering: he produced HIDE PEANUT as often as PEANUT HIDE. But then he started to use a fairly fixed ordering of putting the action before the object, as HIDE PEANUT, BITE TOMATO, a rule apparently picked up from his trainers.

But he also invented rules. If he wanted someone to chase or tickle him, he would specify the action CHASE or TICKLE via a lexigram (keyboard symbol), then make a pointing gesture to the person he wanted to chase or tickle him.

Perhaps most impressive of all was Kanzi's comprehension of spoken language. On one occasion, he was asked to throw his ball in the river – a novel request – which he promptly obeyed. On another occasion he was asked to give an onion to Panbanisha, his half-sister. He looked around for an onion patch, pulled up a bunch, and handed them to Panbanisha. Overall, Kanzi's trainers estimated that he correctly responded to 74 per cent of spoken sentences.

Kanzi is therefore a highly intelligent, sociable creature. But his 'language' is not significantly more advanced than that of the other primates discussed in this chapter. And like them, he used symbols primarily to obtain items he wanted, mainly food. The notion of talking for the sake of talking is largely a human attribute.

Let us now summarize our conclusions on these primates. We need to recognize, perhaps, that having language is not an 'all or nothing' matter. It is misleading to 'treat language like virginity – you either have it or you don't' (Miles 1983: 44). All the apes we have discussed can cope with arbitrary symbols and semanticity, and display some displacement and creativity in their 'speech'. They therefore have a grasp of some design characteristics of language which hitherto had been regarded as specifically human. However, their ability does not extend much further. The animals show little evidence of structure, they merely display a preference for placing certain symbols first or last in a sequence.

We cannot therefore agree with Lana's trainers, who assert that 'neither tool-using skills nor language serve qualitatively to separate man and beast any more' (Rumbaugh 1977: 307), nor with the researcher who has claimed that 'The Berlin Wall is down, and so is the wall that separates man from chimpanzee' (Bates 1993: 178). Chomsky may be right, therefore, when he points out that the higher apes 'apparently lack the capacity to develop even the rudiments of the computational structure of human language' (Chomsky 1980: 57). Or, put more simply, 'we have . . . presented evidence for the existence [in child language] of certain general cognitive processes – falling under two overall headings of intention reading and pattern-finding – that account for the acquisition process.' (Tomasello 2003: 295). These cognitive skills seem to be either lacking or incomplete in non-humans.

Note finally that even though intelligent animals seem *capable* of coping with some of the rudimentary characteristics of human language, they do not seem *predisposed* to cope with them. As one commentator noted: 'As with watching a circus horse walk on its hind legs, I could not escape the feeling that a species ill-adapted to symbolic communication was struggling with an unnatural task' (Marshall 1987: 310). The situation is parallel to that found among birds. Some birds are able to learn the songs of a different species. But they find the task a difficult one. When the birds are removed from the alien species, and placed among their own kind, they learn their normal song with extreme rapidity. They seem to have an innate predisposition towards one kind of song rather than another (Thorpe 1963). Many animals have special, biologically ordained skills:

> Alligators, for example, have a special set of sensors on the skin of their faces that respond sensitively to the slightest disturbance of the surface of a body of water in which the alligator is mostly immersed. Catching (and eating) the sources of such disturbance is one of the alligator's most useful (and characteristic) skills, and there is no serious doubt that this skill results from specific, inherited aspects of the animal's biology. Similarly, the use of language to communicate is one of humankind's most useful and characteristic skills, for which a comparable account is no less plausible.
>
> (Anderson 2004: 56)

The apparent ease with which humans acquire language, compared with other apes, supports the suggestion that they are innately programmed to do so. The next chapter examines whether there is any biological evidence for this apparently unique adaptation to language.

3

GRANDMAMA'S TEETH
Is there biological evidence for innate language capacity?

'O grandmama, what big teeth you have!' said Little Red Riding Hood.
'All the better to eat you with, my dear,' replied the wolf.

If an animal is innately programmed for some type of behaviour, then there are likely to be biological clues. It is no accident that fish have bodies which are streamlined and smooth, with fins and a powerful tail. Their bodies are structurally adapted for moving fast through the water. The same is true of whales and dolphins, even though they evolved quite separately from fish. Similarly, if you found a dead bird or mosquito, you could guess by looking at its wings that flying was its normal mode of transport.

However, we must not be over-optimistic. Biological clues are not essential. The extent to which they are found varies from animal to animal and from activity to activity. For example, it is impossible to guess from their bodies that birds make nests, and, sometimes, animals behave in a way quite contrary to what might be expected from their physical form: ghost spiders have tremendously long legs, yet they weave webs out of very short strands. To a human observer, their legs seem a great hindrance as they spin and move about the web. On the other hand, the orb spider, which has short legs, makes its web out of very long cables, and seems to put a disproportionate amount of effort into walking from one side of the web to another (Duncan 1949, quoted in Lenneberg 1967: 75). In addition, there are often inexplicable divergences between species which do not correlate with any obvious differences in behaviour. The visible sections of the ear differ in chimps, baboons and men – but there is no discernible reason behind this. However, such unpredictability is not universal, and need not discourage us from looking for biological clues connected with speech – though we must realize that we are unlikely to find the equivalent of a large box labelled 'language'.

Changes in the form of the body or structural changes are the most direct indications of innate programming. But we must also take into consideration physiological adaptations – changes in the bodily functions, such as rate of heartbeat and breathing. The first part of this chapter looks at parts of the human body where adaptations related to language are likely to be found. The organs used to produce and plan it are examined – the mouth, vocal cords, lungs and the brain.

The second part of the chapter is slightly different. It considers aspects of language where complex neuromuscular sequencing is involved. It becomes clear that the co-ordination required is perhaps impossible without biological adaptations.

MOUTH, LUNGS AND GREY MATTER

If we look at the organs used in speech, humans seem to be somewhere in the middle between the obvious structural adaptation of birds to flying, and the apparent lack of correlation between birds and nest-building. That is, the human brain and vocal tract have a number of slightly unusual features. By themselves, these features are not sufficient to indicate that people can talk. But if we first assume that all humans speak a language, then a number of puzzling biological facts fall into place. They can be viewed as partial adaptations of the body to the production of language.

For example, human teeth are unusual compared with those of other animals. They are even in height, and form an unbroken barrier. They are upright, not slanting outwards, and the top and bottom set meet. Such regularity is surprising – it is certainly not needed for eating. Yet evenly spaced, equal-sized teeth which touch one another are valuable for the articulation of a number of sounds, S, F, and V, for example, as well as SH (as in shut), TH (as in thin) and several others. Human lips have muscles which are considerably more developed and show more intricate interlacing than those in the lips of other primates. The mouth is relatively small, and can be opened and shut rapidly. This makes it simple to pronounce sounds such as P and B, which require a total stoppage of the airstream with the lips, followed by a sudden release of pressure as the mouth is opened. The human tongue is thick, muscular and mobile, as opposed to the long, thin tongues of monkeys. The advantage of a thick tongue is that the size of the mouth cavity can be varied allowing a range of vowels to be pronounced.

It seems, then, that humans are naturally geared to produce a number of different sounds rapidly and in a controlled manner. Their mouths possess features which either differ from or appear to be missing in the great apes. In all, one cannot help agreeing with the comment of a nineteenth-century writer:

> What a curious thing speech is! The tongue is so serviceable a member (taking all sorts of shapes just as it is wanted) – the teeth, the lips, the roof of the mouth, all ready to help; and so heap up the sound of the voice into the solid bits which we call consonants, and make room for the curiously shaped breathings which we call vowels!
>
> (Oliver Wendell Holmes)

Another important difference between humans and monkeys concerns the larynx, which contains the 'voice box' or 'vocal cords'. Strangely, it is simpler in structure than that of other primates. But this is an advantage. Air can move freely past and then out through the nose and mouth without being hindered by other appendages. Biologically, streamlining and simplification are often indications of specialization for a given purpose. For example, hooved animals have a reduced number of toes, and fish do not have limbs. So the streamlining of the human larynx may be a sign of adaptation to speech. But we pay a price for our specialized larynx. A monkey can seal its mouth off from its windpipe and breath while it is eating. Humans cannot do this, so food can get lodged in the windpipe, sometimes causing them to choke to death.

We now come to the lungs. Although there is no apparent peculiarity in the structure of our lungs, our breathing seems to be remarkably adapted to speech. In most animals the respiratory system is a very finely balanced mechanism. A human submerged under water for more than two minutes will possibly drown. Anyone who pants rapidly and continuously for any length of time faints and sometimes dies. Yet during speech the breathing rhythm is altered quite noticeably without apparent discomfort to the speaker. The number of breaths per minute is reduced. Breathing-in is considerably accelerated, breathing-out is slowed down. Yet people frequently talk for an hour or more with no ill-effects. A child learning to play the flute or trumpet has to be carefully instructed in breathing techniques – but no one has to instruct a 2-year-old in the breathing adaptations required for talking. It is impossible to tell which came first – speech or breathing adaptations. As the biologist Eric Lenneberg inquired (1967: 81), do donkeys say *hee-haw* on inspired and expired air so efficiently because of the way their breathing mechanisms were organized, or did the *hee-haw* come first? The answer is irrelevant. All that matters to us is that any child born in the twentieth century has a breathing mechanism apparently biologically organized for speech.

It seems, then, that there are clear indications in the mouth, larynx and lungs that we speak 'naturally'. However, let us now consider the human brain. To what extent is this programmed for speech? The answer is unclear. Our brain is very different in appearance from that of other animals. It is heavier, with more surface folding of the cortex, the outer layer of 'grey matter' which surrounds the inner core of nerve fibres – though grey matter is actually pink in live humans, it goes grey after death. Of course, size alone is not particularly important. Elephants and whales have bigger brains than humans, but they do not talk. But elephants and whales also have bigger bodies, so some people have suggested that it is the brain–body ratio which matters. At first sight, this seems a promising approach. It appears quite reasonable to suggest that a high brain–body ratio means high intelligence, which in turn might be a prerequisite for language, especially when we find that the brain of an adult human is more than 2 per cent of his or her total weight, while that of an adult chimp is less than 1 per cent. But such ratios can be very misleading. Some animals are designed to carry around large reserves of energy which makes their bodies enormously heavy. Camels, for example, are not necessarily more stupid than horses just because they have huge humps.

But even apart from problems such as this, brain–body ratio cannot be a decisive factor as far as language is concerned, since it is possible to find young chimpanzees and human children who have similar brain–body ratios – yet the child can talk and the chimp cannot. Even more convincing is a comparison between a 3-year-old chimp and a 12-year-old nanocephalic dwarf – a human who because of a genetic defect grows to a height of around 760 mm (or 2 feet 6 inches).

	Brain (kg)	Body (kg)	Ratio
Human, age 13	1.35	45	1 : 34
Human dwarf, age 12	0.4	13.5	1 : 34
Chimp, age 3	0.4	13.5	1 : 34

Source: Lenneberg 1967: 70

Although the chimp and the dwarf have exactly the same brain and body weights (and so, of course, the same brain–body ratio), the dwarfs speak, in a somewhat limited fashion, but the chimps do not. These figures show conclusively that the difference between human and chimp brains is a *qualitative*, not a *quantitative* one.

Superficially, the brains of a chimp and a human have certain similarities. As in a number of animals, the human brain is divided into a lower section, the *brain stem*, and a higher section, the *cerebrum*. The brain stem keeps the body alive by controlling breathing, heartbeats and so on. A cat with the upper section of its brain removed but with the brain stem intact could still swallow milk, purr, and pull its paw away from a thorn when pricked. The higher section, the cerebrum, is not essential for life. Its purpose seems to be to integrate an animal with its environment. This is the part of the brain where language is likely to be organized.

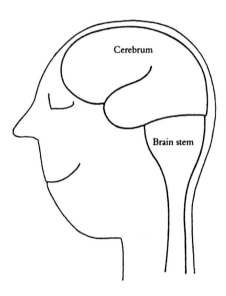

The cerebrum is divided into two halves, the *cerebral hemispheres*, which are linked to one another by a series of bridges. The left hemisphere controls the right side of the body, and the right hemisphere the left side.

But the two hemispheres do not function identically. This was first discovered over a hundred years ago. A Frenchman, Marc Dax, read a paper at Montpellier in 1836, pointing out that paralysis of the right side of the body was often associated with loss of speech, while patients whose left side was paralysed could usually talk normally. This suggested that the left hemisphere controlled not only the right side of the body, but *speech* also. Dax's hypothesis turned out to be correct. Speech in the majority of humans is the concern of the *left*, not the right hemisphere. But it was a long time before this was reliably confirmed. Until relatively recently, statistics could only be drawn up by chance observations, when researchers managed to note cases of people in whom loss of speech was associated with right-side paralysis. But in the twentieth century more sophisticated methods were adopted. One is the sodium amytal test developed by Wada in the 1940s. In this test the patient was asked to count out loud while a barbiturate (sodium amytal) was injected into an artery carrying blood to one side of the brain. If this was the hemisphere used in speech, the patient lost all track of his counting and experienced severe language difficulties for several minutes. If it was not, the patient could resume normal counting almost immediately after the injection. Although this test was effective, it also carried an element of risk. So it was only used when brain surgery was advisable (as in severe epilepsy) and the surgeon wished to know whether he was likely to disturb vital speech areas. If so, he was unlikely to operate.

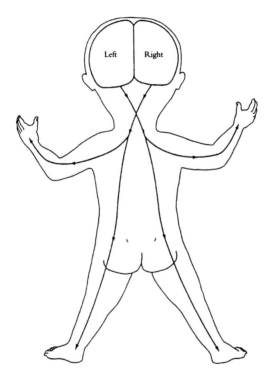

Simpler and less invasive methods for discovering which hemisphere controls language are now the norm. The first was the use of dichotic listening tests (Kimura 1967; Obler and Gjerlow 1999). The subject wears headphones, and is played two different words simultaneously, one into each ear. For example, he or she might hear six in one ear, and two in the other. Most people can report the word played to the right ear (which is directly linked to the left hemisphere) more accurately than the word played to the left ear (linked to the right hemisphere). It is clear that this is not simply due to an overall preference for sounds heard in the right ear, because for non-linguistic sounds the left ear is better. If different tunes are played simultaneously into each ear, subjects will identify the tune played into the left ear better than the one directed into the right ear. We conclude that the left hemisphere is better at processing linguistic signals – and so is normally the dominant one for speech.

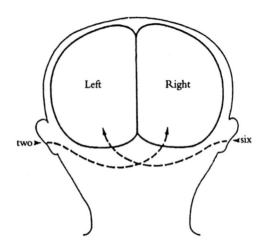

A further technique is tachistoscopic (fast-view) presentation. An image is presented very fast to either the left or right visual field (the area that can be seen to left or right without moving the head or eyes). A linguistic stimulus will normally be processed faster if it is presented to the right visual field, which is then transferred to the left (usually language dominant) hemisphere.

In another twentieth-century technique, electrodes are attached to the skull in order to measure the amount of electrical activity in the area beneath (as will be discussed later). Spoken words produce a greater response in the left hemisphere, whereas noises such as mechanical clicks arouse a greater response in the right (Rosenfield 1978).

The results of the observations and tests described above are surprisingly consistent. The majority of normal human beings – perhaps as many as 90 per cent – have speech located primarily in the left hemisphere. This cannot be due to chance.

A further related discovery is that the location of speech centres in the left hemisphere seems to be linked to right-handedness. That is, most humans are right-handed, and most people's speech is controlled by the left hemisphere. In the nineteenth century it was commonly assumed that left-handers must have speech located in the right hemisphere, and this seemed to be confirmed by a report in 1868 by the influential neurologist John Hughlings Jackson that he had discovered loss of speech in a left-hander who had sustained injury to the right side of the brain. But this viewpoint turns out to be false.

Surprisingly, most left-handers also have language controlled predominantly by the left hemisphere, though the picture is not completely straightforward. Of the relatively few people who do not have their speech centres located in the right hemisphere, more are left-handed than right-handed.

Location of speech centres	Right-handers	Left-handers
Left hemisphere	90% or more	70–90%
Right hemisphere	10% or less	10–30%

(Figures averaged from Penfield and Roberts 1959; Zangwill 1973; Milner, *et al.* 1964.)

These figures indicate two things: first, it is normal for speech and handedness to be controlled by the same hemisphere, and it has been suggested that speech and writing problems are found more frequently in children where the two are not linked. Second, there is a strong tendency for speech to be located in the left hemisphere even when this appears to disrupt the standard linking of speech and handedness.

Some work has been directed at finding out if *all* speech processing must be located in one hemisphere or whether subsidiary linguistic abilities remain in the non-dominant hemisphere. One group of researchers at Montreal, Canada, found ten patients who had speech abilities in both halves of the brain. The sodium amytal test disturbed speech whichever side of the brain it was injected. Interestingly enough, all these patients were either left-handed or ambidextrous (Milner, *et al.* 1964).

Other studies suggest that the right hemisphere contains a limited potential for language which is normally latent, but which can be activated if needed. Patients who have had the whole of the left hemisphere removed are at first without speech. But after a while, they are likely to acquire a limited vocabulary, and be able to comprehend a certain amount, though they always have difficulty in producing speech (Kinsbourne 1975). The right hemisphere is not useless, however. Patients with right hemisphere damage have difficulty with intonation, and in understanding jokes and metaphors (Caplan 1987).

Perhaps the most widely reported experiments on this topic are those involving 'split brain' patients (Gazzaniga 1970, 1983). In cases of severe epilepsy it is sometimes necessary to sever the major links between the two hemispheres. This means that a patient has virtually two separate brains, each coping with one half of the body independently. A patient's language can be tested by dealing with each hemisphere separately. An object shown to the *left* visual field is relayed only to the *right* (non-language hemisphere). Yet sometimes the patient is able to name such an object. This indicates that the right hemisphere may be able to cope with simple naming problems – but it seems unable to cope with syntax. However, the results of these experiments are disputed. Some people have suggested that the information is being transferred from one hemisphere to the other by a 'back route' after the major links have been severed.

This lateralization or localization of language in one half of the brain, then, is a definite, biological characteristic of the human race. At one time, it was thought to develop gradually. But later research indicated that it may be present at birth (Kinsbourne and Hiscock 1987). Even foetuses have been claimed to show traces of it, with some areas of the left hemisphere being bigger than the right (Buffery 1978). The issue is an important one for psycholinguists, since it has sometimes been argued that the period of lateralization coincides with a 'critical period' for language acquisition (to be discussed in Chapter 4).

Although most neurologists agree that language is mainly restricted to one hemisphere, further localization of speech is still controversial. A basic difficulty is that until recently all the evidence available was derived from brain-damaged patients. And injured brains may not be representative of normal ones. After a stroke or other injury the damage is rarely localized. A wound usually creates a blockage, causing a shortage of blood in the area beyond it, and a build-up of pressure behind it. So detailed correlations of wounds with speech defects cannot often be made, especially as a wound in one place may trigger off severe speech problems in one person, but only marginally affect the speech of another. This suggests to some neurologists that speech can be 're-located' away from the damaged area – it has (controversially) been suggested that there are 'reserve' speech areas which are kept for use in emergencies. This creates an extremely complex picture. Like a ghost, speech drifts away to another area just as you think you have located it. But these problems have not deterred neurologists – and some progress has been made.

Until fairly recently, observation and experiment were the two main methods of investigation. Observation depended on unfortunate accidents and post-mortems. A man called Phineas Gage had an accident in 1847 in which a four-foot (over a metre long) iron bar struck and entered the front left-hand section of his head, then exited through the top. Gage kept the bar as a souvenir, until his death, twenty years later. The bar and skull are now preserved in a museum at the Harvard Medical School. Although Gage's personality changed for the worse – he became unreliable and unpredictable – his language was unaffected. This suggests that the front part of the brain is not crucially involved in language. Conversely, a French surgeon named Broca noted at a post-mortem in 1861 that two patients who had had severe speech defects (one could only say *tan* and *sacré nom de Dieu*) had significant damage to an area just in front of, and slightly above, the left ear – which suggested that this area, now named 'Broca's area', is important for speech.

The experimental method was pioneered in the 1950s by two Canadian surgeons, Penfield and Roberts (1959). They were primarily concerned with removing abnormally functioning cells from the brains of epileptics. But before doing this they had to check that they were not destroying cells involved in speech. So, with the patients fully conscious, they carefully opened the skull, and applied a minute electric current to different parts of the exposed brain. Electrical stimulation of this type normally causes temporary interference. So if the area which controls leg movement is stimulated, the patient is unable to move his or her leg. If the area controlling speech production is involved, the patient is briefly unable to speak.

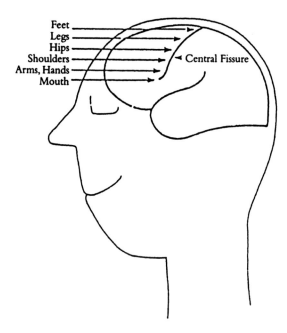

There are obvious disadvantages in this method. Only the surface of the brain was examined, and no attempt was made to probe what was happening at a deeper level. The brain is not normally exposed to air or electric shocks, so the results may be quite unrepresentative. But in spite of the problems involved, certain outline facts became clear long ago.

First of all, it was possible to distinguish the area of the brain which is involved in the actual articulation of speech. The so-called 'primary somatic motor area' controls all voluntary bodily movements and is situated just in front of a deep crack or 'fissure' running down from the top of the brain. The control for different parts of the body works upside down: control of the feet and legs is near the top of the head, and control of the face and mouth is further down.

The bodily control system in animals works in much the same way – but there is one major difference. In humans, a disproportionate amount of space is allotted to the area controlling the hands and mouth.

But the sections of the brain involved in the actual articulation of speech seem to be partly distinct from those involved in its planning and comprehension. Where are these planning and comprehension areas? Experts disagree. Nevertheless, perhaps the majority of neurologists agree that some areas of the brain are statistically likely to be involved in speech planning and comprehension. Two areas seem to be particularly relevant: the neighbourhood of *Broca's area* (in front of and just above the left ear); and the region around and under the left ear, which is sometimes called *Wernicke's area* after the neurologist who first suggested this area was important for speech (in 1874). Damage to Wernicke's area often destroys speech comprehension, and damage to Broca's frequently hinders speech production – though this is something of an over-simplification, since serious damage to either area usually harms all aspects of speech (Mackay *et al.* 1987).

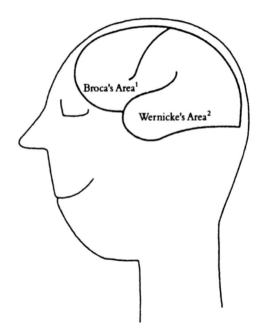

[1] Broca's Area covers approximately the space under the s of Broca's and the A of *Area*
[2] Wernicke's Area is roughly the space directly above the word *Wernicke's*.

Particularly puzzling are cases of damage to Broca's or Wernicke's area where the patient suffers no language disorder. Conversely, someone's speech may be badly affected by a brain injury, even though this does not apparently involve the 'language areas'. There may simply be more variation in the location of brain areas than in the position of the heart or liver. A particular function may be:

> narrowly localized in an individual in a particular area . . . localized equally narrowly in another area in another individual, and carried out in a much larger area . . . in the third. The only constraint seems to be that core language processes are accomplished in this area of neocortex.
>
> (Caplan 1988: 248)

A further problem is that neurologists do not necessarily agree on the exact location of Broca's and Wernicke's areas, though the boundaries are more contentious than the central regions (Stowe *et al.* 2005). In addition there are deeper brain interconnections about which little is known.

Comparisons with the brains of other primates, incidentally, show that humans have a disproportionately large area at the front of the brain, sometimes referred to as the 'prefrontal cortex', though it is unclear how much of this involves language, and how much more general interconnections.

Luckily, brain scans can now supplement our information. From the 1970s onward, these have moved forward in leaps and bounds. First, and prior to 'proper' scans was the EEG (electroencephalograph) which showed the numerous electrical impulses in the brain, and the general state of alertness of a patient, but was unable to provide precise mappings. Then came so-called CT or CAT scans, short for 'X-ray computed tomography'. The tissues within the brain (and the body) differ in density, so a tumour (for example) might appear as an extra dense portion, and these differing densities showed up on the X-rays.

Next PET scans were developed, short for 'positron emission tomography'. These recorded blood flow. Blood surges in the brain when someone uses language, just as extra blood is pumped into the arms and hands when someone plays the piano. Radioactive water was injected into a vein in the arm. In just over a minute, the water accumulated in the brain, and could show an image of the blood flow in progressively more difficult tasks. In one experiment, subjects were first asked to look at something simple, such as a small cross on a screen, and the blood flow was measured. Then, some English nouns were shown or spoken. As a next stage, the subjects were asked to speak the word they saw or heard. Finally, they were asked to say out loud a verb suitable to the noun: for example, if they had heard the word HAMMER, then HIT might be appropriate (Posner and Raichle 1994).

The results showed strong differences between the various tasks. Simply repeating involved only the areas of the brain which dealt with physical movement. But both Broca's and Wernicke's areas became active when subjects consciously accessed word meaning and chose a response. In short, comprehension and production cannot be split apart in the way it was once assumed. In production, selecting a verb was the most complex task, and involved several areas – though with practice, the activity grew less, and became more like that of nouns. So practice not only makes it all easier, but actually changes the way the brain organizes itself. In another experiment, subjects were presented with lists of verbs, and asked to provide the past tense. Regular past tenses such as CLIMBED, WISHED showed different blood flow patterns from irregular ones such as CAUGHT, HID (Jaeger et al. 1996).

The brain, it appears, relies on tactics similar to those used by a sprinter's muscles, with an increase in oxygen in any area where neurons show extra activity – though a basic problem is the tremendous amount happening at any one moment. Pinpointing only the activity relevant to speech is difficult, especially as deeper connections are turning out to be as important as those near the surface. However, techniques are improving all the time. These enable the ebb and flow in blood vessels to be monitored continuously.

More recently, attention has been directed particularly towards ERPs 'event related potentials', and MRI 'magnetic resonance imaging'. These techniques are non-invasive, in that nothing needs to be injected into the body, which can simply be scanned. They are therefore potentially safer, and can be used with a wider range of people.

ERPs monitor electrical activity in the brain, following some stimulus (an 'event') such as reading a sentence. Electrodes are placed on the scalp, and the reaction, the ERP ('event related potential') is measured. The brain responds differently to syntactic and semantic ill-formedness, for example, showing that a division between the two has some type of 'reality' for speakers of English (Kutas and van Petten 1994).

MRI ('magnetic resonance imaging') exploits the finding that human heads and bodies contain hydrogen atoms which can be (temporarily and safely) re-aligned by means of the MRI machine's magnetic field. Images of the brain are produced by taking photos of cross-sectional 'slices'. These are far clearer and more precise than any previous attempts at picturing the brain. They confirm that a huge amount of activity takes place continuously.

The brain is therefore like an ever-bubbling cauldron, seething non-stop. Neurons are organized into complex networks: 'The language areas may be understood as zones in which neurons participating in language-related cell assemblies cluster to a much higher degree than in other areas' (Müller 1996: 629). But connections matter quite as much as locations, with far more buzzing between areas than was previously realized. So connectionism is the general name for this type of theory about how the mind works, largely inspired by all this work on the brain. Multiple parallel links are turning out to be the norm in any mental activity, and especially in language. 'Mental operations appear to be localized, but performance of a complex task requires an integrated ensemble of brain regions' (Fiez *et al.* 1992: 169).

PATTING ONE'S HEAD AND RUBBING THE STOMACH

As all this new work confirms, a type of biological adaptation which is not so immediately obvious – but which is on second sight quite amazing – is the 'multiplicity of integrative processes' (Lashley 1951) which take place in speech production and comprehension.

In some areas of activity it is extremely difficult to do more than one thing at once. As schoolchildren discover, it is extraordinarily hard to pat one's head and rub one's stomach at the same time. If you also try to swing your tongue from side to side, and cross and uncross your legs, as well as patting your head and rubbing your stomach, the whole exercise becomes impossible. The occasional juggler might be able to balance a beer bottle on his nose, twizzle a hoop on his ankle and keep seven plates aloft with his hands – but he is likely to have spent a lifetime practising such antics. And the exceptional nature of these activities is shown by the fact that he can earn vast sums of money displaying his skills.

Yet speech depends on the simultaneous integration of a remarkable number of processes, and in many respects what is going on is considerably more complex than the juggler's manoeuvres with his beer bottle, plates and hoop.

In speech, three processes, at the very least, are taking place simultaneously: first, sounds are actually being uttered; second, phrases are being activated in their phonetic form ready for use; third, the rest of the sentence is being planned. And each of these processes is possibly more complicated than appears at first sight. The complexities involved in actually pronouncing words are not immediately apparent. One might assume that in uttering a word such as GEESE one first utters a G-sound, then an EE-sound, then an S–sound in that order. But the process is much more involved.

First, the G-sound in GEESE differs quite considerably from the G in GOOSE. This is because of the difference in the following vowel. The speaker appears to anticipate (subconsciously) the EE or OO and alter the G accordingly. Second, the vowel in GEESE is shorter than in a word such as GEEZER. The speaker is anticipating the voiceless hissing sound of S in GOOSE rather than the voiced, buzzing sound of Z in GEEZER, since in English (and some other languages) vowels are shortened before voiceless sounds (sounds which do not involve vibration of the vocal cords).

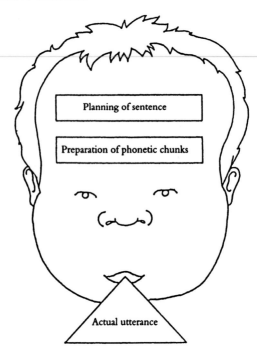

Therefore a speaker does not just utter a sequence of separate elements:

```
1     2     3
G.    EE.   SE.
```

Instead he executes a series of overlapping actions in which the preceding sound is significantly influenced by the sound which follows it:

```
G...
      EE...
           SE...
```

Such overlapping requires considerable neuromuscular co-ordination, particularly as the rate of speech is often quite fast. A normal person often utters over 200 syllables a minute. Meanwhile, simultaneously with actually uttering the sounds, a speaker is activating phrases of two or three words in advance in their phonetic form. This is shown by slips of the tongue, in which a sound several words away is sometimes accidentally activated before it is needed. The linguist who once said PISS AND STRETCH in a lecture for 'pitch and stress' was already thinking of the final -SS of 'stress' when he started to say the first word. And the person who said ON THE NERVE OF A VERGEOUS BREAKDOWN had also activated the syllable 'nerve' before she needed it.

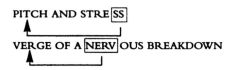

If humans only spoke in three or four word bursts, perhaps the prior activation of phrases would not be very surprising. What is surprising is that this activation is going on at the same time as the planning of much longer utterances. Lenneberg (1967: 107) likens the planning of an utterance to laying down a mosaic:

> The sequence of speech sounds that constitute a string of words is a sound pattern somewhat analogous to a mosaic; the latter is put together stone after stone, yet the picture as a whole must have come into being in the artist's mind before he began to lay down the pieces.

Sometimes, sentences are structurally quite easy to process as in THE BABY FELL DOWNSTAIRS, THE CAT WAS SICK, AND I'VE RESIGNED. At other times they are considerably more complex, requiring the speaker and the hearer to remember quite intricate interdependencies between clauses. Take the sentence IF EITHER THE BABY FALLS DOWNSTAIRS OR THE CAT IS SICK, THEN I SHALL EITHER RESIGN OR GO MAD. Here, IF requires a dependent THEN, EITHER requires a partner OR. In addition, FALLS must have the right ending to go with BABY, and IS must 'agree' with CAT – otherwise we would get *IF EITHER THE BABY FALL DOWNSTAIRS OR THE CAT ARE SICK . . . This whole sentence with its 'mirror-image' properties must have been planned considerably in advance.

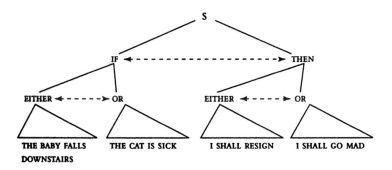

These examples show that in most human utterances, the amount of simultaneous planning and activity is so great that it seems likely that humans are specially constructed to deal with this type of coordination. But what type of mechanism is involved? In particular, how do humans manage to keep utterances in the right order, and not utter them in an incoherent jumble, as they think of them? How do most people manage to say RABBIT quite coherently, instead of BARIT or TIRAB – examples of misordering found in the speech of brain-damaged patients?

Lenneberg (1967) suggests that correct sequencing is based on an underlying rhythmic principle. Everybody knows that poetry is much easier to remember than prose because of the underlying 'pulse' which keeps going like the ticking of a clock:

I WANDERED LONELY AS A CLOUD
(ti-tum-ti-tum-ti-tum-ti-tum)

THAT FLOATS ON HIGH O'ER VALES AND HILLS
(ti-tum-ti-tum-ti-tum-ti-tum)
                                        Wordsworth

There may be some underlying biological 'beat' which enables humans to organize language into a temporal sequence. Breakdown of this beat might also account for the uncontrollable acceleration of speech found in some illnesses such as Parkinson's disease. Lenneberg suggests that one-sixth of a second may be a basic time unit in speech production. He bases his proposals on a number of highly technical experiments, and partly on the fact that around six syllables per second seems to be the normal rate of uttering syllables. However, some people have queried the notion of a fixed 'pacemaker', and suggested that the internal beat can be re-set at different speeds (Keele 1987). This may be correct, since with practice speech can be speeded up, though the relative length of the various words remains the same (Mackay 1987).

INTELLIGENCE, SEX AND HEREDITY

Can studies of the brain clarify how language relates to intelligence? A bit, but not very much. Intelligence is a complex fabric of interwoven skills. Exactly where (if anywhere) each is located is highly controversial. The most we can say is that certain aspects of intelligence, such as judgements of space and time, are largely independent of language. Sufferers of a strange disorder known as Williams Syndrome lack spatial awareness, and find it hard to draw a picture of an elephant or a bicycle. Instead, they draw bits and pieces which they cannot assemble. In contrast, their speech is fluent: 'What would you do if you were a bird?' one sufferer was asked. 'I would fly where my parents could never find me. Birds want to be independent' was the answer (Bellugi, et al. 1991: 387).

Sex differences in the brain are also important for language. Women, on average, have greater verbal fluency, and can more easily find words that begin with a particular letter. Men are better at spatial tasks and mathematical reasoning. These variations probably reflect different hormonal influences on developing brains (Kimura 1992).

Heredity is another topical issue (Gopnik 1997; Stromswolo 2001; Fisher 2006). Can language defects be handed down from generation to generation? Dyslexia, or 'word blindness', often runs in families. So does another puzzling language problem. Several families have been found of whom a proportion of their members cannot put endings on words, the most famous of whom are known as the 'KE family' (Gopnik 1994; Gopnik et al. 1997). ZACKO was given as the plural of the nonsense word ZAT by one sufferer, and ZOOPES as the plural of the nonsense word ZOOP. Those affected have to learn each plural separately, and they find it impossible to learn a general rule such as 'Add-S'. They also find it hard to use pronouns, and tend to repeat full nouns, as: 'The neighbours phone the ambulance because the man fall off the tree. The ambulance come along and put the man into the ambulance' (Gopnik and Crago 1991). At first, optimistic researchers hoped that they had found a gene for language, and even provisionally labelled it the SPCH1 gene. Later, it was realized that the affected members in the KE family (and some other families) had a cluster of language problems, as well as some non-linguistic ones. The defective gene, eventually labelled FOXP2, is still being investigated by researchers, and the details are proving complex (Lal et al. 2001). As well as difficulties with inflections, the affected family members are unable to break down words into their constituent sounds, and they also have problems with the sequencing of mouth movements.

MIND-READING AND MIRROR NEURONS

As researchers puzzle over exactly why humans are such competent language users, new findings have emerged, which may turn out to be of vital importance. Humans have an ability to 'mind-read', to put themselves into another person's shoes, as it were, and envisage their mental state (p. 27). Mind-reading is an awareness that develops with age: 3-year-olds are typically unable to achieve it, but 4-year-olds can normally do so without difficulty. This trait is lacking in those who suffer from the mental disorder of autism, a condition sometimes known as 'mindblindness' (Baron-Cohen 1999; Ramachandran and Oberman 2006). There seem to be layers of mind-blindness. Chimps have some inkling of mind-reading (Chapter 2), though not the same level of awareness as normal humans. This has led researchers to probe into the neurological background behind this ability

An intriguing discovery is that of so-called 'mirror neurons', which according to some researchers, may underlie the ability to understand another person's intentions, and also the ability to imitate. Mirror neurons have been found both in humans and monkeys. An Italian neuroscientist, Giacomo Rizzolatti, is credited with their discovery (Rizzolatti and Arbib 1998). He noticed that a section of the frontal lobe of a monkey's brain fired when it performed certain actions, such as reaching for an object or putting food in its mouth. But bizarrely, the same neurons would fire when it watched another monkey performing the same actions. Rizzolatti labelled these 'mirror neurons' and speculated that he may have identified the neurological basis of mind-reading. Later work has emphasized the importance of mirror neurons in imitation, a skill at which humans seem to be better than apes, and may be crucial in language learning (Rizzolatti et al. 2006), and also their possible role in the evolution of language (Stamenov 2002).

We do not yet know all the details, but the overall picture is clear. Humans are physically adapted to language in a way that snails, sheep and even apes are not. Their vocal organs, lungs and brains are 'preset' to cope with the intricacies of speech in much the same way that monkeys are pre-set to climb trees, or bats to squeak. Chapter 4 gives further evidence of this biological programming by showing that language follows an inner 'time-clock' as it emerges and develops.

4

PREDESTINATE GROOVES
Is there a pre-ordained language 'programme'?

There once was a man who said, 'Damn!'
It is born in upon me I am
An engine that moves
In predestinate grooves,
I'm not even a bus, I'm a tram.
                                    Maurice Evan Hare

Language emerges at about the same time in children all over the world. 'Why do children normally begin to speak between their eighteenth and twenty-eighth month?' asks one researcher:

> Surely it is not because all mothers on earth initiate language training at that time. There is, in fact, no evidence that any conscious and systematic teaching of language takes place, just as there is no special training for stance or gait.
>
> (Lenneberg 1967: 125).

This regularity of onset suggests that language may be set in motion by a biological clock, similar to the one which causes kittens to open their eyes when they are a few days old, chrysalises to change into butterflies after several weeks, and humans to become sexually mature at around 13 years of age. However, until relatively recently, few people had considered language within the framework of biological maturation. But in 1967 Eric Lenneberg, then a biologist at the Harvard Medical School, published an important book, entitled *The Biological Foundations of Language*. Much of what is said in this chapter is based on his pioneering work.

THE CHARACTERISTICS OF BIOLOGICALLY TRIGGERED BEHAVIOUR

Behaviour that is triggered off biologically has a number of special character-istics. In the following pages we shall list these features, and see to what extent they are present in language. If it can be shown that speech, like sexual activities and the ability to walk, falls into the category of biologically sched-uled behaviour, then we shall be rather clearer about what is meant by the claim that language is 'innate'.

Exactly how many 'hallmarks' of biologically controlled behaviour we should itemize is not clear. Lenneberg lists four. The six listed below were obtained mainly by subdividing Lenneberg's four:

1 The behaviour emerges before it is necessary.
2 Its appearance is not the result of a conscious decision.
3 Its emergence is not triggered by external events (though the surrounding environment must be sufficiently 'rich' for it to develop adequately).
4 Direct teaching and intensive practice have relatively little effect.
5 There is a regular sequence of 'milestones' as the behaviour develops, and these can usually be correlated with age and other aspects of development.
6 There may be a 'critical period' for the acquisition of the behaviour.

Let us discuss these features in turn. Some of them seem fairly obvious. We hardly need to set about testing the first one, that 'the behaviour emerges before it is necessary' – a phenomenon sometimes pompously labelled the 'law of anticipatory maturation'. Language develops long before children need to communicate in order to survive. Their parents still feed them, clothe them and look after them. Without some type of inborn mechanism, language might develop only when parents left children to fend for themselves. It would emerge at different times in different cultures, and this would lead to vastly different levels of language skills. Although children differ enormously in their ability to knit or play the violin, their language proficiency varies to a much lesser extent.

Again, little explanation is needed for the second characteristic of biologi-cally triggered behaviour: 'Its appearance is not the result of a conscious decision.' Clearly, a child does not suddenly think to herself, 'Tomorrow I am going to start to learn to talk.' Children acquire language without making any conscious decision about it. This is quite unlike a decision to learn to jump a 4-foot height, or hit a tennis ball, when a child sets herself a target, then organizes strenuous practice sessions as she strives towards her goal.

The first part of feature (3) also seems straightforward: 'The emergence of the behaviour is not triggered by external events.' Children begin to talk even when their surroundings remain unchanged. Most of them live in the same house, eat the same food, have the same parents, and follow the same routine. No specific event or feature in their surroundings suddenly starts them off talking. An inner biological clock is ticking away, set for the right time.

We know for certain that language cannot emerge before it is programmed to emerge. Nobody has ever made a young baby talk – though it seems that there is nothing much wrong with the vocal cords of a newborn infant, and from 5 or 6 months onwards it can 'babble' a number of the sounds needed in speech. Yet children utter few words before the age of 18 months. They have to wait for some biological trigger. The 'trigger' appears to be connected with brain growth. Two-word utterances, which are usually regarded as the beginning of 'true language', begin just as a massive spurt in brain growth slows down. Children do not manufacture any new brain cells after birth. They are born with millions, perhaps billions. At first the cells are not all interconnected, and the brain is relatively light (about 300g). From birth to around 2 years, many more cells interconnect, and brain weight increases rapidly. By the age of 2, it weighs nearly 1000g (Lenneberg 1967).

However, there is one aspect of biologically scheduled behaviour that is sometimes misunderstood: although no external event *causes* the behaviour, the surrounding environment must be sufficiently 'rich' for it to develop adequately. Biologically programmed behaviour does not develop properly in impoverished or unnatural surroundings. We have the apparent paradox that some types of 'natural' behaviour require careful 'nurturing'. Just as Chris and Susie, two gorillas reared away from other gorillas in Sacramento Zoo, were unable to mate satisfactorily, according to an item in the London *Evening Standard* – so an impoverished linguistic environment is likely to retard language acquisition. Children brought up in institutions, for example, tend to be backward in speech development. Lenneberg noted that children raised in an orphanage will begin to talk at the same time as other non-institutionalized children. But their speech will gradually lag behind the norm, being less intelligible, and showing less variety of construction. A less obvious example of linguistic impoverishment was suggested by Basil Bernstein, then a sociologist at London University's Institute of Education. He claimed controversially that children from certain types of family may be language deprived (Bernstein 1972). They may be unable to learn language adequately because they do not have sufficient data at their disposal. He claimed that such families use informal and elliptical speech, in contrast to the more formal and explicit language of households where children learn more quickly. For example, 'Hop it' in one family may correspond to 'Go outside and play, and stop worrying me, I'm busy' in another. As one man described it:

> The words may be limited in number . . . there is a perpetual exchange of pebbled phrases: 'Ah well, some folk are like that; she's nowt but mutton dressed as lamb.' For most of what is said is not said by words but by tone of voice, by silences, by look, gesture and most keenly by touching.

The same man describes the cultural shock of school, where he was faced with 'an unending rush of words, multitudinous, fresh, and ordered in different ways' (Brian Jackson in the *Daily Telegraph* colour supplement). Children seem to need this 'unending rush of words', and those who are deprived of it may lag behind in their development. Luckily the problem is usually only temporary. Language-impoverished children tend to catch up quickly once their verbal environment is enriched: the biological factor takes over as soon as the environment enables it to do so.

In fact, relatively few children are truly deprived, according to more recent research. In many cases, the supposedly 'language impoverished' children were just puzzled for a time when they were exposed to a dialect or accent unlike their own.

Let us now turn to the fourth characteristic of biologically triggered behaviour, 'Direct teaching and intensive practice have relatively little effect.' In activities such as typing or playing tennis, a person's achievement is often directly related to the amount of teaching they receive and the hours of practice they put in. Even people who are not 'naturally' superb athletes can sometimes win tennis tournaments through sheer hard work and good coaching. But the same is not true of language, where direct teaching seems to be a failure. Let us consider the evidence for this.

When one says that 'direct teaching is a failure', people smile and say, 'Of course – whoever tries to *teach* a child to speak?' Yet many parents, often without realizing it, try to persuade their children to imitate them. They do this in two ways: first, by means of overt correction, second, by means of unconscious 'expansions'.

Overt correction is not necessarily successful. One psychologist attempted over a period of several weeks to persuade his daughter to say OTHER + noun instead of OTHER ONE + noun. The interchanges went somewhat as follows:

Child: WANT OTHER ONE SPOON, DADDY.
Father: YOU MEAN, YOU WANT THE OTHER SPOON.
Child: YES, I WANT OTHER ONE SPOON, PLEASE DADDY.
Father: CAN YOU SAY 'THE OTHER SPOON'?
Child: OTHER . . . ONE . . . SPOON.
Father: SAY 'OTHER'.
Child: OTHER.
Father: 'SPOON'.
Child: SPOON.
Father: 'OTHER SPOON'.
Child: OTHER . . . SPOON. NOW GIVE ME OTHER ONE SPOON?

(Braine 1971: 161)

Another researcher tried vainly to coax a child into saying the past tense form HELD:

Child: MY TEACHER HOLDED THE BABY RABBITS AND WE PATTED
         THEM
Adult: DID YOU SAY YOUR TEACHER HELD THE BABY RABBITS?
Child: YES.
Adult: WHAT DID YOU SAY SHE DID?
Child: SHE HOLDED THE BABY RABBITS AND WE PATTED THEM.
Adult: DID YOU SAY SHE HELD THEM TIGHTLY?
Child: NO, SHE HOLDED THEM LOOSELY.

(Cazden 1972: 92)

So forcing children to imitate is likely to be a dismal failure. Children cannot be trained like parrots. And repeated nagging corrections may even hinder a child's progress. The mother of 17-month-old Paul had high expectations, and repeatedly corrected his attempts at speech. He lacked confidence, and his progress was slow. But the mother of 14-month-old Jane was an accepting person who responded uncritically to everything Jane said. Jane made exceptionally fast progress, and knew eighty words by the age of 15 months (Nelson 1973: 105).

Yet the matter is not quite as simple as at first sight. The now famous 'other one spoon' and 'holded the baby rabbits' dialogues show that corrections are unhelpful if the child's attention is at the time focused strongly on matters other than the language. Later work has shown that kindly made corrections from a sensitive caregiver can enable a child to learn language faster. This will be discussed in Chapter 7.

Equally unsuccessful is the second type of coaching often unconsciously adopted by parents – the use of 'expansions'. When talking to a child an adult

continuously 'expands' the youngster's utterances. If the child says, THERE
GO ONE, a mother is likely to expand this to 'Yes, there goes one.' MOMMY
EGGNOG becomes 'Mommy had her eggnog', and THROW DADDY is
expanded to 'Throw it to Daddy.' Children are exposed to an enormous
number of these expansions. They account for perhaps a third of parental
responses. Two researchers note:

> The mothers of Adam and Eve responded to the speech of their children with
> expansions about 30 per cent of the time. We did it ourselves when we talked
> with the children. Indeed, we found it very difficult to withhold expansions. A
> reduced or incomplete English sentence seems to constrain the English-
> speaking adult to expand it into the nearest properly formed complete
> sentence.
>
> (Brown and Bellugi 1964: 144)

At first researchers were uncertain about the role of expansions. Then
Courtney Cazden carried out an ingenious experiment using two groups of
children, all under 3½ (Cazden 1972). She exposed one group to intensive
and deliberate expansions, and the other group to well-formed sentences
which were not expansions. For example, if a child said, DOG BARK, an
expanding adult would say, 'Yes, the dog is barking.' An adult who replied
with a nonexpanded sentence might say 'Yes, he's trying to frighten the cat'
or 'Yes, but he won't bite', or 'Yes, tell him to be quiet.' After 3 months the
rate of progress of each group was measured. Amazingly, the expansion group
were *less advanced* than the other group, both in average length of utterance and
grammatical complexity.

Several explanations of this unexpected result have been put forward.
Perhaps adults misinterpret the child's intended meaning when they expand.
Erroneous expansions could hinder his learning. Several 'wrong' expansions
have been noted. For example:

Child: WHAT TIME IT IS?
Adult: UH HUH, IT TELLS WHAT TIME IT IS.

Alternatively, a certain degree of novelty may be needed in order to capture
children's attention, since they may not listen to apparent repetitions of their
own utterances. Or it may be that expansions over-restrict the data children
hear. Their speech may be impoverished because of an insufficiently rich
verbal environment. As we noted earlier, a child *needs* copious and varied
samples of speech.

The last two explanations seem to be supported by a Russian experiment
(Slobin 1966a: 144). One group of infants was shown a doll, and three

phrases were repeatedly uttered, 'Here is a doll . . . Take the doll . . . Give me the doll.' Another group of infants was shown the doll, but instead, thirty different phrases were uttered, such as 'Rock the doll . . . Look for the doll.' The total number of words heard by both groups was the same, only the composition differed. Then the experimenters showed the children a selection of toys, and asked them to pick out the dolls. To their surprise, the children in the second group, the ones who had heard a richer variety of speech, were considerably better at this task.

We may conclude then that parents who consciously try to 'coach' their children by simplifying and repeating may be actually interfering with their progress. It does not pay to talk to children as if one was telling a foreign tourist how to get to the zoo. Language that is impoverished is harder to learn, not simpler. Children appear to be naturally 'set' to extract a grammar for themselves, provided they have sufficient data at their disposal. Those who get on best are those who are exposed to a rich variety of language – in other words, those whose parents talk to them in a normal way.

But what does 'talk in a normal way' mean? Here we need to clear up a misunderstanding which seems to have originated with Chomsky. He has claimed that what children hear 'consists to a large extent of utterances that break rules, since a good deal of normal speech consists of false starts, disconnected phrases and other deviations' (Chomsky 1967: 441). Certainly, children are likely to hear some deviant sentences. But later research indicated that the speech children are exposed to is not particularly substandard. Adults tend to speak in shorter sentences and make fewer mistakes when they address children. There is a considerable difference between the way a mother talks to another adult, and the way she talks to her child. One researcher recorded a mother talking to an adult friend. Her sentences were on average fourteen to fifteen words long, and she used several polysyllabic medical terms:

'I was on a inhalation series routine. We wen' aroun' from ward to ward. People, are, y'know, that get all this mucus in their chest, and it's very important to breathe properly an' to be able to cough this mucus up and out an' through your chest, y'know as soon as possible. And we couldn't sterilize the instruments 'cause they were plastic.'

But when she spoke to her child the same mother used five-or six-word sentences. The words were shorter, and referred to things the child could see or do:

COME LOOK AT MOMMA'S COLORIN' BOOK.
YOU WANNA SEE MY COLORING BOOK?
LOOK AT MY COLORING BOOK.
LOOKIT, THAT'S AN INDIAN, HUH?

IS THAT AN INDIAN?
CAN YOU SAY INDIAN?
TALK TO ME.
(Drach, quoted in Ervin Tripp – 1971)

Most parents automatically simplify both the content and syntax when they talk to children. This is not particularly surprising – after all, we do not address bus conductors and boyfriends in the same way. The use of language appropriate to the circumstances is a normal part of a human's language ability.

Speech to children in different cultures is so similar that it might even 'have an innate basis in pan-human child-care behavior' according to the controversial claim of one researcher (Ferguson 1978: 215). 'Motherese', as it is sometimes called, tends to consist of short, well-formed sentences spoken slowly and clearly. We shall discuss the relationship between the structure of adult speech and children's progress in Chapter 7. Here we have simply pointed out that direct teaching does not accelerate the speed of learning and might even be a hindrance.

But this is perhaps an over-simplification. Correction *can* help, if the young learner is currently thinking through the problem corrected. Youngsters 'tune in' to different aspects of their language as they progress. If a child is tussling with so-called 'reflexives', and its parents are sensitive enough to notice this, then correction may be worthwhile, as in the following dialogue:

Child: HE WIPED HIM
Adult: HE WIPED HIMSELF
Child: YES, HE WIPED HIMSELF
(Saxton 2000: 229)

In short, correction which ties in with a child's linguistic level may be more useful than was once assumed.

Let us now return to the question of practice. What is being claimed here is that practice alone cannot account for language acquisition. Children do not learn language simply by repetition and imitation. Two types of evidence support this view.

The first concerns the development of 'inflections' or word endings. English has a number of very common verbs which have an 'irregular' past tense form (e.g. CAME, SAW, WENT) as opposed to the 'regular' forms such as LOVED, WORKED, PLAYED. It also has a number of irregular plurals such as FEET and MICE, as well as the far more numerous plurals ending in -S such as CATS, GIRAFFES and PYTHONS. Quite early on, children learn correct past tense and plural forms for common words such as CAME, SAW and FEET. Later, they abandon these correct forms and replace them with overgeneralized 'regular' forms such as COMED, SEED and FOOTS (Ervin 1964). The significance of this apparent regression is immense. It means that language acquisition cannot possibly be a straightforward case of 'practice makes perfect' or of simple imitation. If it were, children would never replace common forms such as CAME and SAW, which they hear and use all the time, with odd forms such as COMED, SEED and FOOTS, which they are unlikely to have come across.

The second type of practice which turns out to be unimportant for language acquisition is spontaneous imitation. Just as adults subconsciously imitate and expand their children's utterances, so children appear to imitate and 'reduce' sentences uttered by their parents. If an adult says 'I shall take an umbrella', a child is likely to say TAKE 'RELLA. Or 'Put the strap under her chin' is likely to be repeated and reduced to STRAP CHIN. At first sight, it looks as if this might be an important mechanism in the development of language. But Susan Ervin of the University of California at Berkeley came to the opposite conclusion when she recorded the spontaneous utterances of a small group of toddlers (Ervin 1964). To her surprise she found that when a child spontaneously imitates an adult, her imitations are not any more advanced than her normal speech. She shortens the adult utterance to fit in with her current average length of sentence and includes the same number of endings and 'little' words as in her non-imitated utterances. Not a single child produced imitations which were more advanced. And one child, Holly, actually produced imitations that were less complex than her spontaneous sentences!

We may conclude, then, that mere practice – in the sense of direct repetition and imitation – does not affect the acquisition of language in a significant way. However, we must be careful that such a statement does not lead to misunderstandings. What is being said is that practice alone cannot account for language acquisition: children do not learn merely by constant repetition of items. In another sense, they do need to 'practise' talking but even this requirement is not as extensive as might be expected. They can learn a surprising amount by just listening. The amount of talking a child needs to do in order to learn language varies considerably. Some children seem to speak very little. Others are constantly chattering, and playing with words. One researcher wrote a whole book on the pre-sleep monologues of her first child Anthony, who murmured paradigms to himself as he prepared for sleep:

GO FOR GLASSES
GO FOR THEM

GO TO THE TOP
GO THROW

GO FOR BLOUSE
PANTS
GO FOR SHOES
(Weir 1962)

To her disappointment, her second child David was nowhere near as talkative although he eventually learned to speak just as well. These repetitious murmurs do not seem to be essential. Children vary enormously in the amount of 'language drills' they engage in (Kuczaj II 1983).

So far, then, we have considered four of the six characteristics of biologically triggered behaviour which were listed at the beginning of this chapter. All these features seem to be present in language. We now come to the fifth feature, 'There is a regular sequence of "milestones" as the behaviour develops, and these can usually be correlated with age and other aspects of development.' (See point 5 on p. 60.) We shall deal with this in a section by itself.

THE PRE-ORDAINED PROGRAMME

All children seem to pass through a series of similar 'stages' as they acquire language. The age at which different children reach each stage or 'milestone' varies considerably, but the relative chronology remains the same. The milestones are normally reached in the same order, though they may be nearer together for some children and farther apart for others.

Consequently, we can divide language development into a number of approximate phases. The chart below is highly over-simplified. The stages overlap, and the ages given are only a very rough guide − but it does give some idea of a child's likely progress.

Language stage	Beginning age
Crying	Birth
Cooing	6 weeks
Babbling	6 months
Intonation patterns	8 months
One-word utterances	1 year
Two-word utterances	18 months
Word inflections	2 years
Questions, negatives	2¼ years
Rare or complex constructions	5 years
Mature speech	10 years

In order to illustrate this progression we shall describe the successive phases which a typical (and non-existent) English child is likely to go through as she learns to speak. Let us call this child *Barbara* a name derived from the Greek word for 'foreigner' and meaning literally 'someone who says bar-bar, who talks gibberish'.

Barbara's first recognizable vocal activity was *crying*. 'The newborn baby comes into the world crying. Unless interrupted by sickness, the production of sounds is constant in human beings, from the first cry to the last breath' (Boysson-Bardies 1999: 37). During the first four weeks of her life, Barbara was truly:

An infant crying in the night:
An infant crying for the light:
And with no language but a cry.
Tennyson

A number of different types of cry could be detected. She cried with hunger when she wanted to be fed. She cried with pain when she had a tummy ache, and she cried with pleasure when she was fed, comfortable and lying in her mother's arms. However, strictly speaking, it is perhaps inaccurate to speak of crying as a 'language phase', because crying seems to be instinctive communication and may be more like an animal call system than a true language. Babies' pain cries are distinguishable from hunger cries everywhere in the world (Lester and Boukydis 1991). So although crying may help to strengthen the lungs and vocal cords (both of which are needed for speech), crying itself perhaps should not be regarded as part of true language development.

Barbara then passed through two reasonably distinct pre-language phases, a *cooing* phase and a *babbling* phase. Early researchers confused these stages and sometimes likened them to birdsong. The nineteenth-century scholar Hippolyte Taine noted of his daughter:

She takes delight in her twitter like a bird, she seems to smile with joy over it, but as yet it is only the twittering of a bird for she attaches no meaning to the sounds she utters.
(Taine 1877, in Bar-Adon and Leopold 1971: 21)

The first of these two phases, *cooing*, began when Barbara was approximately 6 weeks old. To a casual observer, she sounded as if she was saying GOO GOO. But cooing is difficult to describe. Some textbooks call it 'gurgling' or 'mewing'. The sound is superficially vowel-like, but the tracings produced on a sound spectrogram show that it is quite unlike the vowels produced by adults. Cooing seems to be universal. It may be the vocal equivalent of arm and leg waving. That is, just as babies automatically strengthen their muscles by kicking their legs and moving their arms about, so cooing may help them to gain control over their vocal apparatus.

Gradually, consonant-type sounds become interspersed in the cooing. By around 6 months, Barbara had reached the babbling stage. She gave the impression of uttering consonants and vowels together, at first as single syllables – but later strung together. The consonants were often made with the lips, or the teeth, so that the sequences sounded like MAMA, DIDIDI, or PAPAPA. On hearing these sounds, Barbara's parents confidently but wrongly assumed that she was addressing them. Such wishful thinking accounts for the fact that MAMA, PAPA and DADA are found as nursery words for mother and father all over the world (Jakobson 1962). Barbara soon learned that a cry of MAMA meant immediate attention – though she often used it to mean 'I am hungry' rather than to refer to a parent. This phenomenon has been noted by numerous researchers. Charles Darwin, for example, remarked that at the age of 1 year his son 'made the great step forward of inventing a word for food, namely, mum but what led him to it I did not discover' (Darwin 1877, in Bar-Adon and Leopold 1971: 28). Another investigator observed that his child called MAMA as a request for a piece of bread being buttered by himself, the father.

Throughout the babbling period Barbara seemed to enjoy experimenting with her mouth and tongue. She not only babbled, she blew bubbles, gurgled and spluttered. Superficially, she appeared to be uttering an enormous variety of exotic sounds. At one time, researchers wrongly assumed that children are naturally capable of producing every possible speech sound. A Canadian psychologist once commented:

> During this period, that peculiarly charming infantile babble begins, which, though only an 'awkward twittering', yet contains in rudimentary form nearly all the sounds which afterwards, by combination, yield the potent instrument of speech. A wonderful variety of sounds, some of which afterwards give the child difficulty when he tries to produce them, are now produced automatically, by purely impulsive exercise of the vocal muscles.
>
> (Tracy 1909, in Bar-Adon and Leopold 1971: 32)

More recent investigators have noted that the variety of sounds used in babbling is not particularly great. But because the child does not yet have complete control over his vocal organs, the noises are often unlike adult sounds, and seem exotic to an untrained observer. In general, babbling seems to be a period when a child experiments and gradually gains muscular control over his vocal organs. Many people claim that babbling is universal. But there are a few puzzling records of children who did not babble, which provide problems for this point of view. All we can say at the moment is that babbling is sufficiently widespread to be regarded as a normal stage of development.

Some investigators have tried to compare babbling babies who have been exposed to different languages. For example, Chinese babbles seem to be easily distinguishable from American, Russian and Arabic ones (Weir 1966). Because Chinese is a language which distinguishes words by means of a change in 'tone' or 'pitch', Chinese babies tend to produce monosyllabic utterances with much tonal variation. American babies produce polysyllabic babbles with intonation spread over the whole sequence. The non-tone babies sound superficially similar – though American mothers could often pick out the American baby, Russians the Russian baby, and Arabs the Arab baby. But the mothers could not distinguish between the babies babbling the other two languages. This research indicates that there may be a 'babbling drift', in which children's babbling gradually moves in the direction of the sounds they hear around them. These findings have been confirmed by several later studies (e.g. Cruttenden 1970; Vihman et al. 1985; Vihman 1996; Boysson-Bardies 1999). For example, French adults can pick out French baby babbles from non-French ones (Boysson-Bardies et al. 1984). In this respect babbling is clearly distinct from crying, which has no discernible relationship with any one language. As one researcher commented:

> The voices of children all over the world do, of course, have much in common; but listening to their babbling and first words, we see that the young language learners have already captured the characteristic colour and tone of their native languages.
>
> (Boysson-Bardies 1999: 68)

A question which perhaps should be asked at this stage is the following: how much can children actually distinguish of their parents' speech? It is sometimes assumed that babies hear merely a general mish-mash of sound, and only gradually notice details. However, infants may be capable of discriminating a lot more than we realize. They seem to be specially pre-set to notice the rhythms and sounds of speech, and probably begin to 'tune in' before birth. French infants as young as four days old can distinguish French from other languages, according to one group of researchers (Mehler et al. 1988). They found this out by giving babies pacifiers (dummies) to suck. It is well known that infants suck more strongly when they are aroused and interested in what they hear. These French newborns sucked at significantly higher rates when exposed to French, than to English or Italian. So they had possibly become acclimatized to the rhythm and intonation of French while still in the womb.

Using the same sucking technique, other investigators (Eimas et al. 1971; Eimas 1985) had already shown that babies between 1 and 4 months old can distinguish between P and B. The investigators started by playing a repeated B sound, then they switched to P. The babies suddenly increased their sucking rate, showing that they had noticed the alteration. So even though infants may not listen carefully to everything their parents say, they may well be capable of hearing a considerable amount from a very young age. Somewhat surprisingly, these results have been replicated with rhesus monkeys and chinchillas (Kuhl and Miller 1974, 1975; Morse 1976), and so may be due to the hearing mechanisms in certain types of mammals, and not just humans alone. In brief, a child's perception may be much sharper than had previously been supposed, even though it may not be equivalent to an adult's for some time (Fourcin 1978).

Simultaneously with babbling, and from around 8 or 9 months, Barbara began to imitate *intonation patterns*. These made her output sound so like speech that her mother sometimes said 'I'm sure she's talking, I just can't catch what she's saying.' An eighteenth-century German researcher observed of this stage: 'He attempted to imitate conversations, to which end he produced a profusion of incomprehensible sounds' (Tiedemann 1782, in Bar-Adon and Leopold 1971: 15). English mothers have noted that their children often use a 'question' intonation, with a rise in tone at the end of the sentence. This may be due to a normal parent's tendency to bend over the child, asking, 'What are you trying to say then?' 'Do you want some milk?' 'Do you know who this is?' and so on.

Somewhere between 1 year and 18 months Barbara began to utter *single words*. She continued to babble as well, though her babbling gradually diminished as true language developed (Stoel-Gammon and Cooper 1984). The number of single words acquired at around this time varies from child to child. Some have only four or five, others have around fifty. As an average child Barbara acquired about fifteen. Many of them were names of people and things, such as UF (woof) 'dog', DABA 'grandma', DA 'doll'.

Then as she neared her second birthday, she reached the more impressive *two-word stage*. From the time Barbara started to put words together she seemed to be in a state of 'language readiness', and mopped up language like a sponge. The most noticeable feature of this process was a dramatic increase in her vocabulary. By the time she was 2½ years old, she knew several hundred words. Meanwhile, there was a gradual but steady increase in her average or mean length of utterance – usually abbreviated to MLU. MLU is calculated in terms of grammatical items or 'morphemes': plural -S and past tense -D, for example, each count as one item and so do ordinary words such as MUMMY and BATH. Compound words such as BIRTHDAY and QUACK-QUACK also count as a single item (Brown 1973: 54). Many, but not all, researchers accept this as a useful gauge of progress – though the child with the longest utterances does not necessarily have the most grammatically advanced, or even the most grammatically correct utterances (Bates et al. 1988; Bennett-Kastor 1988).

The fact that a steady increase in MLU occurs from the age of around 2 onwards has been shown by Roger Brown of Harvard University, who carried out a detailed study of the speech development of three unacquainted children, Adam, Eve and Sarah – though he found that the chronological age at which different children reached an MLU stage differed considerably (Brown *et al.* 1968; Brown 1973). A comparison of Adam and Eve showed that Eve outstripped Adam by far. Eve's MLU was two items at around 20 months, three at 22 months and four at 28 months. Adam was over 26 months old before he achieved an MLU of two items. He was nearly 3 years old before his MLU reached three items and 3½ before it reached four items – a whole year behind Eve.

If we assume that Barbara is not as advanced as Eve, but ahead of Adam, she possibly had an MLU of two items a little before her second birthday, an MLU of three items at 2½, and four items around her third birthday.

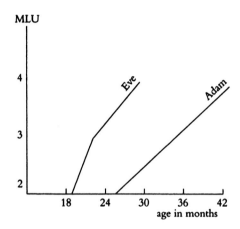

In the early part of the two-word stage, when she was around 2 years old, Barbara's speech was 'telegraphic'. She sounded as if she was sending urgent telegrams to her mother: WANT MILK, WHERE DUCK? As in a real telegram, she tended to preserve the nouns and verbs in the correct order, but omitted the 'little' words such as THE, A, HAS, HIS, AND. She also left out word endings, such as the plural -S or past tense -D, as in TWO SHOE and MILK SPILL.

How much do children understand at this time? Most parents confidently claim that children understand much more language than they can produce. But dog-owners sometimes make the same assumption about their pets, so how can anyone know for sure? Psychologists have discovered that children prefer pictures that match what they are hearing. This has inspired an ingenious experiment. A child is read out a sentence which corresponds to one of two pictures being shown on two television screens in front of him (Hirsh-Pasek and Golinkoff 1996). For example, the youngster might be shown a popular TV character, such as Cookie Monster, one of a family of 'Muppets' who feature in the American children's programme *Sesame Street*. Cookie Monster is a large fluffy creature who is covered in blue fur, has big bulging eyes and a voracious appetite for chocolate cookies. On one screen, Cookie Monster would be made to tickle Big Bird, another character from the same show. On the other screen, Big Bird would be tickling Cookie Monster. Then a sentence would be played, either 'Look! Cookie Monster is tickling Big Bird!' or 'Look! Big Bird is tickling Cookie Monster!' If the child understands the difference between the sentences, he or she tends to show a preference for the screen which matches the picture, and the time taken to focus on this can be measured. Such experiments have confirmed parental and researchers' intuitions, that children's comprehension is normally ahead of their production.

To return to Barbara, once the two-word stage is firmly in place, then, gradually, the 'little' words and inflections are added. 'All these, like an intricate work of ivy, begin to grow up between and upon the major construction blocks, the nouns and verbs' (Brown 1973: 249).

In this aspect of language, Barbara is following the same path of development as the Harvard child Adam, but at a slightly earlier age (Brown 1973: 271). Between the ages of 2 and 3½, Barbara acquired the following grammatical forms:

Age 2	Progressive -ING	I SINGING
	Plural -S	BLUE SHOES
	Copula AM, IS, ARE	HE IS ASLEEP
	Articles A, THE	HE IS A DOCTOR
Age 3	3rd person singular -S	HE WANTS AN APPLE
	Past tense -D	I HELPED MUMMY
	Full progressive AM, IS, ARE + -ING	I AM SINGING
	Shortened copula	HE'S A DOCTOR
	Shortened progressive	I'M SINGING

It is important to distinguish between the *emergence*, or first appearance of an ending, and its *acquisition*, its reliable use in the places where an adult would expect to find it. An ending can be considered acquired if it occurs in at least 90 per cent of the contexts where it is needed (Brown 1973: 258).

The actual age at which Barbara acquired each form is not significant because it varies widely from child to child. What is important and interesting is the *order* of acquisition. The sequence seems surprisingly similar among English-speaking children. Roger Brown noted that in the unacquainted Harvard children, the developmental order of these grammatical forms was 'amazingly consistent'. There were one or two minor variations: Sarah, for example, acquired the progressive -ING after the plural, whereas Adam and Eve acquired it before. But in all the children, both the progressive -ING and the plural -S occurred before the past tense, the third person singular -S, and the copula AM, IS, ARE.

Perhaps even more surprising, is the fact that in all the Harvard children the copula AM, IS, ARE as in I AM A DOCTOR developed before AM, IS, ARE when it was part of the progressive construction, for example, I AM SINGING. And the shortened copula as in HE'S A BEAR came before the shortened progressive, for example HE'S WALKING. This is quite an astonishing discovery. Although we might expect children to go through similar general lines of development, there seems to be no obvious reason why a variety of English children should correspond so closely in their acquisition of specific items. Possible reasons for this phenomenon will be discussed in Chapter 7.

A similar consistency of order is found in the acquisition of more complicated constructions, such as questions and negatives. For example, in the acquisition of WH- questions (questions beginning with WHAT, WHY, WHERE, WHO, etc.), we can safely assume that Barbara, like Adam, Eve and Sarah, went through three intermediate stages before she acquired them perfectly (Klima and Bellugi 1966). First of all, soon after her second birthday, she placed the WH-word in front of the rest of the sentence:

WHAT	MUMMY DOING?
WHY	YOU SINGING?
WHERE	DADDY GO?

A second stage occurred three or four months later when she added an auxiliary verb such as CAN or WILL to the main verb:

WHERE	YOU	WILL GO?
WHY	KITTY	CAN'T SEE?
WHY	YOU	DON'T KNOW?

Finally, before she was 3, she realized that the subject noun must change places with the auxiliary and produced correct sentences such as:

WHERE	WILL YOU	GO?
WHY	CAN'T KITTY	SEE?
WHY	DON'T YOU	KNOW?

Once again, the rather surprising finding that all English children tend to follow a similar pattern will be discussed later. As already noted, the actual *age* at which each stage is reached is irrelevant. It is the order which matters.

By the age of 3½, Barbara, like most children, was able to form most grammatical constructions – and her speech was reasonably intelligible to strangers. Her constructions were, however, less varied than those of an adult. For example, she tended not to use the 'full' passive such as THE MAN WAS HIT BY A BUS. But she was able to converse quite adequately on most topics.

By 5, she gave the superficial impression of having acquired language more or less perfectly. But this was an illusion. Language acquisition was still continuing, though more slowly. The grammar of a child of 5 differs to a perhaps surprising degree from adult grammar. But the 5-year-old is not usually aware of his shortcomings. In comprehension tests, children readily assign interpretations to the structures presented to them – but they are often the wrong ones. 'They do not, as they see it, fail to understand our sentences. They understand them, but they understand them wrongly' (Carol Chomsky 1969: 2). To demonstrate this point, the researcher showed a group of 5- to 8-year-olds a blindfolded doll and said: 'Is this doll hard to see or easy to see?' All the 5- and 6-year-olds said HARD TO SEE, and so did some of the 7- and 8-year-olds. The response of 6-year-old Lisa was typical:

Chomsky:	IS THIS DOLL EASY TO SEE OR HARD TO SEE?
Lisa:	HARD TO SEE.
Chomsky:	WILL YOU MAKE HER EASY TO SEE?
Lisa:	IF I CAN GET THIS UNTIED?
Chomsky:	WILL YOU EXPLAIN WHY SHE WAS HARD TO SEE?
Lisa: (to doll)	BECAUSE YOU HAD A BLINDFOLD OVER YOUR EYES.

Some psychologists have criticized this particular test. A child sometimes believes, ostrich-fashion, that if his own eyes are covered, others will not be able to see him. And he may be partly switching to the doll's viewpoint when he says a blindfolded doll is hard to see. But a re-run of this experiment using wolf and duck puppets, and sentences such as:

THE WOLF IS HARD TO BITE .
THE DUCK IS ANXIOUS TO BITE.

confirmed the original results (Cromer 1970). Children of 5 and 6 just do not realize that pairs of sentences such as THE RABBIT IS NICE TO EAT and THE RABBIT IS EAGER TO EAT have completely different underlying meanings.

In fact, the gap between child and adult speech lasts longer than was once realized. Detailed experiments on French children's understanding and use of the articles LE/LA 'the' and UN/UNE 'a' have shown quite surprising differences between child and adult usage, which remained in some cases up till the age of 12 (Karmiloff-Smith 1979).

But the discrepancies between Barbara's speech and that of the adults around her gradually disappeared over the next few years. By the age of about 11, Barbara exhibited a command of the structure of her language comparable to that of an adult. At the age of puberty, her language development was essentially complete, apart from vocabulary. She would continue to accumulate lexical items throughout her life.

The language milestones we have outlined tend to run parallel with physical development. Clearly, there is no essential correlation between language and motor development, since there are numerous examples of children who learn to talk, but never walk, and vice versa. However, researchers are agreed that in normal children the two often go together. Language stages are often loosely linked to physical milestones. The gradual change of cooing to babbling occurs around the time an infant begins to sit up. Children utter single words just before they start to walk. Grammar becomes complex as hand and finger co-ordination develops.

We now need to discuss one final point. Is it crucial for children to develop language at the age they normally do? According to the sixth and final characteristic of maturationally controlled behaviour, there may be a 'critical period' for its acquisition, though this is not essential. Is this true of language? Let us consider this matter.

IS THERE A 'CRITICAL PERIOD'?

Are humans like chaffinches? Or like canaries? Both these birds have to partially learn their songs. But a chaffinch's song becomes fixed and unalterable when it is around 15-months old. If the young bird has not heard any chaffinch song before that time, it never learns to sing normally (Thorpe 1972). But canaries can continue to alter their song for years (Nottebohm 1984; Marler 1988). Lenneberg argued that humans, like chaffinches, have a narrow 'critical period' set aside by nature for the acquisition of language. In his view, it lasts from toddler time to adolescence:

> Between the ages of two and three years language emerges by an interaction of maturation and self-programmed learning. Between the ages of three and the early teens the possibility for primary language acquisition continues to be good . . . After puberty, the ability for self-organization and adjustment to the physiological demands of verbal behaviour quickly declines. The brain

behaves as if it had become set in its ways and primary, basic skills not acquired by that time usually remain deficient for life.

(Lenneberg 1967: 158)

At one time, Lenneberg's views were widely accepted. Children clearly start talking at about the age of 2. And it seemed plausible that language ability ceased at around 13. Almost everybody can remember how difficult it was to learn French at school. Even the best pupils had a slightly odd accent, and made numerous grammatical mistakes. It was comforting to believe that there was a biological explanation for this. On closer inspection, however, the matter is not so clear cut.

Lenneberg appears to be right in outline, but wrong in some details. The early part of life is indeed important for language, though it all starts earlier than he assumed. Lenneberg argued for a link between a critical period and lateralization, the specialization of language to one side of the brain (Chapter 3). This process, in his view, happened slowly, between the ages of 2 and 14. He was probably wrong about this. Lateralization is established much earlier than he suggests. Even babies under a year old show some evidence of it. In one experiment, 5- and 6-month-old infants were presented with sounds and lip movements which were sometimes synchronized, sometimes not. They seemed to notice the synchrony only when the direction of their gaze showed that they were using their left hemisphere (MacKain et al. 1983). So lateralization is evident in the first few months of life. And as soon as young children can be tested with dichotic listening (Chapter 3), around age 2½ or 3, they seem to be using their left hemisphere for language (Kinsbourne and Hiscock 1987).

Lenneberg also claimed that if a child under the age of 2 sustained severe damage to the left (language) hemisphere of the brain, speech would develop normally, though it would be controlled by the right hemisphere. The 'critical period' had in his view not yet begun. But he was wrong to assume that children under 2 would not be affected by left hemisphere damage. On the contrary, babies who have had this half of their brain removed in the first year of life have considerable language problems (Dennis 1983; Vargha-Khadem and Polkey 1992). Severe left hemisphere injury usually results in permanent linguistic impairment, whatever the age of the patient.

But Lenneberg is right that a huge language surge occurs at around the age of 2. And his claim that the language of younger children is less severely impaired by brain damage than the speech of older ones appears to be true (Vargha-Khadem et al. 1985). This is not surprising. Young brains have greater powers of recovery. Infant monkeys with brain damage recover faster than older ones (Goldman-Rakic 1982).

But does language come to a shuddering halt around adolescence, as Lenneberg believed? The cases of three socially isolated children, Isabelle,

Genie and Chelsea, provide superficial support for this view. All three were cut off from language until long after the time they would have acquired it, had they been brought up in normal circumstances.

Isabelle was the illegitimate child of a deaf mute. She had no speech, and made only a croaking sound when she was found in Ohio in the 1930s at the age of 6½. Mother and child had spent most of the time alone in a darkened room. But once found, Isabelle's progress was remarkable:

> Isabelle passed through the usual stages of linguistic development at a greatly accelerated rate. She covered in two years the learning that ordinarily occupies six years. By the age of eight and a half, Isabelle was not easily distinguishable from ordinary children of her age
>
> (Brown 1958: 192)

Genie, however, was not so lucky. She was not found until she was nearly 14. Born in April 1957, she had lived most of her life in bizarre and inhuman conditions:

> From the age of twenty months, Genie had been confined to a small room . . . She was physically punished by her father if she made any sounds. Most of the time she was kept harnessed into an infant's potty chair; otherwise she was confined in a homemade sleeping bag in an infant's crib covered with wire mesh.
>
> (Curtiss et al. 1974: 529)

When found, she was totally without language. She began acquiring speech well after the onset of adolescence – after the proposed 'critical period'.

Although she learnt to speak in a rudimentary fashion, she progressed more slowly than normal children (Curtiss 1977). For example, ordinary children go through a stage in which they utter two words at a time (WANT MILK, MUMMY PLAY), which normally lasts a matter of weeks.

Genie's two-word stage lasted for more than five months. Again, ordinary children briefly pass through a phase in which they form negative sentences by putting the word NO in front of the rest of the utterance, as in NO MUMMY GO, NO WANT APPLE. Genie used this primitive form of negation for over two years. Normal children start asking questions beginning with words such as WHERE, WHAT, at the two-word stage (WHERE TEDDY?). Genie found this kind of question impossible to grasp, occasionally making inappropriate attempts such as WHERE IS STOP SPITTING? The only aspect of speech in which Genie outstripped normal children was her ability to learn vocabulary. She knew many more words than ordinary children at a comparable stage of grammatical development. However, the ability to memorize lists of items is not evidence of full language capacity, even the chimps Washoe and Sarah found this relatively easy. The rules of grammar are crucially important, and this is what Genie found difficult. Her slow progress compared with that of Isabelle seemed to provide evidence in favour of a 'cut-off' point for language acquisition. We must be cautious, however. Two individual cases cannot provide firm proof, especially as each is problematical. Isabelle was not studied by linguists, so her speech may have been more deficient than was reported. Genie, on the other hand, showed some evidence of brain damage. Tests suggested that her left hemisphere was atrophied, which meant that she was functioning with only one half of her brain, the half not usually associated with language. The final chapter of Genie's story is depressing. Her mother removed her from the care of those who conversed with her. Left hospitalized and alone, she stopped talking. 'It's a fated case', commented one of her psychiatrists. 'You have a second chance in a situation like that – a chance to rescue the child. But you don't get a third chance, and that's the situation now' (Rymer 1993: 223).

Chelsea was another late starter (Curtiss 1988). She is an adult with hearing problems who started learning language in her early thirties. Like Genie, her vocabulary is good, but her syntax is poor. She says things such as: THE WOMAN IS BUS THE GOING, ORANGE TIM CAR IN, BANANA THE EAT. Chelsea's strange syntax could be due to her late start. But it might also be because of her defective hearing. So neither Genie nor Chelsea provides convincing proof of a 'cut-off' point for language acquisition. Each of them has severe non-linguistic problems, which could account for their rudimentary language.

According to Lenneberg, further evidence in favour of a critical period is provided by mentally handicapped children, in particular, Down's syndrome cases (Lenneberg 1967). These follow the same general path of development as normal children, but much more slowly. Lenneberg claimed that they never catch up because their ability to learn language slows down dramatically at puberty. But some researchers have disputed this claim, arguing that the children's language ceases to develop through lack of stimulation. Moreover, further work suggests that Down's syndrome children have a built-in endpoint to their ability. They may reach this ceiling at any age, though often quite a long time before adolescence (Gleitman 1984).

To summarize so far, all the arguments for a sudden onset or final endpoint of the supposed critical period are unconvincing. It may be better to speak of a 'sensitive period' – a time early in life when acquiring language is easiest, and which tails off gradually, though never entirely.

Early exposure to language is therefore important. Most of us envy the linguistic ability of young children exposed to two or more languages. They grow up fluent in all of them. Older children hardly ever sound like native-born speakers, even when they are talking the same language. Six Canadians whose families moved to Britain demonstrate this. The youngest, age 7 when he arrived, was eventually almost indistinguishable from his English peers. But those over the age of 14 'appear to be heading for life-times with non-native accents' (Chambers 1995: 163).

Sign language also shows the need for an early start. Deaf children who have deaf parents start signing earlier, and end up more proficient than deaf young-sters with hearing parents. Nicaragua's deaf community dramatically demon-strates the advantage of starting young. Here, young deaf signers have developed a partial sign language into a 'full' one in under 20 years (Kegl 1994). Before 1980, signing in Nicaragua was minimal, a hotchpotch of different signs. Some 15 or so years later, a whole language had emerged. An outline system learned by the first generation was picked up and elaborated by the next generation. A 7-year-old deaf boy called Santos, for example, learned rudimentary signing from his deaf aunt and uncle. He soon progressed beyond them: 'His signing was the most fluid and fluent signing I have seen in Nicaragua' commented one researcher (Senghas 1994: 38), adding that 'older signers can look to younger children like Santos who lead the way'. These Nicaraguan signers show how fast humans can acquire and even devise a language system for themselves when they are young. Ildefonso, a deaf languageless adult from rural Mexico had far more trouble acquiring signs (Schaller 1995).

But some questions remain. First, is the sensitive period a specifically linguistic one, as Lenneberg suggested, or a more general one? This is unclear, though several neurologists favour the latter: 'The period between age two and the onset of puberty is one of extreme neural plasticity. There is, however, little . . . that suggests a specifically linguistic type of mechanism' is a typical comment (Müller 1996). Further work needs to be done on this.

A second question is this: how does child sensitivity to language work, given how difficult language learning seems to be for most adults? A 'natural sieve' hypothesis is one idea. Very young children may be able to extract only certain limited features from what they hear, and may automatically filter out many complexities (Newport 1991). Later learners may have lost this inbuilt filter, and be less able to cope as everything pours over them simultaneously. A 'tuning-in' hypothesis is another, overlapping possibility. At each age, a child may be attuned to some particular aspect of language (Locke 1997). Infants may be tuned in to the sounds, older children to the syntax, and after age ten, the vocabulary remains a major concern (Aitchison 1997).

Selective attention of this type fits in well with what we know about biologically programmed behaviour. Children are innately guided to pick out certain features from the sound-stream (or sign-stream), just as bees are instinctively guided to pick out flowers. Some learning is involved for bees, because flowers are so different from one another. But bees end up flying to clover and roses, rather than to postboxes or lamp posts, just as children acquire language, rather than donkey hee-haws or the twitter of blackbirds (Gould and Marler 1987).

In this chapter, therefore, we have shown that language seems to have the characteristics of biologically programmed behaviour. It emerges before it is necessary, and its emergence cannot be accounted for either by an external event, or by a sudden decision taken by the child. Direct teaching and intensive practice have relatively little effect. Acquisition follows a regular sequence of milestones which can be loosely correlated with other aspects of the child's development. In other words, there is an internal mechanism both to trigger it off and to regulate it. There is a sensitive period for acquiring it, with early exposure a strong advantage, since younger brains have more plasticity.

However, it would be wrong to think of language as something which is governed only by internal mechanisms. These mechanisms require external stimulation in order to work properly. The child needs a rich verbal environment during the acquisition period.

This suggests that the so-called nature–nurture controversy mentioned in Chapter 1 may be misconceived. Both sides are right: nature triggers off the behaviour, and lays down the framework, but careful nurture is needed for it to reach its full potential. The dividing line between 'natural' and 'nurtured' behaviour is by no means as clear cut as was once thought. In other words, language is 'natural' behaviour – but it still has to be carefully 'nurtured' in order to reach its full potential. In modern terminology, the behaviour is *innately guided*. Or, as another writer expressed it in the title of his book, we should be talking about *Nature via Nurture* (Ridley 2003).

But, although we have now shed considerable light on the general problem of innateness, and the difficulty of separating natural from nurtured behaviour, we have not yet tried to answer the crucial question, exactly what, if anything, could be innate? We noted in Chapter 1 that Chomsky argued in favour of postulating a 'rich internal structure'. What in his opinion does this structure consist of? And what do Chomsky's opponents say? This is the topic considered in the next chapter.

5

A BLUEPRINT IN THE BRAIN?
Could any linguistic information conceivably be innate?

There are very deep and restrictive principles that determine the nature of human language and are rooted in the specific character of the human mind.
Chomsky, *Language and Mind*

Young children must learn . . . the set of linguistic conventions used by those around them . . . for any given language . . . The human species is biologically prepared for this prodigious task . . ., but this preparation cannot be too specific, as human children must be flexible enough to learn not only all of the different words and conventional expressions of any language but also all the different types of abstract constructional patterns . . . It thus takes many years.
Tomasello, *Constructing a Language*

It is relatively easy to show that humans are innately predisposed to acquire language. The hard part is finding out exactly *what* is innate. People have indulged in speculation about this for centuries. Over two thousand years ago the Egyptian king Psammetichus had a theory that if a child was isolated from human speech, the first word he spontaneously uttered would come from the world's oldest inhabitants. Naturally he hoped this would be Egyptian. He gave instructions for two newborn children to be brought up in total isolation. When eventually the children uttered the word BEKOS, Psammetichus discovered to his dismay that this was the Phrygian word for 'bread'. He reluctantly concluded that the Phrygians were more ancient than the Egyptians.

Nobody takes Psammetichus's theory seriously today – especially as the few reliable accounts we have of children brought up without human contact indicate that they were totally without speech when they were found. The famous French boy, Victor of Aveyron, who was discovered naked rooting for acorns in the Caune woods in 1797, did not speak Phrygian or any other language. He merely grunted like an animal.

Although the speculations of Psammetichus can safely be ignored, the ideas of Noam Chomsky on the topic of innateness were for a long time taken seriously. He claimed that for language acquisition to be possible, a child must be endowed with a 'rich internal structure', and the biological evidence examined in the last two chapters suggest that his ideas cannot be summarily dismissed. Chomsky's notion of a rich innate schema contrasted strongly with the point of view popularly held earlier in the century that children are born with 'blank sheets' as far as language is concerned. Consequently, some people considered Chomsky as someone who had set out to shock the world with outrageous and novel proposals. But Chomsky denied this. He pointed out that he was following in the footsteps of eighteenth-century 'rationalist' philosophers, who believed in the existence of 'innate ideas'. Such philosophers held that 'beyond the peripheral processing mechanisms, there are innate ideas and principles of various kinds that determine the form of the acquired knowledge in what may be a rather restricted and highly organized way' (Chomsky 1965: 48). Descartes, for example, suggested that when a child sees a triangle, the imperfect triangle before his eyes immediately reminds him of a true triangle, since we already possess within us the idea of a true triangle.

But leaving philosophical predecessors aside, what exactly does (or did) Chomsky regard as innate? In his words: 'What are the initial assumptions concerning the nature of language that the child brings to language learning, and how detailed and specific is the innate scheme?' (Chomsky 1965: 27).

Chomsky gave an explicit account of his early views in his (now outdated) linguistic classic *Aspects of the Theory of Syntax* (1965), though he has repeated them in a number of other places with minor variations. But in recent years he has changed his mind on various points, sometimes quite fundamentally. His later views were set out in *Knowledge of Language: Its Nature, Origin and Use* (1986), later ones still in *The Minimalist Program* (1995) and further views in *On Nature and Language* (2002). The following account begins with his 1965 statements. It then explains why he came to regard these as unsatisfactory, and outlines his more recent ideas. It then discusses why Chomsky's ideas are gradually fading from the forefront of research, and those of later scholars, such as Michael Tomasello, are taking over.

CHOMSKY'S EARLY IDEAS: LAD AND LAS

Chomsky has never regarded his proposals on the matter of innateness as definitive: 'For the present we cannot come at all close to making a hypothesis that is rich, detailed and specific enough to account for the fact of language acquisition' (1965: 27). Nevertheless, his ideas were specific enough to be interesting.

Chomsky started out with the basic assumption that anybody who acquires a language is not just learning an accumulation of random utterances but a set of 'rules' or underlying principles for forming speech patterns: 'The person who has acquired knowledge of a language has internalized a system of rules that relate sound and meaning in a particular way' (Chomsky 1972b: 26). These 'rules' enable a speaker to produce an indefinite number of novel utterances, rather than straight repetitions of old ones. As we saw in Chapters 1 and 2, an essential characteristic of language is its creativity. People do not just run through a repertoire of stereotyped phrases when they speak. Instead, they are continually producing novel utterances such as 'My baby swallowed four ladybirds', or 'Serendipity upsets me'. But where do the rules come from? How do speakers discover them? Somehow, children have to construct their own set of rules from the jumble of speech they hear going on around them. This is a formidable task. Chomsky pointed out that children are to some extent in the same situation as a linguist faced with an unknown language. Both child and linguist are surrounded by a superficially unintelligible confusion of sound which they must somehow sort out.

So let us first consider how a linguist deals with this unknown language situation. She possibly starts by finding simple sound sequences which refer to single objects, such as TREE, NOSE, CONGER EEL. But this stage is not particularly interesting from a syntactic point of view. Learning a few dozen vocabulary items is a relatively simple task, as is clear from the ease with which the chimp Washoe managed to do this. In addition, Genie, the Californian teenager discussed in Chapter 4, found the acquisition of vocabulary easy – it was the grammatical rules that slowed her down. For a linguist working on an exotic language, the interesting stage is likely to come when she starts to notice recurring syntactic patterns among the data. As soon as she has found some, she begins to make guesses or *hypotheses* concerning the principles which underlie the patterns. For example, suppose she repeatedly finds the utterances WOKKI SNIZZIT, WOKKI UGGIT and WOKKI SNIFFIT. She might hazard, as a first guess that the sequence WOKKI always has to be followed by a sequence which ends in -IT. But if, later, she finds utterances such as LUKKIT WOKKI and UKKING WOKKI, she would have to abandon her original, oversimple theory, and form a new, more complex hypothesis to account for the fresh data. She continues this process of forming hypotheses, testing them, then abandoning them when they prove inadequate until, ideally, she has compiled a set of rules which can account for all the possible sequences of the language she is studying.

Children, according to Chomsky (1965), construct an internalized grammar in the same way. They look for regularities in the speech they hear going on around them, then make guesses as to the rules which underlie the patterns. Their first guess will be a simple one. The second amended hypothesis will be more complex, the third, more elaborate still. Gradually their mental grammar will become more sophisticated. Eventually their internalized rules will cover all the possible utterances of the language. Fodor (1966: 109) described the situation clearly:

> Like the scientist, the child finds himself with a finite body of observations, some of which are almost certain to be unsystematic. His problem is to discover regularities in these data that, at the very least, can be relied upon to hold however much additional data is added. Characteristically the extrapolation takes the form of the construction of a theory that simultaneously marks the systematic similarities among the data at various levels of abstraction, permits the rejection of some of the observational data as unsystematic, and automatically provides a general characterization of the possible future observations.

If this hypothesis-testing view of language acquisition is correct, children must be endowed with an innate *hypothesis-making device* which enables them, like miniature scientists, to construct increasingly complex hypotheses.

However, there are a number of differences between a linguist working on an unknown language, and a child acquiring language for the first time. The linguist has always had considerably more help at his disposal. He could say to a native speaker of the language he is working on, 'Does LEGLESS DADDY-LONG-LEGS make sense?' 'Is ATE UP IT grammatical?' 'Is PLAYING CARDS ambiguous?' and so on. The child cannot do this. Yet the amazing fact remains: it is the child who acquires the complete grammar. No linguist has ever written a perfect grammar of any language. This suggests that by itself, an internal hypothesis-making device is not sufficient to account for the acquisition of language. The child must have some extra knowledge at his disposal. It cannot be knowledge about any particular language because babies learn all languages with equal ease. A Chinese baby brought up in England will learn English as easily as an English baby in China will learn Chinese. The wired-in knowledge must, therefore, said Chomsky, consist of *language universals*. Children learn language so fast and efficiently because they 'know' in outline what languages look like. They know what is, and what is not, a possible language. All they have

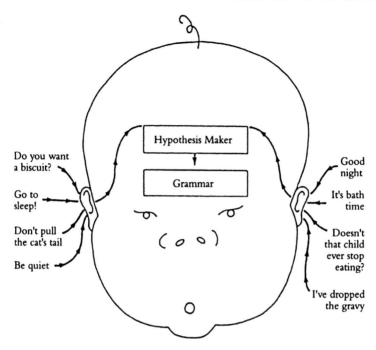

to discover is which language they are being exposed to. In Chomsky's words, his theory:

> attributes tacit knowledge of linguistic universals to the child. It proposes that the child approaches the data with the presumption that they are drawn from a language of a certain antecedently well-defined type, his problem being to determine which of the (humanly) possible languages is that of the community in which he is placed.
>
> (Chomsky 1965: 27)

The child is perhaps like a pianist waiting to sight-read a piece of music. The pianist will know in advance that the piece will have a rhythmic beat, but she will not know whether it is in two, three or four time until she sees it. She will know that the notes are within a certain range – but she will not know in what order or combinations they come. But it is not very satisfactory to speak airily of 'innate linguistic universals'. What *are* these shadowy phenomena?

Language universals, Chomsky suggested (1965), are of two basic types, *substantive* and *formal*. Substantive universals represent the fundamental 'building blocks' of language, the substance out of which it is made, while formal universals are concerned with the form or shape of a grammar. An analogy might make this distinction clearer. If, hypothetically, Eskimos were born with an innate knowledge of igloo-building they would have *two* kinds of knowledge. On the one hand, they would know in advance that the *substance* out of which igloos are made is ice and snow, just as thrushes automatically know that their nests are made of twigs, not bricks or worms or glass. On the other hand, their innate knowledge of igloo-building would include the information that igloos are round in *shape*, not square or diamond-shaped or sausage-like, just as thrushes instinctively build round nests, not ones shaped like bathtubs.

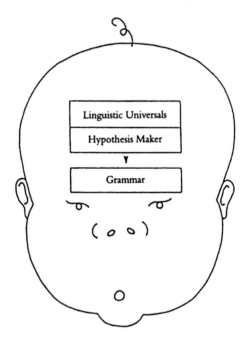

To return to the substantive universals of human language, a child might know instinctively the possible set of sounds to be found in speech. She would automatically reject sneezes, belches, hand-clapping and foot-stamping as possible sounds, but accept B, O, G, L, and so on. She would dismiss PGPGPG as a possible word, but accept POG, PIG, PEG or PAG.

But the idea of *substantive* universals was not particularly new. For a long time linguists had assumed that all languages have nouns, verbs and sentences even though the exact definitions of these terms is in dispute. And for a long time linguists have been trying to identify a 'universal phonetic alphabet' which 'defines the set of possible signals from which signals of a particular language are drawn' (Chomsky 1972b: 121). Such a notion is not very surprising, since humans all possess similar vocal organs. More revolutionary were the *formal* universals proposed by Chomsky. These were concerned with the form or shape of a grammar, including the way in which the different parts relate to one another.

According to Chomsky, children would 'know' in advance how their internalized grammar must be organized. It must have a set of *phonological* rules for characterizing sound patterns and a set of *semantic* rules for dealing with meaning, linked by a set of *syntactic* rules dealing with word arrangement.

SEMANTIC RULES	SYNTACTIC RULES	PHONOLOGICAL RULES

Furthermore, children would instinctively realize that in its rules language makes use of *structure-dependent* operations. This, as noted in Chapter 1 involves at least two types of knowledge: first, an understanding of hierarchical structure – the notion that several words can fill the same slot as one:

COWS	EAT	GRASS
LARGE BROWN COWS	HAVE EATEN UP	THE GRASS

Second, it involves a realization that each slot functions as a unit that can be moved around (though with minor extra adjustments):

3	2	1
THE GRASS	HAS BEEN EATEN	UP BY LARGE BROWN COWS

Furthermore (as outlined in Chapter 1) Chomsky at one time assumed that every sentence had an 'inner' hidden *deep structure* and an outer manifest *surface structure*. The two levels of structure were linked by rules known as *transformations*. As he explained:

> The grammar of English will generate, for each sentence, a deep structure, and will contain rules showing how this deep structure is related to a surface structure. The rules expressing the relation of deep and surface structure are called 'grammatical transformations'.
>
> (Chomsky 1972b: 166)

According to this view, several sentences that were quite different on the surface could be related to *one* deep structure. The four sentences:

CHARLES CAPTURED A HEFFALUMP.
A HEFFALUMP WAS CAPTURED BY CHARLES.
IT WAS A HEFFALUMP WHICH CHARLES CAPTURED.
WHAT CHARLES CAPTURED WAS A HEFFALUMP.

were all related to a similar underlying structure.

Deep structure (simplified)

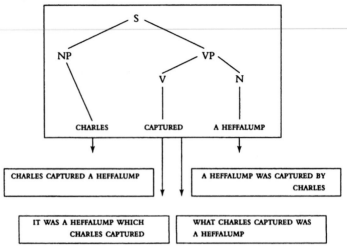

Alternatively, different deep structures could undergo transformations which made them similar on the surface, as in:

THE RABBIT IS READY TO EAT.

which could either mean that the rabbit was hungry, or that it was about to be eaten.

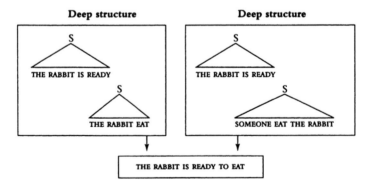

Chomsky assumed that children would somehow 'know' about deep structures, surface structures and transformations. They would realize that they had to reconstruct for themselves deep structures which were *never* visible on the surface.

To summarize so far, we have been outlining Chomsky's 'classic' (1965) viewpoint. He assumed that children were endowed with an innate hypothesis-making device, which enabled them to make increasingly complex theories about the rules which would account for the language they heard going on around them. In making these hypotheses, children were guided by an inbuilt knowledge of language universals. These provided a 'blueprint' for language, so that the child would know in outline what a possible language looked like. This involved, first, information about the 'building blocks' of language, such as the set of possible sounds. Second, it entailed information about the way in which the components of a grammar were related to one another, and restrictions on the form of the rules. In particular, Chomsky argued that children automatically knew that language involved two levels of syntax – a deep and a surface level, linked by 'transformations'. And (as he later argued) children also knew about some innately inbuilt constraints on the form sentences could take. With this help a child could speedily sift through the babble of speech he heard around him, and hypothesize plausible rules which would account for it.

Children needed to be equipped with this information, he claimed, because the 'primary linguistic data' (the data children are exposed to) was likely to be 'deficient in various respects' (1965: 201). It consisted (he controversially assumed) 'of a finite amount of information about sentences, which, further-more, must be rather restricted in scope . . . and fairly degenerate in quality' (1965: 31).

But another problem arose. There may be more than one possible set of rules which will fit the data. How does a child choose between them? At one time, Chomsky suggested that children must in addition be equipped with an *evaluation* procedure which would allow them to choose between a number of possible grammars, that is, some kind of measure which would enable them to weigh up one grammar against another, and discard the less efficient. This was perhaps the least satisfactory of Chomsky's proposals, and many psycholinguists regarded it as wishful thinking. There were no plausible suggestions as to how this evaluation procedure might work, beyond a vague notion that a child might prefer short grammars to long ones. But even this was disputed, since it is equally possible that children have very messy, complicated grammars, which only gradually become simple and streamlined (e.g. Schlesinger 1967). So the problem of narrowing down the range of possible grammars was left unsolved.

According to Chomsky (1965 version), then, a hypothesis-making device, linguistic universals and (perhaps) an evaluation procedure constituted an innately endowed Language Acquisition Device (LAD) or Language Acquisition System (LAS), (LAD for boys and LAS for girls, as one linguist facetiously remarked). With the aid of LAD any child could learn any language with relative ease – and without such an endowment language acquisition would be impossible.

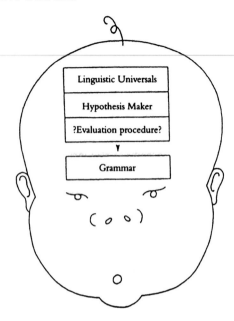

Over the years, Chomsky realized that he needed to specify further restrictions on his grammar, of which (he assumed) children were 'naturally' aware. Youngsters would know that there were constraints on the ways in which deep structures could be altered by the transformational rules. They would be automatically aware of some quite complex constraints on rearrangement possibilities. For example, consider the sentence:

IGNATIUS HAS STOLEN A PIG.

If we wanted to ask which pig was involved, we would normally bring the phrase about the pig to the front:

WHICH PIG HAS IGNATIUS STOLEN?

But supposing the original sentence had been:

ANGELA KNOWS WHO HAS STOLEN A PIG.

It would then be impossible to bring the 'pig' phrase to the front. We could not say:

*WHICH PIG ANGELA KNOWS WHO HAS STOLEN?

According to Chomsky 'some general principle of language determines which phrases can be questioned' (1980: 44), and children would somehow 'know' this.

However, this relatively straightforward system disappeared from Chomsky's later writings. What made him change his mind, and what did he propose instead?

CHOMSKY'S LATER VIEWS: SETTING SWITCHES

Suppose children knew in advance that the world contained two hemispheres, a northern and a southern. In order to decide which they were in, they simply needed to watch water swirling down the plughole of a bath, since they were pre-wired with the information that it swirled one way in the north, and another way in the south. Once they had observed a bath plughole, then they would automatically know a whole lot of further information: an English child who discovered bathwater swirling clockwise would know that it had been placed in the northern hemisphere. It could then predict that the sun would be in the south at the hottest part of the day, and that it would get hotter as one travelled southwards. An Australian child who noticed water rotating anticlockwise would immediately realize the opposite.

This scenario is clearly science fiction. But it is the sort of situation Chomsky then envisaged for children acquiring language. They were pre-wired with a number of possible options which language might choose. They would need to be exposed to relatively little language, merely some crucial trigger, in order to find out which route their own language had chosen. Once they had discovered this, they would automatically know, through pre-programming, a considerable amount about how languages of this type work.

Let us consider how Chomsky hit on such an apparently bizarre idea.

Learnability remained Chomsky's major concern. How is language learnable, when the crumbs and snippets of speech heard by children could not possibly (in Chomsky's view) provide sufficient clues to the final system which is acquired? There seemed no way in which the child could narrow down its guesses sufficiently to arrive at the grammar of a human language. The learnability problem has also been called the 'logical problem of language acquisition': how, logically, do children acquire language when they do not have enough information at their disposal to do so?

The logical answer is that they have an enormous amount of information pre-wired into them: the innate component must be considerably more extensive than was previously envisaged. Children, therefore, are born equipped with *Universal Grammar*, or UG for short: 'UG is a characterization of these innate, biologically determined principles, which constitute one component of the human mind – the language faculty' (Chomsky 1986: 24).

This is 'a distinct system of the mind/brain' (1986: 25), separate from general intelligence.

UG was envisaged as more structured than the old and somewhat vaguer notion of innate universals. It was 'a computational system that is rich and narrowly constrained in structure and rigid in its essential operations' (1986: 43). Let us see how it differed.

Imagine an orchestra, playing a symphony. The overall effect is of a luscious tropical jungle, a forest of intertwined melodies. Yet, if one looks at the score, and contemplates the various musical instruments, one gets a surprise. Each instrument has its own limitations, such as being confined to a certain range of notes. Most of the instruments are playing a relatively simple tune. The overall, intricate Turkish carpet effect is due to the skilled interaction of numerous simple components.

In 1986, then, Chomsky viewed UG and language as something like an orchestra playing a symphony. It consisted of a number of separate components or *modules*, a term borrowed from computers. Chomsky noted: 'UG . . . has the modular structure that we regularly discover in investigation of cognitive systems' (1986: 146). Within each module, there were sets of principles. Each principle was fairly straightforward when considered in isolation. The principles became complex when they interacted with those from other modules.

The general framework was not at that time entirely new. He still retained the notion of deep and surface structure (or D-structure and S-structure as he started to call them). But the number of transformations was drastically reduced – possibly to only one! But this one, which moved structures about, was subject to very severe constraints. Innate principles specified what could or could not happen, and these were quite rigid. Chomsky's major concern, therefore, was in specifying the principles operating within each module, and showing how they interacted.

How many modules were involved, and what they all did, was never fully specified. But the general idea behind the grammar was reasonably clear. For example, one module might specify which items could be moved, and how far, as with the word WHO, which can be moved to the front of the sentence:

WHO DID SEBASTIAN SAY OSBERT BIT?

Another might contain information as to how to interpret a sentence such as:

SEBASTIAN SAID OSBERT BIT HIM INSTEAD OF HIMSELF.

This would contain principles showing why SEBASTIAN had to be linked to the word HIM, and OSBERT attached to the word HIMSELF. These two types of principles would interact in a sentence such as:

WHO DID SEBASTIAN SAY OSBERT BIT INSTEAD OF HIMSELF?

Most of the principles, and the way they interleaved, were innately specified and fairly rigid.

However, a narrowly constrained rigid UG presented another dilemma. Why are not all languages far more similar? Chomsky argued that UG was only partially 'wired-up'. There were option points within the modules, with switches that could be set to a fixed number of positions, most probably two. Children would know in advance what the available options are. This would be pre-programmed and part of a human's genetic endowment. A child would there-fore scan the data available to him or her, and on the basis of a limited amount of evidence would know which way to throw the switch. In Chomsky's words:

> We may think of UG as an intricately structured system, but one that is only partially 'wired-up'. The system is associated with a finite set of switches, each of which has a finite number of positions (perhaps two). Experience is required to set the switches. When they are set the system functions.
>
> (Chomsky 1986: 146)

Chomsky supposed that the switches must be set on the basis of quite simple evidence, and that a switch, once set in a particular direction, would have quite complex consequences throughout the language. These conse-quences would automatically be known by the child.

As an example, Chomsky suggested that children might know in advance that language structures have one key word, or *head*. They then had to find out the position of the subsidiary words (or *modifiers*). These could be placed either before or after the head. In English, heads are generally placed before modifiers:

Head	Modifier
DROP	THAT SLIPPER!
DOWN	THE DRAIN

So we get sentences such as:

THE DOG DROPPED THE SLIPPER DOWN THE DRAIN.

A language such as Turkish would reverse this order, and say the equivalent of THAT SLIPPER DROP, THE DRAIN DOWN. The end result is that Turkish looks quite different on the surface. It would say, as it were:

THE DOG THE DRAIN DOWN THE SLIPPER DROPPED.

However, this superficial strangeness is to a large extent the result of one simple option, choosing to place modifiers on a different side of the head.

UG, then, was envisaged as a two-tier system: a hard-wired basic layer of universal *principles*, applicable to all languages, and a second layer which was only partially wired in. This contained a finite set of options which had to be decided between on the basis of observation. These option possibilities were known as *parameters*, and Chomsky spoke of the need 'to fix the parameters of UG' (Chomsky 1981: 4). The term *parameter* is a fairly old mathematical one, which is also used in the natural sciences. In general, it refers to a fixed property which can vary in certain ways. For example, one might talk of 'temperature' and 'air pressure' as being 'parameters' of the atmosphere. So in language, a parameter is a property of language (such as head position, discussed above) whose values could vary from language to language.

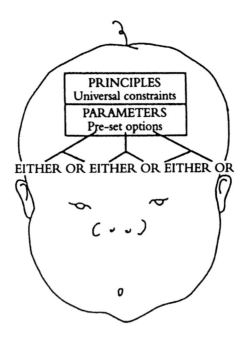

We were therefore dealing with 'a system of unifying principles that is fairly rich in deductive structure but with parameters to be fixed by experience' (Chomsky 1980: 66). The interlocking nature of the system would ensure that minor alterations would have multiple consequences: 'In a tightly integrated theory with a fairly rich internal structure, change in a single parameter may have complex effects, with proliferating consequences in various parts of the grammar' (Chomsky 1981: 6). In particular, 'a few changes in parameters yield typologically different languages' (Chomsky 1986: 152). This whole idea has become known as the 'principles and parameters' or 'P and P' approach.

Once the values of the parameters are set, 'the whole system is operative' (Chomsky 1986: 146), and a child has acquired its *core language*. Only minor peripheral elements now remain to be learned:

> Suppose we distinguish *core language* from *periphery*, where a core language is a system determined by fixing values for the parameters of UG, and the periphery is whatever is added on in the system actually represented in the mind/brain of a speaker-hearer.
>
> (Chomsky 1986: 147)

In this system 'what we "know innately" are the principles of the various subsystems . . . and the manner of their interaction, and the parameters associated with these principles. What we learn are the values of the parameters and the elements of the periphery' (Chomsky 1986: 150).

Children had relatively little to do in this type of system: 'We view the problem of language acquisition as . . . one of fixing parameters in a largely determined system' (Chomsky 1986: 151). Indeed, many of the old rules which children had to learn just appeared automatically, because the principles underlying them were there already. Take the 'rule' that objects follow verbs, as in THROW THE BALL, EAT YOUR CAKE. The child might 'know' that languages behave consistently as far as heads and modifiers are concerned (as discussed above). Once the 'head' parameter is set, then the rule appears without any tedious learning, as does the rule that prepositions precede nouns, as in IN THE BATH, ON THE TABLE. As Chomsky noted: 'There has been a gradual shift of focus from the study of rule systems . . . to the study of systems of principles, which appear to occupy a much more central position in determining the character and variety of possible human languages' (Chomsky 1982: 7–8). If this minimal effort by the child is correct, then it makes sense to think of the language system as a 'mental organ', which grows mainly by itself, in the same way that the heart grows in the body. Chomsky became increasingly concerned with understanding the principles which underlay this growth.

PARING IT DOWN STILL FURTHER

Chomsky tried to become like a biologist who no longer looks in turn at a human heart, then at a human elbow, but instead aims to understand the body as a whole. Or, as he suggested, he was like someone trying to go beyond the simple observation that apples fall to the ground because that is where apples inevitably end up, and instead, tries to understand the principle of gravity. In his words:

> If we are satisfied that an apple falls to the ground because that is its natural place, there will be no serious science of mechanics. The same is true if one is satisfied with traditional rules for forming questions, or with the entries in the most elaborate dictionaries, none of which come close to describing simple properties of these linguistic objects.
>
> (Chomksy 1995a: 387)

Increasingly, then, he tried to find the basic principles behind the tangled jungle of individual linguistic rules: 'The task is to show that the apparent richness and diversity of linguistic phenomena is illusory . . . the result of interaction of fixed principles under slightly varying conditions' (Chomsky 1995a: 389).

He therefore pared his proposals down to what he called a Minimalist Program, which contained hypotheses about the bare bones of language. This pared-down version retained basic switch-setting (p. 109), with its 'principles' and 'parameters', but two levels of structure were abolished. D-structure (once deep structure) and S-structure (once surface structure) no longer appeared as separate strata. The wordstore (lexicon) fed into a 'computational system', which checked that word combinations fitted in with basic principles. The wordstore also fed into a 'spell-out' which sifted through anything likely to affect the pronunciation. The endpoint was meaning on the one hand, and pronunciation on the other.

This bare-bones system remained in its preliminary stages. But the principles which guided the system were perhaps the most interesting part, though they remained sketchy. They were basically principles of 'economy' or simplicity. For example, one of these was 'Shortest Move'. If one of two chunks of structure needed to be moved, then the one which moved least far must be selected. Take the sentence:

FENELLA PERSUADED ALPHONSE TO BUY A GREEN PARROT.

Suppose you wanted to check who was persuaded, and what was bought:

FENELLA PERSUADED WHO TO BUY WHAT?

Normally, any WH-word (word beginning with WH- such as WHO, WHAT) has to be brought to the front of the sentence. But only one can be moved. So here you have to choose. Should it be WHO or WHAT? Or doesn't it matter? In fact, it matters very much. You can say:

WHO DID FENELLA PERSUADE TO BUY WHAT?

But not:

*WHAT DID FENELLA PERSUADE WHO TO BUY?

Only the WH-word nearest to the front can be moved, which ties in with Chomsky's 'Shortest Move' principle.

This, then, was the type of principle which Chomsky hoped to identify – though his goal remained elusive. As he admitted:

> Current formulation of such ideas still leaves substantial gaps. It is, further-more, far from obvious that language should have anything like the character postulated in the minimalist program, which is just that: a research program concerned with filling the gaps and asking how positive an answer we can give to the question how 'perfect' is language?
>
> (Chomsky 1995a: 390)

But if Chomsky is so unsure, does anybody else know? Chomsky's increasingly broad and general claims about language brought him closer to people he originally disagreed with, those who argued that the broad general principles of language are indistinguishable from the broad general principles of human cognition in general. So where do we go from here?

Maybe the answer is to turn back from such huge abstract ideas, and to look again at the nitty-gritty of how humans actually use language. According to Michael Tomasello, 'how children learn language is not a logical problem but an empirical problem.' (Tomasello 2003: 328). In his opinion, we need to turn to a usage-based approach, one which explores how human children combine inherited talents and learned skills as they acquire language. He explains: 'The human capacity for language is best seen as a conspiracy of many different cognitive, social-cognitive, information-processing, and learning skills, some of which humans share with primates and some of which are unique products of human evolution' (Tomasello 2003: 321).

The next step is perhaps to look at child language, and see what can be gleaned from the way children learn to talk. This will be the topic of the next two chapters.

6

CHATTERING CHILDREN
How do children get started on learning to speak?

They can't talk straight
Any more than they can walk straight.
Their pronunciation is awful
And their grammar is flawful.
  Ogden Nash, *It must be the milk*

According to Ogden Nash, the behaviour of children and drunks is equally confusing. Linguists would perhaps agree with him. Listening to infants speaking is like being in topsy-turvy land. The problems of children faced with adult language sometimes seem trivial to a linguist who is trying to decipher infant burbles. But far worse than the problem of decipherment is the difficulty of interpreting the utterances. One writer remarked that writing about the acquisition of language:

> is somewhat like the problem of reconstructing a dinosaur while the bones are still being excavated. It can happen that after you have connected what you earnestly believe are the hind legs you find that they are the jaw bones.
>
> (McNeill 1970: vii)

Consequently, before we consider the main topic of this chapter – how children get started on learning to speak – we must outline some of the problems of interpretation which arise when linguists attempt to analyse child language. We shall do this by considering one-word utterances.

BA, QUA, HA AND OTHER ONE-WORD UTTERANCES

One-word utterances present a microcosm of the difficulties faced by linguists examining child language. Consider the following situation. Suppose a child says BA when she is in the bath, again says BA when given a mug of milk, and also says BA to the kitchen taps. How are we to interpret this? There are at least four possible explanations.

The first possibility is that the child is simply naming the objects to prove she knows them, but has overgeneralized the word BA. That is, she has learnt the name BA for 'bath' and has wrongly assumed that it can apply to anything which contains liquid. A typical example of this type of overgeneralization was noted by one harassed mother in a letter to the London *Evening Standard*:

> My baby is Moon-struck. She saw the moon in the sky at six o'clock last week and ever since she's gaped at the sky shouting for the moon. Now she thinks anything that shines is the moon; street lamps, headlights, even the reflected light bulb in the window. All I hear is yells about the moon all day. I love my baby but I'm so ashamed. How does one get patience?

However, this plain overgeneralization interpretation may be too simple a view of what is happening when the child says BA. A second, and alternative, explanation has been proposed by the famous Russian psychologist Vygotsky (1893–1934). He suggested that when children overgeneralize they do so in a quite confusing way. They appear to focus attention on one aspect of an object at a time. One much quoted example concerns a child who used the word QUA to refer to a duck, milk, a coin and a teddy bear's eye (Vygotsky 1962: 70). QUA 'quack' was, originally, a duck on a pond. Then the child incorporated the pond into the meaning, and by focusing attention on the liquid element, QUA was generalized to milk. But the duck was not forgotten, since QUA was used to refer to a coin with an eagle on it. Then, with the coin in mind, the child applied QUA to any round coin-like object, such as a teddy bear's eye. Vygotsky called this phenomenon a 'chain complex' because a chain of items is formed, all linked by the same name. If he is correct, then in the case of BA, we can suggest that the child originally meant 'bath'. Then, by focusing her attention on the liquid elements she generalized the word to 'milk'. Meanwhile, remembering the bath taps, she used BA to mean 'kitchen taps' (see diagram on p. 102).

Yet even Vygotsky's 'chain complex' interpretation seems oversimple in the view of some researchers. A third, and less obvious, point of view is that of

David McNeill, a psychologist at the University of Chicago. He argued that one-word utterances show a linguistic sophistication which goes far beyond the actual sound spoken. He claimed that the child is not merely involved in naming exercises, but is uttering *holophrases*, single words which stand for whole sentences. For example, BA might mean 'I am in my bath' or 'Mummy's fallen in the bath'. He justifies his viewpoint by claiming that misuse of words shows evidence of grammatical relationships which the child understands, but cannot yet express. For example, a 1-year-old child said HA when something hot was in front of her. A month later she said HA to an empty coffee cup and a turned-off stove. Why did she do this? McNeill suggested that:

> by misusing the word the child showed that 'hot' was not merely the label of hot objects but was also something said of objects that could be hot. It asserted a property.
>
> (McNeill 1970: 24)

He also claimed that the same child understood the notion of location because she pointed to the empty top of the refrigerator, where bananas were normally kept, and said NANA. He concluded that 'there is a constant emergence of new grammatical relations, even though no utterance is ever longer than one word' (McNeill 1970: 23). So, McNeill might perhaps suggest that BA, when applied to kitchen taps and milk, showed an understanding of location: 'There are taps like this on the bath tub', 'There is liquid like this in the bath.'

McNeill claimed that children understand a wide variety of grammatical relationships and that one-word utterances are sentences in embryo. This seems over-imaginative to many researchers. However, the idea that single-word utterances may be more than mere labels has also been examined by Lois Bloom, a researcher at Columbia University, who put forward a fourth possibility (Bloom 1973).

After a careful analysis of the single words spoken by her daughter, Allison, she suggested that there is no simple answer to the problem of interpretation because the meaning of a one-word utterance varies according to the age of the child. For example, when Allison said MUMMY at the age of 16 months, she seemed to mean, simply, 'That's Mummy'. But at the age of 19 months she appeared to be trying to express some kind of interaction between Mummy and the surrounding environment, as when she pointed to her mother's cup and said, MUMMY.

However, Bloom was unable to tell exactly what kind of interaction was intended. Did Allison mean 'That's Mummy's cup', or was she saying 'Mummy's drinking from a cup too'? Because of this intrinsic ambiguity, Bloom was cautious about assigning specific meanings to BA-type words which relate either to objects, or to interaction between objects. She was more optimistic about the interpretation of words such as NO, MORE and A'GONE in which 'conceptual notions are so conveniently tied to the actual words in the child's speech' (Bloom 1973: 140). For example, Allison showed by her use of the words NO and A'GONE that she could cope with the notion of non-existence. Bloom, therefore, concluded (perhaps not surprisingly) that single words are grammatically fairly uninteresting. Their importance lies in the light they throw on a child's conceptual representation of experience.

Other researchers have tried to analyse what the child is trying to do with one-word utterances (e.g. Wells 1974; Halliday 1975; Griffiths 1986). If a child says GA, is she simply naming an object such as a cat? Is she asking for the cat? Or is she trying to control the actions of her parents by telling them to let the cat in? All of these are possible. The probable 'translation' may even depend on the temperament of the child. Some children simply enjoy naming things, others prefer to use words to get the attention of the adults around them.

An extra reason for caution is that some youngsters may not even realize that they are 'naming' things when they first utter words (McShane 1979, 1980). They may simply be taking part in a ritual game. Many middle-class parents sit down with their children and leaf through picture books, naming the objects which appear on each page, such as 'apple', 'ball', 'cat', 'duck', and so on. The child may shriek BA delightedly when she reaches the page with the round blue blob in the middle, but may not for some weeks realize that this sequence of sounds is actually the 'name' of a certain type of round object, a ball. As McShane put it: 'The child first learns the words and later learns that these words are names' (1979: 890). The sudden realization that things have names appears to lead to a surge of 'labelling' everyday objects such as CAR, MILK, BALL, APPLE, followed by a surge of 'describing', with the use of words such as BLUE, GONE, BROKE, HIT. This in turn, he suggested, leads to the beginning of structured speech. His suggestion is supported by others: 'This burgeoning store of comprehended words triggers or reinforces the activation of analytical mechanisms' (Locke 1997: 276).

But the situation is by no means clear cut. Some children go through this sudden 'naming insight' stage, others seem to know that things have names before they start to utter any words (Harris et al. 1988). And occasionally, the 'single word' stage may even be missed out. There are reports of a working-class black community in Pennsylvania where it is considered odd to talk to babies, and parents make no attempt to interpret children's early babbles as labels. These children often begin to communicate by picking up whole phrases, which they use with a wide range of intonations and meanings. One toddler, Teegie, used 'You shut up' to mean 'No', 'Leave me alone', 'Give me that', and 'Take it, I don't want it' (Heath 1983). But these children learned language perfectly well via this route. A young child is 'faced with having to discover what talking is all about' (Griffiths 1986: 281), and there seems to be no one way in which this realization comes about.

This brief excursus has by no means exhausted the views on one-word utterances found in the literature. It does, however, illustrate one important point: when the data are so confusing, it is no wonder that differences of opinion abound in child language studies. All researchers, to some extent, see what they want to see. This accounts for the extraordinarily diverse view-points which arise over apparently simple issues.

Having pointed out the type of problem that is likely to arise, we must now return to the main topic of this chapter, which is the following: how do children get started on learning to speak? We shall consider this question by looking first at children's two-word utterances. We shall then go on to examine how children acquire more complicated aspects of language such as word endings and negation.

TWO-BY-TWO

There are basically two ways of analysing two-word utterances. We may choose either the 'Let's pretend they're talking Martian' technique or the 'Let's guess what they're trying to say' method. In the first, linguists approach the child's speech as if it were an unknown exotic language. Having freed their minds of preconceived notions connected with their knowledge of English, they write a grammar based entirely on the word patterns they discern in the child's speech. In the second method, linguists try to provide an interpreta-tion of what the child is saying by using their knowledge of the language and by observing the situation in which the words were uttered.

In their earliest attempts at analysing two-word utterances, linguists followed the 'Let's pretend they're talking Martian' technique. Martin Braine (1963), of the University of California at Santa Barbara, listed all the two-word utterances produced by three 2-year-olds, Steven, Gregory and Andrew. The results were superficially puzzling. There were a number of inexplicable sequences such as MORE TAXI, ALLGONE SHOE, NO BED, BUNNY DO, IT DOGGIE. Such utterances could not be straight imitations, as it is unlikely that any adult ever said MORE TAXI, ALLGONE SHOE or BUNNY DO. Anyway, straight imitation would put too great a strain on the child's memory. Braine counted over 2,500 different combinations uttered by one child. Are these then just accidental juxtapositions? Apparently not.

To his surprise, Braine noted that the combinations did not seem to be random. Certain words always occurred in a fixed place, and other words never occurred alone. Andrew, Steven and Gregory all seemed to have adopted a simple though genuine pattern when they put two words together. They had two distinct classes of word in their speech. One class contained a small number of words such as ALLGONE, MORE, THIS, NO. These words occurred frequently, never alone, and in a fixed position. They were labelled *pivots*, because the utterance appeared to pivot round them. The other class contained many more words which occurred less frequently, but in any position and sometimes alone. These words often coincided with adult nouns such as MILK, SHOE, BUNNY and so on. They are sometimes called *open* class words, since an 'open' class is a set of words which can be added to indefinitely.

For example, Steven always used WANT, GET, THERE, IT as pivots in first position, and DO as a pivot in second position. His open class words included a wide variety of names such as BABY, CAR, MAMA, DADA, BALL, DOLL, BUNNY, HORSIE. Steven seemed to have adopted a pattern which said, 'A sentence consists of *either* a type 1 pivot followed by an open class word ($P^1 + O$), *or* an open class word followed by a type 2 pivot ($O + P^2$)':

Pivot 1	Open
WANT	BABY
GET	BALL
THERE	BOOK
IT	DADDY

Open	Pivot 2
BUNNY	DO
DADDY	

Several other researchers who independently tried the exotic language technique confirmed this phenomenon by finding other children who formed word combinations in the same way as Andrew, Steven and Gregory (Brown and Fraser 1964; Miller and Ervin 1964). For a time, linguists were quite excited. They thought they might have discovered a universal first grammar, a so-called *pivot grammar*. But, alas, disillusion gradually crept in. One by one, researchers noted that a number of children did not fit into this simple pattern. Although all children showed strong preferences for placing certain words in a particular position in an utterance, these preferences were not always strong enough to be regarded as genuine 'rules'. In addition, some children used so-called pivots such as MORE, NO, by themselves, which disagreed with Braine's finding that pivot words do not occur alone. And other children confused the picture by having pivot constructions as only a small portion of their total utterances.

Perhaps the biggest difficulty for pivot grammar was the appearance of utterances such as MUMMY SOCK, DADDY CAR, KITTY BALL, which occur in the speech of many children. Here two *open* class words seem to be juxtaposed, with no pivot in sight! Braine dismissed this problem by saying that O + O constructions were a second stage, which occurred only *after* the P + O and O + P phase. But this does not seem to be true of all children. Of course, there is nothing wrong with stating that some youngsters make sentences which can be P + O, O + P or O + O. It just does not tell us very much to say that 'As well as pivot constructions, almost any other two words can occur together.' But even if such empty statements were acceptable, it is not necessarily correct to assume that O + O utterances are random juxtapositions. There may be more reason behind them than appears at first sight, and the words may be related to one another in a highly structured way. It is quite inadequate to characterize a sentence such as DADDY CAR as O + O, since such a description cannot distinguish between several possible interpretations:

1   'Daddy is washing the car.'
2   'That's Daddy's car.'
3   'Daddy is under the car.'

Pivot grammars, therefore, were not as much use as was once hoped. They only described the rules used by a small number of children – or perhaps, more accurately, they characterized only a small portion of the output of most children. If one used pivot grammars in order to answer the question 'Are two-word utterances structured?', the answer would be: 'Partially – children use pivot constructions but supplement them by apparently combining open class words at random.'

Disillusioned by the pivot grammars which resulted from the 'Let's pretend he's talking Martian' technique, later linguists tended to favour the second 'Let's guess what they're trying to say' approach. This is more time-consuming, since researchers must note not just the utterances themselves, but also the accompanying actions. Luckily, what young children say usually relates directly to what they do and see:

If an adult or an older child mounts a bicycle, there is no need for him to inform anyone who has seen him do it that he has done it. But a young child who mounts a tricycle will often 'announce' the fact: *I ride trike!*

(Bloom 1970: 9)

One of the first linguists to make a careful study of two-word utterances following this method was again Lois Bloom (1970, 1991; Bloom *et al.* 1975). She kept a careful account of the actions accompanying the utterances of three children, Kathryn, Eric and Gia, and provided convincing interpretations of what they were trying to say. For example, it was quite clear what 21-month-old Kathryn meant on the two occasions when she uttered the words MOMMY SOCK. The first time, she said it as she picked up her mother's sock, indicating that she meant 'This is Mummy's sock'. The second time was when her mother was putting Kathryn's sock on Kathryn, so Kathryn was saying 'Mummy is putting on my sock for me.' Two-year-old Gia said LAMB EAR apparently meaning 'That's the lamb's ear' when her mother pointed to the ear on a toy lamb, and said, 'What's this?' She said GIRL BALL when looking at a picture of a girl bouncing a ball, and presumably meant 'The girl is bouncing a ball.' She said FLY BLANKET when a fly settled on her blanket, probably meaning 'There is a fly on my blanket.'

There is a possible objection to these interpretations. Is Bloom not reading too much into these utterances? Perhaps Gia was just saying 'That is a lamb and an ear', 'That is a girl and a ball.' 'That is a fly and a blanket.' Or perhaps she was just bringing up a 'topic' of conversation, and then making a 'comment' about it: 'I'm talking about a fly, and it has involved itself with my *blanket*', 'I'm referring to a *girl* who is connected with a *ball*.' This type of suggestion was first put forward in the mid-1960s to explain two-word utterances (Gruber 1967).

How can one eliminate these possibilities? The answer is that the highly consistent word order made it unlikely that the sequences were random juxtapositions. Whenever Gia seemed to be expressing location she put the object she was locating first, and the location second: FLY BLANKET 'The fly is on the blanket', FLY BLOCK 'The fly is on the block', BLOCK BAG 'The block is in the bag.' When she referred to subjects and objects, she put the subject first, and the object second: GIRL BALL 'The girl is bouncing the ball', GIRL FISH 'The girl is playing with a fish.' And she expressed possession by putting the possessor first, the possession second: LAMB EAR 'That's the lamb's ear', GIA BLUEYES 'That's Gia's doll, Blueyes.' If Gia was accidentally juxtaposing the words we would expect BLANKET FLY or EAR LAMB as often as FLY BLANKET or LAMB EAR. And the possessive sentences make it highly unlikely that Gia was using a 'topic' and 'comment' construction. It would be most odd in the case of GIA BLUEYES to interpret it as 'I am talking about myself, Gia, and what I want to comment on is that I have a doll Blueyes.'

Of course, Gia was expressing these relationships of location, possession, and subject–object in the same order as they are found in adult speech. But the important point is that she seemed to realize automatically that it was necessary to express relationships consistently in a way Washoe the chimp perhaps did not. She seemed to *expect* language to consist of recurring patterns, and seemed naturally disposed to look for regularities. But before stating conclusively that Gia's utterances were patterned, we must consider one puzzling exception. Why did Gia say BALLOON THROW as well as THROW BALLOON when she dropped a balloon as if throwing it? Why did she say BOOK READ as well as READ BOOK when she was looking at a book? Surely this is random juxtaposition of the type we have just claimed to be non-existent? A closer look at Gia's early utterances solves the mystery.

In her earliest two-word sequences, Gia *always* said BALLOON THROW and BOOK READ. She had deduced wrongly that the names of people and objects precede action words. This accounts for 'correct' utterances such as GIRL WRITE and MUMMY COME as well as 'mistakes' such as BALLOON THROW and SLIDE GO, when she placed some keys on a slide. Soon she began to have doubts about her original rule, and experimented, using first one form, then the other. Utterances produced at a time when the child is trying to make up her mind have aptly been labelled 'groping patterns' by one linguist (Braine 1976). Eventually, after a period of fluctuation, Gia acquired the verb–object relationship permanently with the correct order THROW BALLOON, READ BOOK.

The consistency which Bloom found in the speech of Kathryn, Eric and Gia, has been confirmed by numerous researchers who have worked independently on other children. In conclusion, then, our answer to the question 'Are two-word utterances patterned?' must be 'Yes'. From the moment they place two words together (and possibly even before) children seem to realize that language is not just a random conglomeration of words. They express each relationship consistently, so that, for example, in the actor–action relationship, the actor comes first, the action second as in MAMA COME, KITTY PLAY, KATHY GO. Exceptions occur when a wrong rule has been deduced, or when a child is groping towards a rule. And even at the two-word stage, children are creative in their speech. They use combinations of words they have not heard before.

However, we have talked so far only about children who are learning English, which has a fixed word order. But some languages have a variable order, and mark grammatical relationships with other devices, such as word endings. How do children cope in these circumstances? The answer varies from language to language (Slobin 1986a). Turkish is a language in which the endings are particularly clear and easy to identify, and Turkish children are reported to adopt consistent endings with variable word order. But in Serbo-Croatian, where word endings are confusing and inconsistent, children prefer to disregard the endings and use a fixed word order to begin with, even though there is variation in the word order used by the adults around them.

In brief, the evidence suggests that children express relationships between words in a consistent way, whether they use word order or devices such as word endings. This raises a further question: do children from different parts of the world express the *same* relationships? Apparently, children everywhere say much the same things at the two-word stage. Roger Brown noted that 'a rather small set of operations and relations describe all the meanings expressed . . . whatever the language they are learning' (Brown 1973: 198). Because of this similarity, psycholinguists at one time hoped that they might be able to make a definitive list of the concepts expressed at this stage, and predict their order of emergence. But it soon became apparent that there was considerable variation between different children, even when they spoke the same language. Every researcher produced a slightly different list, organized in a slightly different order.

Perhaps the best-known list was that of Brown (1973: 173). He suggested a set of eight 'minimal two-term relations', supplemented by three 'basic operations of reference', as set out in the chart below.

Relations	1	Agent action	MUMMY PUSH
	2	Action and object	EAT DINNER
	3	Agent and object	MUMMY PIGTAIL
	4	Action and location	PLAY GARDEN
	5	Entity and location	COOKIE PLATE
	6	Possessor and possession	MUMMY SCARF
	7	Attributive and entity	GREEN CAR
	8	Demonstrative and entity	THAT BUTTERFLY
Operations	9	Nomination	THIS (IS A) TRUCK
	10	Recurrence	MORE MILK
	11	Non-existence	ALLGONE EGG

The examples here show clearly that young children can cope with different types of meaning relationships. But to what extent do these two-word utterances embody specifically linguistic knowledge? At one time, certain psycholinguists thought that children were born with an inbuilt understanding of some basic grammatical relations. For example, it was claimed that the child who said DRINK MILK showed an innate knowledge of the verb–object relationship (McNeill 1966, 1970). However, most people have now shifted away from this viewpoint. As one researcher noted, the assumption that children understand grammatical relationships in a way comparable to adults is 'an act of faith based only on our knowledge of the adult language' (Bowerman 1973: 187). We must admit that these early utterances do not show any firm evidence of specific linguistic knowledge. They merely reveal an awareness that meaning relationships need to be expressed consistently.

This leaves us with a considerable problem. If we assume that two-word utterances show linguistic knowledge (which would be fanciful) then we have to specify exactly what kind of linguistic grammar we are dealing with. If, on the other hand, we do not regard them as showing evidence of grammar, then we have to find out when children start having a primitive syntax. In this case, we have to assume that language learning is a discontinuous process. Children start with one kind of system, and then shift over to another, syntactic one. We may be dealing with a tadpole-to-frog phenomenon (Gleitman and Wanner 1982), in which the immature tadpole behaves rather differently from the mature frog.

A number of researchers support the notion of discontinuity. Perhaps children initially use their general cognitive ability to express meaning relationships in a consistent way. When they have acquired a certain number, they start to sort them out in their mind. This possibly triggers an inbuilt syntactic capacity. We shall discuss this possible switch-over to syntax in Chapter 7.

GETTING STARTED

We need to ask a further question. How do children set about acquiring these early utterances? Do they discover how to express one concept at a time? Or do they deal with several simultaneously? A psycholinguist who examined this question was Martin Braine, of pivot grammar fame. Braine found that children coped with several concepts at the same time, but used each one in a very restricted set of circumstances (Braine 1976). For example, just prior to his second birthday, his own son, Jonathan, could express possession, (MUMMY SHOE), recurrence (MORE JUICE) and attribution (BIG DOG), but only with a narrow range of words. In the case of possession, the only possessors were MOMMY and DADDY. Jonathan had apparently acquired a formula for dealing with possession, but a formula of very limited scope, MOMMY or DADDY + object, as in MOMMY SHOE 'Mummy's shoe', DADDY PIPE 'Daddy's pipe.' Jonathan's formula for dealing with recurrence was even more limited, consisting of the word MORE + object. He used this whenever he wanted more food, as in MORE JUICE, or when he noticed more than one of something, as in MORE BEE. His attribution formula consisted of the words BIG or LITTLE + object, as in BIG PLANE, BIG DOG, LITTLE LAMB, LITTLE DUCK.

Gradually, Jonathan expanded the range of words he used in each formula. Approximately one month later, he had added extra names to his possession formula, as in ELLIOT COOKIE 'Elliot's cookie', ANDREW BOOK 'Andrew's book'. He extended his recurrence formula with the words TWO and OTHER, as in TWO SPOON, OTHER BALL 'There's another ball'. He also attributed the colours RED, GREEN, BLUE to objects as in RED BALLOON, as well as the properties OLD and HOT, as in OLD COOKIE, HOT TEA. Somewhat unexpectedly, he also included the word HURT in his attribution formula, producing phrases such as HURT KNEE, HURT HAND, HURT FLY. At around this time he started to express a new concept, that of location, though he restricted the object located mainly to the word SAND, as in SAND EYE 'sand in my eye', SAND TOE 'sand on my toe'. He also began to produce actor–action phrases, in which he usually chose the word DADDY as actor, as in DADDY WORK, DADDY SLEEP. The emergence of Jonathan's limited scope formulae is set out in the diagram below.

Possession	Recurrence	Attribution	Location	Actor–Action
Stage 1 MUMMY SHOE DADDY PIPE etc.	MORE JUICE BEE	BIG PLANE LITTLE LAMB		
Stage 2 MUMMY SHOE DADDY BREAD ELLIOT JUICE ANDREW BOAT etc.	MORE TOY OTHER BALL TWO SPOON etc.	BIG LION LITTLE BOY RED BALLOON OLD COOKIE HOT TEA HURT KNEE etc.	SAND EYE TOE etc.	DADDY WORK SLEEP WALK etc.

Source: Simplified, from Braine 1976.

Do all children acquiring language behave like Jonathan? Braine examined the early utterances of a number of other children, and concluded that each one had adopted a 'limited scope formulae' approach at the two-word stage, though the actual formulae varied from child to child. Numerous children seem to go about learning language in a roughly similar fashion, even though there is considerable individual variation in the precise track they follow.

However, there may be more variation than Braine realized at the time. It is possible that most of the children studied in the 1960s were subconsciously picked out because they were easy to understand. And they were easy to understand because they fitted in with our preconceptions about what happens as children learn to talk – that they learn single words, then put these words together. But reports then came in of children who do not behave like this. Some learn whole sequences of sounds, then only gradually break them down into words, as with a child called Minh (Peters 1977, 1983). Minh's words were often fuzzy and indistinct, but he paid considerable attention to intonation patterns. Over time, his words became separate and distinct, but he did not go through the gradual building-up process found in the speech of many children. As one researcher noted: 'There is no one way to learn language. Language learning poses a problem for the child, and, as with other complex problems, there is no single path to a solution' (Nelson 1973: 114).

Where does all this leave us? There is no rigid universal mould into which all early utterances will fit, even though children express the same kind of things at the two-word stage. Moreover, these two-word utterances are patterned in the sense that children express meaning relationships such as actor–action, location and possession consistently. But we have not been able to show that these are essentially grammatical relationships that are being expressed. Consequently, in order to assess the claim that children's language is patterned in a strictly linguistic sense, we must look at later aspects of language acquisition – at the development of word endings and more complex constructions such as the rules for negation in English.

THE CASE OF THE WUG

The case of the wug

THIS IS A WUG

'Wugs' you should say, if you understand the rules which underlie English plurals. And that is the reply given almost unanimously by a group of children who were shown this picture. The researcher wanted to prove that they hadn't just memorized each plural as they heard it, but had an internalized 'rule' which could apply even to words they had never heard (Berko 1958).

And it wasn't just wugs the children coped with correctly, so no one could argue that they misunderstood the word as 'bugs'. Another picture showed a man standing on the ceiling, with the words: 'This is a man who knows how to bing. He is binging. He did the same thing yesterday. Yesterday he − ?' 'Binged' said nearly all the children tested. Admittedly, they had higher results for words they already knew. More children got the plural of GLASS right than the plural of a nonsense word TASS (TASS and GLASS rhyme in American English, having the same vowel as the word MASS). But no one can doubt that they were applying 'rules' (linguistic patterns) which they had worked out for themselves.

An even more striking example of the child's ability to generalize patterns is the development of irregular verbs such as COME and CAME, GO and WENT, BREAK and BROKE. As noted in Chapter 4, children start by acquiring the correct irregular forms for the past tense, CAME, WENT, BROKE. Some of these are acquired fairly early, since they are very common words (Ervin 1964; Slobin 1971a). One might suppose that practice makes perfect, and that these words would remain correctly formed. But not at all. As soon as children learn the regular past tense for words such as HELPED, PLAYED, WALKED and WASHED, they give up using the correct irregular form, and start using the overgeneralized forms COMED, GOED, BREAKED. And when they re-acquire the irregular verbs, they first produce semi-regular forms which have a normal ending, as in LOST, LEFT (Slobin 1971a). All this indicates that children have a strong tendency to look for and apply 'rules' (linguistic patterns), at least as far as English noun and verb endings are concerned.

This mastery of past tenses has been simulated on a computer, which went through the same stages as young children. A 'learning network' was presented with sets of verbs, some regular, some irregular. It connected together verbs and endings by picking up on the frequency of the forms it was exposed to. First, it learned the irregular verbs, then it started to over-regularize them, with forms such as GO-ED and HIT-ED. Finally, it correctly mastered the past tenses of almost all the verbs fed into it (Plunkett 1995; Elman et al. 1996).

Two opposing conclusions could be drawn from this: either language learning is straightforward, graspable even by a well-programmed computer; or word endings are a small and not very difficult part of language: even Genie, the deprived teenager could handle them (Chapter 3). It is perhaps not surprising that children are able to generalize plurals and past tenses. After all, word endings tend to rhyme. Children are known to have a fascination for rhymes, and they frequently make up little poems such as 'I am a bug, sitting on a rug, warm and snug, with my mug.' So the extension of an -S from BUGS, MUGS and RUGS to WUGS is not particularly startling.

Incidentally, not all children add on endings straightforwardly. A partially blind child, Seth, acquired his word endings via 'phonological toeholds'. He reproduced the rhythm of the words, and often placed an indistinct 'filler' sound where a syllable should be. But these became accurate endings only gradually (Peters and Menn 1993).

What further evidence of linguistic patterns can we find? We can note that from the moment children place three or more words together, they seem to show an instinctive awareness of *hierarchical structure*, the realization that several words can fill the same structural 'slot' as one:

THAT	FLOWER
THAT	A BLUE FLOWER

PUT	HAT	ON
PUT	THE RED HAT	ON

However, the sentences just quoted look like ordinary adult ones with a few words left out. This means that we need more evidence to test the claim that children are operating with an internalized set of 'rules' which do not correspond to the adult ones. Several researchers have hunted for this evidence, and claim to have found it. Ursula Bellugi of Harvard University noted: 'We have found several periods where the child's sentences show systematic deviations from adult language, as if they were constructed according to a different set of rules' (Bellugi 1971: 95). She and Edward Klima analysed the development of negatives and interrogatives by studying the utterances produced by the now famous Harvard trio Adam, Eve and Sarah (Klima and Bellugi 1966). As already noted in Chapter 4, the families of these children were totally unacquainted and independent of one another, and each child heard a different set of sentences as 'input'. Nevertheless, the children passed through surprisingly similar stages in their progress towards adult constructions. Each phase was characterized by identifiable patterns and the utterances could not be regarded merely as bad imitations of adult speech. The children seemed to be devising hypotheses to account for the regularities in the speech they heard around them. The development of negative sentences, outlined below, shows this clearly.

At first, Adam, Eve and Sarah seemed to be using a primitive self-instruction, 'Put NO or NOT in front of the whole sentence.'

Neg	Sentence
NO	WANT STAND HEAD
NO	FRASER DRINK ALL TEA
NO	PLAY THAT

But this phase did not last long. Next came the realization that the negative goes inside rather than in front of the sentence. The children devised a new 'rule' which said, 'Put the negative after the first noun phrase and before the rest of the sentence.'

NP	Neg	Rest of sentence
HE	NO	BITE YOU
THAT	NO	MUMMY
I	CAN'T	CATCH YOU
I	DON'T	SIT ON CROMER COFFEE

At this stage, CAN'T and DON'T seemed to be treated as alternatives to NO. The children had not yet realized that they consisted of two elements. To them, CAN'T and DON'T were single negative units which could be substituted for NO or NOT. However, this substitution was not completely free. Just as in correct adult speech you never find CAN -ING (e.g. *I CAN SINGING) or DON'T -ING (e.g. *I DON'T SMOKING) – so the children never said * I CAN'T CATCHING YOU or *I DON'T CRYING. They had grasped the fact that CAN'T and DON'T do not occur before verbs ending in -ING.

The next stage came when the children realized that CAN'T and DON'T contained two separate elements, CAN + NOT, DO + NOT. This was guaranteed by the fact that CAN and DO began to occur in the children's speech in non-negative sentences. This led to a more sophisticated negative rule in which the negative was placed in the third slot in a sentence, after the noun and auxiliary or copula and before the rest of the sentence.

The difference between this and the standard adult rule was that the children had not yet realized that the tense need only be included once.

NP	Aux (or Cop)	Neg	Rest of the sentence
PAUL	CAN	N'T	HAVE ONE
YOU	DO	N'T	WANT SOME SUPPER
I	DID	N'T	SPILLED IT
YOU	DID	N'T	CAUGHT ME
I	AM	NOT	A DOCTOR
THAT	WAS	NOT	ME

A final stage occurred when the children amended sentences such as YOU DIDN'T CAUGHT ME to YOU DIDN'T CATCH ME.

So, independently, Adam, Eve and Sarah each went through similar intermediate stages in their acquisition of the negative:

1	Neg + Sentence
	NO WANT STAND HEAD
2	NP + Neg + VP
	HE NO BITE YOU
3	NP + Aux + Neg + Rest of Sentence
	I DID N'T CAUGHT IT

Each of these can be regarded as a hypothesis to account for the rules of negation in English. The first is a simple hypothesis. The second is slightly less simple, and the third is almost the same rule as that used by adults. Klima and Bellugi are justified in their remark that 'It has seemed to us that the language of children has its own systemacity, and that the sentences are not just an imperfect copy of those of an adult' (Klima and Bellugi 1966: 191).

So Chomsky (1965) may be superficially right to regard the child as a miniature scientist who makes successive hypotheses to account for the data. But there is one major difference. When a scientist discards a hypothesis, he abandons it totally, and works only with the new one he is testing. Children do not behave like this. The stages do not follow one another cleanly and suddenly – they overlap quite considerably. As Klima and Bellugi note: 'A characteristic of child language is the residue of elements of previous systems' (Klima and Bellugi 1966: 194). For example, beside I AM NOT A DOCTOR, IT'S NOT COLD, and THAT WAS NOT ME, the children still produced sentences such as THIS NOT ICE CREAM, I NOT CRYING, PAUL NOT TIRED.

This type of fluctuation is noticeable in all aspects of child language. For example, Roger Brown noted, in the case of word endings, that children do not 'abruptly pass from total absence to reliable presence. There is always a considerable period, varying in length, in which production-where-required is probabilistic' (Brown 1973: 257). When he analysed the speech of the child Sarah, he found extraordinary swings in her use of the suffix -ING. At the age of 2 years she used it correctly 50 per cent of the time in sentences such as I (AM) PLAYING. But 6 months later this had dropped to 20 per cent. One month after this it shot up to 80 per cent, then went down again to around 45 per cent. She was over 3 years old before -ING occurred steadily and correctly in all her utterances.

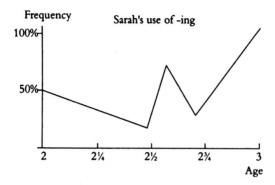

And it is not only production of speech which fluctuates, but comprehension also. Richard Cromer tested children's understanding of constructions such as THE WOLF IS TASTY TO BITE, THE WOLF IS HAPPY TO BITE, THE DUCK IS HORRIBLE TO BITE. Using glove puppets of a wolf and a duck, he asked the subjects to show him who was biting whom. To his surprise he concluded that 'children may be very inconsistent in their answers from one day to the next' (Cromer 1970: 405).

What causes this baffling inconsistency? There may be more than one reason. First, children make mistakes. Just as adults make grammatical errors such as DIDN'T YOU SAW BILL? instead of 'Didn't you see Bill?' or 'Didn't you say you saw Bill?', so do children. But this does not mean the utterances are random jumbles of words. The patterns are there, despite lapses. A second reason for inconsistency may be selective attention. Children may choose to concentrate on one aspect of speech at a time. If Sarah was working out rules for plurals one month, she may have ignored the -ING ending temporarily. As a schoolboy learning Latin said, 'If I get the verb endings right, you can't expect me to get the nouns right as well!'

However, mistakes and selective attention cannot account completely for the extreme fluctuations in Sarah's use of -ING. Linguists have realized that inconsistency is a normal transitional stage as children move from one hypothesis to the next. It seems to occur when a child has realized that her 'old' pattern is wrong or partially wrong, and has formulated a new one, but remains confused as to the precise instances in which she should abandon her older primitive rule (Cromer 1970). For example, Cromer suggested that when they hear sentences such as THE DUCK IS READY TO BITE, children start out with a rule which says 'The first noun in the sentence is doing the biting.' As they get older, they become aware that this simple assumption does not always work. But they are not quite sure why or when their rule fails. So they experiment with a second rule, 'Sometimes it is the first noun in the sentence which is doing the biting, but not always.'

When a child has made an inference that is only partially right, he can get very bewildered. Partially correct rules often produce right results for the wrong reasons, as in sentences such as I DON'T WANT IT, where DON'T is treated as a single negative element. A further example of the confusion caused by a partially effective rule was seen in the Harvard child Adam's use of the pronoun IT. He produced 'odd' sentences such as MUMMY GET IT LADDER, SAW IT BALL, alongside correct ones such as GET IT, PUT IT THERE. He appeared to be treating IT as parallel in behaviour to THAT which can occur either by itself, or attached to a noun: BRING ME THAT, BRING ME THAT BALL.

| BRING ME | IT (BALL) |
| BRING ME | THAT (BALL) |

( ) Parentheses denote optional items.

But this was not the only wrong conclusion Adam reached. He also wrongly assumed that IT had an obligatory -S when it occurred at the beginning of a sentence, so he produced IT'S FELL, IT'S HAS WHEELS, as well as superficially correct utterances such as IT'S BIG. Presumably this error arose because Adam's mother used a large number of sentences starting with IT'S . . .: IT'S RAINING, IT'S COLD and so on. When Adam's 'funny' rules produced correct results half the time, it is not surprising that he took time to abandon them.

Perhaps the situation will become clearer if we look in detail at the emergence of one particular wrong word ending in the speech of one child. Consider the following utterances produced by a child named Sally when she was nearly 3:

ME MADEN THAT
ME TIPPEN THAT OVER
ME HADEN STAWBERRIES AT LUNCHTIME
ME JUST BUYEN IT
SOMETHING MAKEN A FUNNY NOISE.

Sally seemed to have decided that one way to deal with the past was to add -EN on to the ends of verbs. How did this strange personal 'rule' emerge? Did Sally just wake up one morning and start saying TIPPEN OVER, BUYEN, MADEN, or what happened? Fletcher (1983) examined Sally's verbs ending in -EN in some detail (her progress was also recorded in Fletcher (1985), where she was called Sophie). He started recording her speech one November when she was almost 2½ years old. She began producing verbs ending in -EN in December. That month, there were three of them: BROKEN (which occurred thirteen times), then FALLEN (once) and TAKEN (once). Note that these three are all forms which actually occur in adult speech, even though Sally used them in her own idiosyncratic way, to denote a simple past tense. In the middle of January a new form, PUTTEN, emerged, alongside the existing three. This was the first non-existent form which she produced. In February, Sally used two more existing forms, GIVEN and EATEN, and eight more invented forms: BOUGHTEN, BUILDEN, RIDEN, GETTEN, CUTTEN, MADEN, WANTEN, TOUGHEN. The peak of Sally's inventiveness came in March when she added on one actual word, WAKEN, and eighteen made-up ones: HADEN, STEPPEN, HURTEN, LEAVEN, BRINGEN, COMEN, DRAWNEN, HITTEN, LETTEN, RUNNEN, WASEN, SEE-EN, ROCKEN, HELPEN, SPOILEN, MAKEN, TIPPEN, HAVEN. In April, there were no new forms noted, but in May nine new invented ones appeared: LETTEN, WRAPPEN, SHOULDEN, HIDEN, WALKEN, BUYEN, CLOSEN, PLAYEN and a strange verb CAVEN, whatever Sally meant by that. In June the real form BITTEN was added. In July, a mere three invented forms emerged, WEAREN, LEAVEN, LIKEN, then in August just one, STAYEN. This was the last of the invented forms. Finally, an actual one, FORGOTTEN, appeared in December. The rise and fall of forms in -EN took just 9 months. This is represented on the graph below.

What can we learn from this? Of course, Sally's speech was not recorded every moment of the day, so there may be some element of chance in the data. But she was probably recorded often enough (two or three times a week) for the sequence of events presented here to be reasonably reliable.

First, Sally seems to have picked out from adult speech several words ending in -EN which actually occur. She may well have heard them in sentences such as YOU'VE BROKEN IT, I'VE TAKEN YOUR DOLL upstairs, and

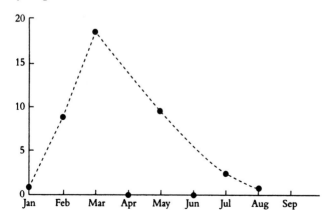

Sally's overgeneralizations in -EN

failing to take notice of the shortened form 'VE (HAVE), she perhaps believed that she was dealing with a simple past tense – though this is speculation. What we do know is that she spent over a month using a small number of actual forms, and one in particular, BROKEN, which kept recurring. She then perhaps experimentally brought in a new one, PUTTEN. Her hypothesis that -EN was a correct ending was probably confirmed by hearing more actual -EN forms, since her next new form was GIVEN. She then became confident in her -EN endings, and had a surge of them in February and March. Soon after, she began to have doubts, and forms in -EN started to tail off, while Fletcher noted that her verbs ending in -ED were gradually increasing at this time, occurring in sentences such as:

ME CALLED IT PEANUT BUTTER.
SOME MILK DRIPPED, DROPPED ON THE FLOOR.

Eventually, the overgeneralized forms in -EN faded away completely. (Sally's overall progress was discussed in Fletcher 1985.)

This scenario suggests that a new construction works its way into a child's speech in a manner similar to that found in language change. In language change, first of all a few words get the new pronunciation, though not every time they occur. Then, when these few have acquired a firm hold, the change spreads rapidly to a large number of other words. Then finally, the change slowly rounds up the stragglers (Aitchison 2001). The word by word progress of a change through the vocabulary is known as lexical diffusion. In the case of Sally, the situation started off normally. The new ending got a firm footing in a few words, then spread rapidly to a large number. But as Sally had made a false hypothesis, the overgeneralized forms gradually decreased in number, then disappeared.

But how did Sally ever discover that her MAKEN, PUTTEN, BUILDEN forms were wrong? Children are not often receptive to correction, as we saw earlier (Chapter 4). So how do they discover their errors? This is a complex problem, which we shall return to in the next chapter. In this case, however, there may be a simple answer. Children seem to expect different words to mean different things, an expectation which has been called 'the principle of contrast' (Clark 1987). When she heard someone say, perhaps, DADDY BUILT THAT SNOWMAN, Sally may have realized that this was equivalent to her own DADDY BUILDEN THAT SNOWMAN. This may have led her to reassess her own 'rule', and eventually emend it.

We must conclude, then, that children are not just copying adult utterances when they speak. They seem to be following rules they devise themselves, and which produce systematic divergences from the adult output. Chomsky (1965) may have been partly on the right track in attributing to children an innate hypothesis-forming device which enables them to form increasingly complex theories about the rules which underlie the patterns of the language they are exposed to. Like scientists, children are constantly testing new hypotheses. But, as we have seen, the scientist metaphor falls down in one vital respect. Scientists, once they have discarded a hypothesis, forget about it and concentrate on a new one. Children, on the other hand, appear to go through periods of experimentation and indecision in which two or more hypotheses overlap and fluctuate: each rule wavers for a long time, perhaps months, before it is finally adopted or finally abandoned.

Also, children's hypotheses often apply only to rather small corners of language at a time. Occasionally one finds a broad sweeping 'rule' such as 'Put NO in front of the sentence to negate it.' But this type of across-the-board generalization is quite rare, and mostly children concentrate on much smaller pieces of structure. Language acquisition is turning out to be a much messier process than was once assumed.

One further point needs to be stressed. Children make the right kind of guesses about language. Their hypotheses are within a rather narrow range of possibilities. They are naturally equipped to have sensible linguistic hunches. This is a great feat, considering how baffled humans are by the vocal communication of other species:

> There were three little owls in a wood,
> Who sang hymns whenever they could.
> What the words were about
> One could never make out,
> But one felt it was doing them good.
>
> (Anon.)

Or, as a psychologist expressed human linguistic ability using somewhat more elegant phrases:

> The fact that the brain can tolerate variation in language transmission and reception, despite different environmental inputs and still achieve the target capacity (being a native speaker of a natural language, perhaps several) provides support for a genetic component underlying language acquisition that is nevertheless biologically 'flexible' (neurologically plastic).
>
> (Petitto 2005: 100)

We can now summarize the main conclusions of this chapter. In spite of difficulties connected with interpreting the data, we have come to some firm conclusions. Children automatically 'know' that language is patterned, and they seem to make a succession of hypotheses about the rules underlying the speech they hear around them. However, these hypotheses overlap and fluctuate in a way that the hypotheses of scientists do not.

We also considered whether there is a universal framework underlying early speech. We noted that children everywhere seem to produce roughly comparable utterances at the two-word stage. However, it would be an exaggeration to claim that this represents a 'universal framework'. All we can say is that children at this stage tend to express similar meaning relationships in a consistent way.

Therefore, in order to assess whether Chomsky was right in his assumption that children learning language make use of fairly specific outline facts which could be inbuilt, we must look in more detail at the way children cope with acquiring speech beyond the two-word stage. We also need to consider whether there are other plausible ways of explaining language development. This will be the topic of the next chapter.

7

PUZZLING IT OUT

Exactly how do children learn language?

Teach your child to hold his tongue, he'll learn fast enough to speak.

Benjamin Franklin

Children learn language so efficiently and so fast because they know in outline how languages behave. So far, it has not been very difficult to show that children have some inkling of what languages are like. They seem to realise that language is rule-governed – that a finite number of principles govern the enormous number of utterances they hear going on around them. They also have an instinctive awareness that languages are hierarchically structured – the knowledge that several words can go in the same structural slot as one. A child might say:

	I LOVE	TEDDY
or	I LOVE	MY TEDDY
or	I LOVE	MY OLD BLUE TEDDY

Furthermore, children realize that language makes use of operations which are structure-dependent, so that each 'slot' in a sentence functions as a unit which can be moved around, as in:

WHERE	MY TEDDY?	
DON'T TAKE	MY TEDDY	AWAY
	MY TEDDY	HERE

However, an inbuilt knowledge that language is rule-governed, that it has a hierarchical structure, and that it makes use of structure-dependent operations by no means explains the whole of language acquisition. We still need to know exactly *how* children develop language ability so efficiently. We would also like to find out *why* many English children follow similar paths in the development of their language. These are mysteries which cannot just be swept aside with vague assumptions of 'innate programming'. We must investigate the matter more fully.

CONTENT CUTHBERT OR PROCESS PEGGY?

Over the past half century, two types of explanation have been put forward to account for the seemingly mysterious nature of language acquisition. First of all, there was Chomsky's *content* approach. Second, an alternative, and possibly more plausible, *process* approach has been proposed. What is the difference between these two? Briefly, a content approach postulates that a child's brain naturally *contains* a considerable amount of specific information about language. A process approach, on the other hand, suggests that children have inbuilt puzzle-solving equipment which enables them to *process* the linguistic data they come across. Each of these approaches has inspired a considerable amount of research. Both therefore need to be looked at carefully.

A content approach, such as Chomsky's, claimed that children come to language learning with certain expectations. They are pre-wired with some quite specific information about language, and so approach the data they hear with advance knowledge. Of course Chomsky has never assumed that this knowledge is ready waiting, the moment the child is born. It takes time to mature. But when the time is right, it requires relatively little exposure to language for the knowledge to emerge. It may be like the growth of teeth or breasts. Given normal surroundings, these appear without any great effort on the part of the acquirer.

However, Chomsky's theory that children innately contain large chunks of specific information about language always was, and still is disputed. Other researchers claim that, instead of possessing advance information, children are born with some sort of processing mechanism which enables them to analyse linguistic data. They suggest that:

the child's mind is somehow 'set' in a predetermined way to process the sorts of structures which characterize human language . . . That is not to say that the grammatical system itself is given as innate knowledge, but that the child has innate means of processing information and forming internal structures, and that when these capacities are applied to the speech he hears he succeeds in constructing a grammar of his native language.

(Slobin 1971b: 56)

The crucial point is this: are children wired with prior knowledge about language, as Chomsky has suggested? Or do they come equipped with special techniques for performing linguistic analysis? Are children's heads loaded with information? Or with puzzle-solving equipment? Are we dealing with a 'Content Cuthbert' or a 'Process Peggy'?

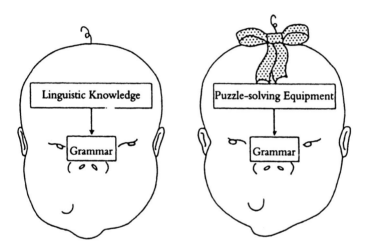

CONTENT CUTHBERT OR PROCESS PEGGY?

In both the content and process approaches the child may end up with the same type of grammar. But in the second case it is the result of analytic procedures. Information was not there at the beginning.

Because the end result may be the same in both cases, it is sometimes claimed that the two points of view are virtually indistinguishable, and should be regarded as two sides of one coin. But there is a crucial difference. Chomsky's content approach presupposes that the pre-wired knowledge is specific to language, and is independent of general intelligence. But the process approach comes in two versions, an intelligent Peggy and a linguistic Peggy. In the intelligent version, Peggy makes use of the same general cognitive abilities as she would to cope with everything else she comes across in the world. In the linguistic version, her processing mechanisms are geared specifically to language. So are we dealing with a Content Cuthbert? an intelligent Process Peggy? or a linguistic Process Peggy? We shall consider each of these possibilities in turn.

DOES CONTENT CUTHBERT EXIST?

If Chomsky was correct, then we would expect to find evidence for Content Cuthbert displayed in at least two ways. First, children would be aware of universal constraints. They could never utter a sentence that would be an impossible one for human languages. Second, they would take dramatic steps forward as they 'set switches' (Chapter 5). Let us see if either of these things happen.

Let us begin with universal constraints. If children are aware of these, then anything quite weird will be ruled out by 'a biological mandate against wild grammars' (Goodluck 1986: 55). This ensures that 'each developing grammar will fall within the bounds of adult language systems as characterized by linguistic theory' (Goodluck 1986: 64).

So do children always obey universal constraints? This might seem a strange question to ask. After all, adults don't produce strange sentences such as:

*WHICH PIG ANGELA KNOWS WHO HAS STOLEN? (p. 92.)

Surely, therefore, we are quite unlikely to find equally odd sentences in child language?

Surprisingly, perhaps, a 3-year old boy called Seth has produced a series of 'forbidden' utterances (Wilson and Peters 1988). Consider the following:

Seth: WE'RE GONNA LOOK AT SOME HOUSES WITH JOHNNIE.
        WHAT ARE WE GONNA LOOK FOR SOME?
        WHAT ARE WE GONNA LOOK FOR SOME WITH JOHNNIE?

Seth appears to have picked on the phrase SOME HOUSES. He has then replaced HOUSES with the word WHAT, and brought this WH-word to the front, but left the word SOME behind. Supposedly, (according to Chomsky) children should know automatically that it is impossible to split up a phrase such as SOME HOUSES, and move half of it away. And this was not an isolated example, so cannot be attributed to a chance mistake. This 'prohibited' construction occurred several times, as when Seth was sorting through magnetic letters:

Seth: IS THIS A FUNNY T?
Father: NO, THAT'S A FUNNY I.
Seth (holding up another):   WHAT IS THIS A FUNNY, DAD?

A possible reason for Seth's extraordinary behaviour is that he is partially blind. Because of this, his father often asked him to finish off sentences, as when playing with the magnetic letters:

Father:	THAT'S A . . .	*Father:*	THAT'S A NICE . . .
Seth:	ALEPH	*Seth:*	OTHER KAF.

So Seth may have assumed that it was necessary to have a word following the verb at the end of a sentence. At the same time, he knew that WH-words had to go to the front. When he combined these two 'rules of thumb', he produced the 'impossible' sentences.

Seth ended up chopping the strange sentences out of his speech, so they were only a small detour on the way to fluent English. But Seth's case suggests that children are not pre-wired with absolute information about language universals from the beginning. They may need to get there gradually, especially if they are in any way disadvantaged, as Seth was.

The gradual acquisition of (presumed) universal constraints is supported by another study, which looked at them from the point of view of comprehension.

One American linguist set out to discover how children understand sentences involving the phrase EACH OTHER (Matthei 1981). Now if you have a sentence such as:

THE BOYS WANTED THE GIRLS TO LIKE EACH OTHER.

the only possible interpretation is that each girl should like all the other girls. Any other interpretation, according to Chomsky, would go against universal constraints. So a number of children between the ages of 4 and 6 were presented with sentences such as:

THE CHICKENS SAID THAT THE PIGS TICKLED EACH OTHER.

They were asked to perform the actions described with farmyard animals. Unfortunately for Chomsky, most of them seemed quite unaware of the proposed constraints. The majority interpreted the sentence as if the chickens and pigs were tickling one another, though a few made the chickens tickle one another. In fact, it has been repeatedly shown that young children often do not pay attention to the syntax, and either answer at random, or utilize a 'probable world strategy', that is, interpret sentences by arranging the words to give the most plausible meaning (Cromer 1976).

Of course, one can always argue that the child really 'knew' about the constraint, but failed to reveal this knowledge. Perhaps the experiment was badly designed, or the youngsters did not fully understand what they had been asked to do. Or perhaps the children were simply 'overloaded', in that they had been asked to cope with too many things at once. A child forced to deal simultaneously with language and non-verbal responses might appear less competent than he or she really is (Hamburger and Crain 1984).

But the most plausible conclusion is that children do not have any firm, fixed beliefs about language as they acquire it. So far, they do not seem to know what to look for, or what to avoid – though some of this knowledge clearly develops over the course of time. Let us now consider Chomsky's later 'switch-setting' views.

DO CHILDREN 'SET SWITCHES'?

Universal Grammar (UG) is partly like a switchboard with its switches in neutral position, according to Chomsky (Chapter 5). Children know in advance about the possible routes which languages can take. But they have to find out which particular option has been selected by the language they are learning. Once they discover this, they flick each switch, and 'the system functions'. Is this true?

Chomsky himself is somewhat vague about how many switches there are, and what they switch. But one possible switch, he has suggested, is 'head position' (Chapter 5). Children might know in advance that linguistic structures have a head (key word), and that languages tend to put the modifiers (words relating to the head) consistently either before or after it. So, to repeat the English example given on p. 95, English children might say:

THE DOG DROPPED(H) THAT SLIPPER(M) DOWN(H) THE DRAIN(M)

with heads (H) preceding modifiers (M), while Turkish children would reverse this order, and say the equivalent of:

THE DOG THE DRAIN(M) DOWN(H) THE SLIPPER(M) DROPPED(H)

with modifiers preceding heads. Does this suggestion work?

At first sight, this is a plausible idea. Children are on the whole consistent in their treatment of heads and modifiers. But on second thoughts, this may be because youngsters are sensitive to the order of the words they hear. There is no need to assume an English child has 'set a parameter' when it says WANT MILK, rather than *MILK WANT. It just listened to its mother saying: 'Do you want some milk?' and remembered the word order. Furthermore, if a switch had been set, we would expect children to iron out various inconsistencies. They should say *AGO TWO WEEKS instead of TWO WEEKS AGO, where the modifier occurs (exceptionally) after the words it modifies. But they show no real signs of behaving like this.

Perhaps the biggest weakness of the switch-setting theory is that no one can agree how many switches there are, nor how exactly they are set (Roeper and Williams 1987). This may be because language acquisition is just too messy a process to be explained by the flick of a switch.

Let us now summarize our conclusions about Content Cuthbert. This approach does not seem to be borne out by the evidence. Children do not appear to have firm advance expectations about language. They do not necessarily steer clear of sentences which are prohibited by language universals. They do not acquire chunks of language by flicking a switch. Of course, Chomskyan language universals may still exist. But they are not there 'ready to go' at a relatively early stage, triggered by simple data, and requiring very little effort on the child's part, as Chomsky has suggested. Let us now consider whether Process Peggy provides a better explanation for language acquisition.

IS PROCESS PEGGY A GENERAL PROBLEM SOLVER?

The most general process approach proposes that Process Peggy simply makes use of a wider set of puzzle-solving abilities which she brings to bear on the world as a whole. Proponents of this viewpoint put forward various non-linguistic factors which they consider to be critical for guiding the child forward through the thickets of language. We shall consider two of these: children's needs and their general mental development.

According to an 'everyday needs' approach, children are by nature sociable little animals who need to interact with other humans. They also have certain material needs, such as MILK or JUICE. They are therefore concerned primarily with interacting with other people, and with getting what they want. They acquire speech in order to help them in this quest (e.g. Donaldson 1978). Within a particular culture, there is relatively little variation in the interests and requirements of different children. Therefore, it is not surprising that children develop language in a parallel fashion, even though they have never met one another.

This viewpoint is certainly borne out by children in the very early stages of development. As we noted in Chapter 6, children all over the world seem to talk about very similar things at the two-word stage. We find requests such as WANT MILK, rejections such as NO WASH, questions such as WHERE DADDY?, and so on, in widely separated children. Some researchers have suggested that this state of affairs lasts throughout the language learning period. They argue that children are concerned primarily with the external world, both with finding out about it, and with getting what they want. As youngsters attempt to learn about and manipulate some aspect of their environment, they look for ways to talk about it. Language, therefore, mirrors the preoccupations of the child at each stage.

In a trivial way, this is undoubtedly true, in that children talk about the things which concern them. But it cannot explain why children proceed to further stages of language development when their own primitive structures have the desired effect. For example, if a child says WHERE KITTY?, she is likely to be told what she wants to know – where the cat is. Why, therefore, should she, and most other children, proceed to (probably) WHERE KITTY GO?, then some weeks or months later to WHERE KITTY HAS GONE? and finally to WHERE HAS KITTY GONE? In brief, the argument that the child learns language in order to help her to manipulate the world does not explain why she does not stop learning as soon as she starts obtaining what she wants, nor why we find similar structural developments in different children.

A child called John provides further problems for the notion that children develop language in order to cope with everyday needs (Blank et al. 1979). John used language creatively, and had a firm grasp of linguistic structures – but he did not use language to communicate. He disliked interacting with others so much that he never spoke directly to anyone, even his parents. He simply talked to himself as he played with his toys: 'Let's go shopping. Where's the money? OK here's the change. Open the door. Pretend it's a shopping centre. OK get elevator. Push button.' John provides evidence against the view that children are sociable beings who cater for their needs by communicating with others.

Let us, therefore, look at another factor, which may be important in understanding the stages by which children acquire language. This is general mental development, or rather, general cognitive development as it is more usually expressed. Some people have suggested that language acquisition is both dependent on it, and caused by it. Like the 'everyday needs' view, such a belief is obviously justified to a limited extent, since 'It is tautological that linguistic development presupposes cognitive development in the uninteresting sense that one cannot express a concept that one doesn't have' (Fodor et al. 1974: 463). Certain concepts seem to be easier for children to grasp than others. For example, English, Italian, Turkish and Serbo-Croatian children were asked to describe where an object such as a nut was placed in relation to one or more other items, such as plates or glasses (Johnston and Slobin 1979; Slobin 1982). They could all cope with the nut being IN, ON, BESIDE or UNDER a plate before they could describe it as being BETWEEN two plates.

It is also true that certain cognitive abilities and language structures tend to emerge at similar times. For example, one researcher claimed that the development of comparative constructions (I AM BIGGER THAN YOU) occurs at a time when the child can recognize that a pint of milk remains the same whether it is poured into a long thin container or a short fat one (Sinclair-de-Zwart 1969). However, the simultaneous development of different abilities does not prove that one is dependent on the other, since in the normal child, many aspects of growth take place at around the same time. As one researcher noted 'Hair growth and language development might be positively correlated, but few psycholinguists would wish to posit interesting links between the two' (Curtiss 1981).

Perhaps the best way to test whether language acquisition and cognitive development are inextricably linked is to search for children who show some discrepancy between cognitive and linguistic abilities. If such a discrepancy can be found, then clearly the link is not an inevitable one. And there are reports of several children whose general cognitive development is unrelated to their grasp of language structure.

Consider Laura, earlier known under the pseudonym Marta (Yamada 1988, 1990). Laura had been a limp, floppy infant. In spite of coming from a loving, supportive home, her general development was delayed. She could not sit alone until she was 15 months old. She was also severely mentally retarded, and as a teenager was unable to perform tasks which even normal 2-year-olds can carry out successfully. When she was given a stack of pictures to sort, she did not separate humans from objects, as normal children tend to do. She did not understand numbers, and did not know her age. Her short-term memory was limited, and she could not repeat back sequences of more than three unrelated items.

In contrast, her speech was fluent and sometimes richly structured, and had apparently been so since around the age of 9. When her speech was studied in her teens, she produced sentences such as:

SHE DOES PAINTINGS, THIS REALLY GOOD FRIEND OF THE KIDS WHO I WENT TO SCHOOL WITH LAST YEAR, AND REALLY LOVED.

She used syntactic structures which are acquired relatively late in normal development, such as 'full' passives as in:

I GOT IT CUT ALREADY BY A MAID (when talking about her hair).
I DON'T WANT TO GET EATEN BY ONE (about crocodiles at the zoo).

Laura was not just repeating back sentences she'd heard, as shown by occasional errors, as in:

WHEN I FIRST WENT THERE THREE TICKETS WERE GAVE OUT BY A POLICE LAST YEAR.

She could also repeat back correctly a sentence such as:

AN APPLE WAS EATEN BY JENI.

This construction is difficult for children who have not acquired the passive. But the passive was not the only advanced construction she had acquired. Consider:

> I SHOULD'VE BROUGHT IT BACK.
> I DON'T LIKE HIM PUTTIN' PAPER TOWELS IN MY MOUTH.
> DID YOU HEAR ABOUT ME NOT GOING TO THIS SCHOOL?
> HE WAS SAYING THAT I LOST MY BATTERY-POWERED WATCH THAT I LOVED.

These all show a considerable degree of linguistic sophistication as far as syntax is concerned.

But Laura's speech was by no means 'normal'. Her utterances were often semantically odd, or inappropriate, as in:

> I WAS 16 LAST YEAR AND NOW I'M 19 THIS YEAR.
> I WAS LIKE 15 OR 19 WHEN I STARTED MOVING OUT O' HOME.
> SHE WAS THINKING THAT IT'S NO REGULAR SCHOOL, IT'S JUST PLAIN OLD NO BUSES.
> WELL, WE WERE TAKING A WALK, MY MOM, AND THERE WAS THIS GIANT, LIKE MY MOTHER THREW A STICK.

In brief, she was able to deal with the structure of language to a perhaps surprising extent, but found it difficult to cope with the type of concepts which language normally expresses.

Genie, the Californian girl whose development was outlined in Chapter 4, illustrates the reverse situation (Curtiss 1977). Genie was able to cope with complex feelings and concepts, but her ability to deal with language structure was minimal. She expressed herself mainly by means of content words strung together with little syntactic structure as in: THINK ABOUT MAMA LOVE GENIE, or DENTIST SAY DRINK WATER. Her utterances were appropriate, and often conceptually sophisticated, even though telegraphic, as in:

Adult:	HOW MANY SIDES DOES A TRIANGLE HAVE?
Genie:	THREE.
Adult:	HOW MANY SIDES DOES A CIRCLE HAVE?
Genie:	ROUND.

As Curtiss noted: 'Genie's semantic sophistication suggests a conceptual level far surpassing what one would imagine from her otherwise rather primitive utterances' (1981: 21) – an impression borne out by her relatively good performance in a wide range of intelligence tests.

Laura, therefore, showed that severe conceptual deficits can exist alongside a surprisingly developed language ability, while Genie illustrated the opposite – that conceptual ability can outstrip language structure. These case studies suggest that cognitive development cannot provide the definitive key to the acquisition of language structure – even though it is clearly important for meaningful communication.

But Laura and Genie are not the only ones who showed a bizarre mismatch between linguistic and general cognitive abilities. Christopher, a multilingual savant, and Kate, a savant poet, are two gifted but disadvantaged individuals whose use of language massively outweighs their other mental abilities. A savant, incidentally, is someone who has exceptional skills in one particular area (Treffert 1989/1990). Judging from the literature, most savants have either musical or mathematical skills. But Christopher and Kate are both savant linguists.

Christopher is a man, now over 40, who is unable to look after himself. Yet he can speak English perfectly well. In addition, he is obsessed by languages other than his own, and can translate fluently from over a dozen. Here is a translation by Christopher from Polish, followed by an accurate version (Smith and Tsimpli 1995: 15):

Christopher's translation: 'I had to take him out of the car strongly and put – he put himself on the floor and opened his eyes – and shut his eyes, not wishing to see what was waiting for him.'

Accurate version: 'I had to throw him into the car with force. He lay down on the floor and closed his eyes, not wishing to see what awaited him.'

Kate is over 40, but her case is equally strange. Her mental age has been assessed at around that of a 7-year-old. She cannot solve even the simplest verbal intelligence test problems, and has huge difficulties using language in everyday situations. Yet she is judged by professionals in English literature to be a highly gifted poet. Over half her poems describe her own problems (Dowker et al. 1996):

I got it;
my disability;
not never to walk from it.
It shares my space,
breathes the same air.
I cannot have a day off.

Or, as she said in another poem:

> I lost the me
> It got under everything
> that was not poems.

Christopher and Kate show that language can not only be spared, but even enriched, when other cognitive abilities are impaired. So far, then, we have argued that language seems to be a special skill. In occasional cases, it can be partially separated from general cognitive ability.

But normal children do not just acquire language by lucky chance. They exploit the helpfulness of those around, and (mostly) pay attention to what they say.

CAREGIVER LANGUAGE

> NO, YOU SHOULDN'T MAKE A HOLE IN THE BOTTOM.
> NO, LET DADDY DO IT FIRST.
> NO, I DON'T THINK YOU'LL BE ABLE TO CUT STRAIGHT.
> NO, DON'T CUT TOO MUCH ON THE FRONT.
> NO, I DON'T THINK YOU SHOULD PUT MORE HOLES IN IT.
> NO, DON'T CUT TWO HOLES.

These six examples of NO placed in front of the sentence occurred in a 15-minute recording session in which 2-year-old Nicholas was 'helping' his father to carve a pumpkin (De Villiers and De Villiers 1979). This construction seemed to be a favourite one for Nicholas's father. Not surprisingly, the majority of Nicholas's early negatives (76 per cent) involved opposition to some suggestion proposed by his parents, and his means of expressing this was by placing NO in front of the sentence, as in NO DADDY DRESS ME.

Faced with such examples, a number of people have suggested that *motherese*, *caretaker language*, or *caregiver language* (speech addressed to children) can solve the mystery of how children acquire language so efficiently. Children, according to this view, absorb and copy the speech they hear around them. They learn so fast, it is claimed, because speech addressed to children is rather different from that to adults (Chapter 4), and so grabs their attention. In many communities, this special way of talking to children begins as soon as the baby is born:

> Wha's a matter, Bobby, yo' widdle tum-tum all empty? Here you are, a growin' boy, and dese folks won't feed you. You tell 'em, they can't just let you cry, not while Aunt Sue is 'round . . . You're a-gonna be a big boy, just

like your daddy. Mamma gonna hafta get some new rompers soon . . . Okay, okay, look, look, there's mamma, she's comin', she gonna get dat bottle right now and get it ready for you. It's a hungry boy, it is.

(Heath 1983: 118)

This stream of speech was addressed to Bobby by a helpful neighbour when he was only a month or so old. It contains many of the characteristics found repeatedly in child-directed speech (Ferguson 1978). It tends to be slower, spoken with higher pitch, and with exaggerated intonation contours. The utterances are shorter, with the average length being approximately one-third of that found in speech addressed to adults (Newport, Gleitman and Gleitman 1977). The sentences are well-formed, simple in structure and repetitious, in that the same lexical items recur, though in slightly different combinations. Special 'baby' words are sometimes used, such as DOGGIE, BIRDIE, GEE-GEE, CHUFF-CHUFF, TUM-TUM. The topic is usually related to the 'here and now' – things that are present both in place and time.

Yet the link between caregiver speech and child language is not always straightforward. And 'repairs' – cases in which caregivers try to 'mend' a communication which has been ignored or misinterpreted – turn out to be too infrequent to be of consistent use. Meanwhile, reformulations such as:

OPEN YOUR MOUTH. OPEN IT.
SPIT OUT THE SNAIL, SPIT THE SNAIL OUT. SPIT IT OUT.
GIVE MUMMY THE SNAIL. GIVE THE SNAIL TO MUMMY.

account for only around 4 per cent of maternal speech, it has been claimed (Shatz 1982).

So is Chomsky right in his belief (outlined in Chapter 5) that what children hear is 'fairly degenerate in quality' (1965: 31)? Or has he never listened to parent–child conversation? Let us consider the matter more carefully.

For a start, it seems reasonable to expect that words and constructions which occur frequently in adult speech will be produced early by children. And this certainly seems to be borne out in some studies. For example, in the development of verbal auxiliaries (words such as *can, will, might, have,* etc.) the order of acquisition roughly follows the frequency of these words in adult speech (Wells 1979).

Statistically, therefore, there is a link between items produced frequently by parents, and those acquired early by the child. But the problem with statistical correlations is that they do not hold for every construction, nor for every child. Furthermore, correlations which are valid for groups of people can sometimes disappear when each individual child and its parents are examined separately (Wells 1979, 1986). We must conclude, therefore, that overall frequency of use is only a rough guide to the order of acquisition, and is by no means a definitive map.

Since simple frequency counts have not proved entirely helpful, some researchers have suggested that motherese directs child language in a more subtle way. They have proposed that parents have an inbuilt sensitivity to their children. According to this view, parents gradually increase the complexity of their speech as the child becomes ready for each new stage. This has sometimes been called the 'fine-tuning' hypothesis (Cross 1977), in the sense that parents subconsciously attune their output to their child's needs. And a few people have claimed that, far from children possessing an innate language learning device, mothers possess an innate language teaching device! Those who support this viewpoint assume that there will be a close correlation between the structure of the mother's speech and that of the child at every stage of development. Is this true?

Research confirms that parents attune their speech to their children's needs, but suggests they attune them to a child's interests, more than to his or her language structure. That is, parents talk about topics which are relevant to the child such as picking up blocks or drinking juice, but show no evidence that they are grading their syntax, or introducing constructions one at a time, as one might expect if they were subconsciously guiding their children from one stage of language to another. There is no sign of a step-by-step programme, except in the broad general sense that as the child gets older, the parents' speech tends to become less repetitious, with longer sentences and more complex subject matter. Moreover, researchers who examined the speech of fifteen mothers interacting with their young daughters, concluded that if one was designing a curriculum for language teaching, motherese was highly unsuitable! (Newport et al. 1977). In a good language teaching programme, you would expect teachers to introduce constructions one at a time and to concentrate first on simple active declarative sentences (TOBY WANTS A BATH, or MARION IS EATING A BUN), then move on to constructions in which words are omitted or the order shifted round as in imperatives (TURN OFF THE TAP! COME HOME!) or questions (WHAT IS TONY EATING? WHY ARE YOU CRYING?). Instead, they found mothers did the reverse. That is, they used all these constructions jumbled together with more questions and imperatives (62 per cent) than declaratives (30 per cent)! Oddly enough, there were more declaratives in the *second* session, six months later, than in the first, and even more in the speech addressed to other adults! These researchers, therefore, assert that 'Motherese is not a syntax-teaching language.'

Children, therefore, have an inbuilt filter which allows them to choose what they pay attention to: 'The child is selective in WHAT he uses from the environment provided; he is selective about WHEN in the course of acquisition he chooses to use it' (Gleitman *et al.* 1984). Child 'uptake' is not matched in any straightforward way with adult input.

A further piece of evidence that uptake matters more than input, is the existence of communities where parents do not modify their speech when talking to infants. In 'Trackton', a working-class black community in the southeast of the USA, adults do not regard babies as suitable partners for regular conversation (Heath 1983). They rarely address speech specifically to very young children. Moreover, Trackton inhabitants find it odd when they hear white people gurgling over infants: 'White folks uh hear dey kids say sump'n, dey say it back to 'em' (Heath 1983: 84). Trackton children are an integral part of family life, so they hear plenty of speech around them. Somehow, they acquire language as efficiently as anyone else.

Adults can, however, help their children by talking about things that interest them, and engaging in joint enterprises (Wells 1979): 'Now, then, Shirley, are you going to help mummy peel the potatoes? Can you get me six out of that basket?' The tendency of girls to be mildly ahead of boys in their language may be due to the different treatment meted out by parents. Girls are often kept in to help with the chores in many families, but boys are sent out to play games. Mothers, rather than footballs, aid progress in language. And sensitive fathers can help their sons too.

Some researchers have queried why the role of caregivers arouses such controversy among those who study it. One finding is that the various types of interaction have been classified in overlapping and confusing ways. Researchers may, as a preliminary step, need to distinguish negative *feedback* from negative *evidence* (Saxton 2000).

Negative feedback is a signal to the child that something is wrong with their utterance, though exactly what is unspecified:

Alex: A PIRATE HITTED HIM ON THE HEAD.
Father: WHAT?

This query prompted Alex to reassess what he had said, and amend this too: 'The pirate hit him on the head' (Saxton 2000: 228) – though Alex must already have known the correct form, because no extra information was provided by his father. Negative evidence, on the other hand, provides the child with the information needed to put the utterance right:

Alex: I SAY IT GOODER.
Father: BETTER.
Alex: BETTER, YEAH. (Saxton 2000: 224).

Where does all this lead us? We now realize that caregiver speech is an important factor which must be taken into consideration when we study child language, and that it is often considerably more coherent and more useful than Chomsky suggests. Yet as Cromer (1981: 65) notes:

> To show that the input signal to many children is far clearer than had been assumed in no way explains how the grammatical structures that the child uses are developed.

Or, in the words of the nineteenth-century German philosopher-linguist Wilhelm von Humboldt: 'Language cannot really be taught . . . One can only offer the thread along which language develops on its own' (quoted in Slobin 1975: 283).

A LINGUISTIC PROCESS PEGGY

Process Peggy, then, is not a general problem-solver. Neither everyday needs nor general intelligence nor caregiver speech can fully account for her special language abilities – though all these factors are important if she is to develop normally. She must be innately programmed to tackle language. In this section, we shall discuss how she might set about her linguistic puzzle-solving.

In the beginning, she possibly uses her general intelligence to get going (Chapter 6). She may behave like a computer, which often needs a fairly general program to start up before it can use a more specific one. Computer operators talk about 'booting up' or 'boot-strapping' a computer – giving it some preliminary commands, which will then allow it to cope with more detailed programs. So some linguists talk about a 'bootstrapping' approach to language (Pinker 1984, 1987).

Linguistic bootstrapping might work as follows. Children learn words such as DOGGY, KITTY, BITE, DRINK, BALL, MILK, which correlate well with actors, actions and objects. They therefore build these up in various semantic relationships (Chapter 6):

KITTY DRINK (ACTOR + ACTION).
DRINK MILK (ACTION + OBJECT).

And they may combine these into longer sequences:

KITTY DRINK MILK (ACTOR + ACTION + OBJECT).

Up to this point, general intelligence may be at work, rather than linguistic ability. The basic scaffolding relies on meaning.

Then they switch over to syntax. Exactly how they do this is disputed. According to one suggestion, syntax begins when children discover some discrepancy in their semantic scaffolding. They may discover that words describing actions such as BITE or DRINK can sometimes be replaced by words such as WANT, GOT, LIKE, which do not involve any kind of deed:

KITTY WANT MILK.
KITTY LIKE MILK.

The child may therefore realize that the 'slot' a word occupies in the sentence matters more than its strict correlation with an action or event in the external world. At this point, the child has acquired a linguistic category, that of verb.

To take a slightly different example, children may notice that different semantic relationships have some underlying structural similarity:

BLUE SOCK 'It's a blue sock' (ATTRIBUTE + OBJECT).
MUMMY SOCK 'It's mummy's sock' (POSSESSOR + OBJECT).

They may notice that both BLUE and MUMMY fall into the same slot, the one in front of SOCK, and combine them in their minds. Once two different types of word have been combined under one heading, this is syntax, not meaning.

To summarize, a possible way of moving from a semantic grammar to a syntactic (linguistic) one is to discover that there is not necessarily a direct correlation between types of word and the world. The child therefore discovers abstract relationships underlying the semantic ones. This is the beginning of syntax. Just as some children have a 'naming-insight' which triggers a surge forward in vocabulary (Chapter 6), so some children may acquire a syntactic insight, which triggers an innate processing device.

Children cannot persist in using meaning to guide them, because language just does not correlate sufficiently with the world around. If children carried on classifying verbs as actions, they would probably make strange overgeneralizations such as:

SHE IS NOISYING.
SHE IS BUSYING.

They would wrongly assume that NOISY and BUSY were verbs, because they describe actions. Similarly, they would fail to recognize words such as LIKE, HATE, GOT as verbs, because they do not involve an action. But children do not seem to have this type of problem (Maratsos 1982).

Somehow, children are specially pre-programmed to notice linguistic regularities, and to give them priority over semantic ones, as shown by children learning French or German (Maratsos 1982). A language such as French has a somewhat odd gender system (by English standards), since every word has to be labelled as masculine or feminine. Sometimes this correlates with natural gender: UN GARÇON 'a boy' (m.), UNE DAME 'a lady' (f.), but at other times it does not, as in UN CANIF 'a knife' (m.), UNE FOURCHETTE 'a fork' (f.). Certain word endings (such as -IEN) are typically masculine, while others (such as -IENNE) are typically feminine. Children pay more attention to this type of information than to matching up gender with the external world. This was demonstrated by an ingenious experiment (Karmiloff-Smith 1979).

The researcher showed children a picture of two little boys, and told them: 'Here are two FORSIENNES.' She then showed them another picture, which had just one of the little boys in it, and asked: 'What's this?' The children replied: 'It's UNE FORSIENNE.' They automatically used the feminine UNE 'a' because this goes with the ending -IENNE. They did not seem bothered that a boy seemed to be assigned to the feminine gender. If they had required language to correlate closely with the world, they should have been puzzled. But they were not. We conclude that linguistic consistency matters more than language–world matching.

OPERATING PRINCIPLES

Children are wired, the linguist Noam Chomsky has argued, with a substantial amount of innate knowledge (Chapter 5). Others have argued that children are simply efficient at sorting out and learning the patterns of any language to which they are exposed. (Tomasello 2003). Let us explore the matter further.

Dan Slobin of the University of California at Berkeley worked on this problem for a number of years, and is regarded as a pioneer in this field. (Slobin 1973, 1982, 1986a–1997b). He started by claiming to have isolated a number of 'operating principles' used by children as they process language. Children find certain types of constructions easier to cope with than others. They begin by acquiring 'easy' constructions, and will then move on to more difficult ones. This commonsense assumption underlies Slobin's pioneering work. We need therefore to find out what constitutes 'difficulty' for a child in linguistic terms. We can learn a certain amount by simply looking at constructions which are acquired early, and seeing what they have in common, after, of course, checking that the frequency of use by adults is not a major factor for the construction in question. For example, children acquire relative clauses (clauses introduced by relative pronouns such as WHO, WHICH, THAT) in a certain order. They produce relative clauses which follow the main clause such as:

MUNGO SAW AN OCTOPUS [WHICH HAD 20 LEGS]

before ones which are placed inside the main clause:

THE OCTOPUS [WHICH HAD 20 LEGS] ESCAPED

even though there seems to be little difference in the frequency with which adults produce these two types. We can also draw certain conclusions from looking at children's errors: why, for example, do children so often leave out the auxiliary verb, as in DADDY (IS) SWIMMING, MUMMY (IS) COOKING? However, the best way of discovering which constructions children find easy, and which difficult, he suggested, may be the study of children speaking different languages, and in particular, bilingual children

Slobin pointed out that children who grow up learning two languages do not normally acquire a particular construction simultaneously in both languages. For example, children who are acquiring Hungarian and Serbo-Croatian as twin native languages use Hungarian locatives (INTO THE BOX, ON THE TABLE) long before they produce the equivalent Serbo-Croatian ones. Clearly, there cannot be any conceptual difficulty connected with the notion of locative, because the Hungarian ones are used in the correct circumstances. We conclude that there must be something intrinsically difficult about Serbo-Croatian locatives from the linguistic point of view.

Let us examine the locatives in these two languages, and then go on to consider Slobin's conclusions (which were based on far more evidence than can be considered here).

The Hungarian locative, on the one hand, is formed by means of a suffix attached to a noun. Each locative expression, INTO, ON, and so on, is a single unambiguous syllable, placed after a noun:

HAJÓBAN 'Boat-in, in the boat'
HAJÓBÓL 'Boat-out-of, (getting) out of the boat'.

The Serbo-Croatian locatives, on the other hand, are not nearly as clear cut. The Serbo-Croatian word U can mean either 'into' or 'in'. You can tell the difference between the two uses of Serbo-Croatian U by looking at the end of the following noun:

U KUCU 'into the house'
U KUCI 'in the house'.

But the situation is further complicated because the noun endings are not used only in conjunction with this preposition, but have other uses as well. Worse still, another preposition, K 'towards', which you might expect to be followed by the same suffix as U 'into', in fact takes a quite different noun ending. So in Serbo-Croatian we find the same prepositional form with more than one meaning, and followed by more than one noun ending. And we find prepositions with similar meanings followed by different noun endings, as well as the same noun endings used for a variety of purposes. No wonder the children get confused!

Slobin concluded that children find some constructions easy to learn and others difficult because they have certain expectations about language. They expect language to be consistent, and assume that there will be one unit of form to match each unit of meaning. They expect words to be systematically modified, especially by means of endings. They assume that word-order is important. They are puzzled by interruptions and rearrangements of linguistic units.

Slobin expresses these expectations as a set of 'operating principles' – self instructions which the child might subconsciously give himself as he attempts to analyse linguistic data. For example:

1 allot one form only to each unit of meaning;
2 pay attention to the ends of words;
3 pay attention to the order of words;
4 avoid interruptions.

Of course, Slobin's list contains many more principles than the four listed above (which appear in a slightly different form in his more recent work). But there is considerable evidence to support his point of view, particularly in respect of the four principles mentioned here. Let us briefly comment on each, giving some examples.

The principle of one form per unit of meaning seems to persist right through the acquisition period. It lies behind children's overgeneralizations. Once a child has correctly identified the plural ending on words such as DUCKS, COWS, HORSES, he naturally assumes that this ending can be extended to other words, as in SHEEPS, MOUSES, GOOSES. Children confidently expect the same plural ending to be applicable everywhere (with minor phonetic variations). Several researchers have noted that children show an inbuilt resistance to using two different forms to mean the same thing (e.g. MacWhinney 1978; Clark 1987). Conversely, children do not like to allot more than one meaning to any word or word-ending. Karmiloff-Smith (1979) has shown that this principle is still at work in children between the ages of 5 and 8. In a study of the acquisition of the articles LE/LA 'the' and UN/UNE 'a' in French, she noted that until around the age of 8 'the child does not place on one word the burden of conveying more than one meaning' (Karmiloff-Smith 1979: 224). For example, French UN/UNE can either mean 'a' or 'one'. When children first became aware of the double meaning, several of them in her experiments tried to invent ways of distinguishing between the two meanings, by altering the syntax. In the following conversation, an 8-year-old correctly says UNE BROSSE for 'a brush', but incorrectly uses the phrase UNE DE BROSSE for 'one brush'. The experimenter had shown the child a picture of a boy in a room with three brushes, and a girl in a room with one brush, and had asked: 'To whom would I say, lend me a brush?' The child replied:

> ... it's the boy because he's got a brush (UNE BROSSE), no it's the girl because she has one brush (UNE DE BROSSE) ... no, the boy because he could give you any of his brushes.
>
> (Karmiloff-Smith 1979)

The second operating principle mentioned above, 'Pay attention to the ends of words' seems to be subconsciously followed even when children are not dealing with specific inflectional endings. When English children confuse two different words, they often get the last part right: THE LION AND THE LEPRECHAUN instead of 'the lion and the unicorn', ICE CREAM TOILET, for 'ice cream cornet' (Aitchison and Straf 1981). And it is well known that children tend to omit or confuse the first syllable of a word, particularly if it is unstressed, as in RITTACK, RIDUCTOR, RIFECTION for 'attack', 'conductor', 'infection' (Smith 1973: 12). But this is not only because the syllable is unstressed. It is also because the syllable occurs at the beginning of the word. In Czech, where initial syllables are stressed, it is the unstressed final syllables which are better remembered by children, according to one researcher (Pašcová 1968, reported in Slobin 1973). And further evidence that suffixes are more salient than prefixes or items placed in front of a word comes from the observataion that English children omit prepositions that are essential to the sentence (e.g. MUMMY GARDEN) at a time when they have already started using the correct endings on words (e.g. DADDY SINGING).

The third operating principle 'Pay attention to the order of words' is illustrated by the consistency with which children preserve the adult word order in English (Chapter 6), while their resistance to alterations in the 'normal' order is shown by their tendency to acquire the process of noun-auxiliary inversion relatively late. As we noted, children produce sentences such as WHERE DADDY HAS GONE? before the correct, inverted form WHERE HAS DADDY GONE?

Finally, the principle 'Avoid interruptions' is shown by the development of the verbal construction known as the progressive. This describes an ongoing action:

POLLY IS SNORING.
ARTHUR IS WHISTLING.

It is a discontinuous sandwich-like construction because the progressive sequence IS . . . ING is interrupted by the verb:

POLLY	IS	SNOR	ING
ARTHUR	IS	WHISTL	ING

It is clear that IS . . . ING functions as a single unit, because when an ongoing action is described we do not find one without the other. English does not have sentences such as:

> *POLLY IS SNORE.
> *ARTHUR WHISTLING.

The Harvard children, Adam, Eve and Sarah all used the -ING part of the progressive early (Brown 1973). Both Adam and Eve acquired it earlier than any other ending. But they all omitted the IS (AM, ARE, etc.) part:

> WHAT COWBOY DOING?
> WHY YOU SMILING?

The full IS . . . ING construction appeared only after a long delay. In both Adam's and Sarah's speech, the gap was longer than 12 months. For a year, it seems, they just did not fully recognize the connection between the IS and the ING. And there appears to be nothing inherently difficult about the phonetic forms AM, IS, ARE. This is shown by the fact that for all three children AM, IS, ARE occurred with nouns, as in:

> HE IS A COWBOY.

some time before AM, IS, ARE, in progressive constructions.

It seems that all three children were puzzled by the discontinuity involved. They assigned -ING to the progressive early, but were baffled by the preceding IS. In other words, discontinuities seem to go against children's natural intuitions about what language is like. This point is again illustrated by the development of relative clauses. As we noted earlier, those which do not interrupt the main clause such as:

> THE FARMER WAS ANGRY WITH THE PIG [WHICH ATE THE TURNIPS].

develop before those which do:

> THE PIG [WHICH ATE THE TURNIPS] ESCAPED.

Moreover, if children are asked to repeat a sentence in which a main clause is interrupted by a relative clause, they tend to alter the sentence in order to avoid this happening. A child asked to repeat the sentence.

THE OWL [WHO EATS CANDY] RUNS FAST.

repeated it as:

THE OWL EAT A CANDY AND HE RUN FAST (Slobin and Welsh 1973).

Operating principles are not the whole answer, however. The four described above cannot account for the whole of acquisition. But as soon as we start adding to them – Slobin eventually listed about forty – then they start to clash with one another. Every time we find one which doesn't work, we can claim it is because another one is in operation, cancelling out the first. This leads to the whole idea being vacuous (Bowerman 1986). Unless we can find out which have precedence, and how children cope in cases of conflict, then we are back at square one – looking for some basic principles which guide children through the morass of possibilities.

Some people have suggested that the principles interact with particular languages. If one operating principle works well, due to the structure of the language concerned, then it is given priority over others (Bates and MacWhinney 1987; MacWhinney 1987, MacWhinney and Bates 1989). For example, English has a fairly rigid word order. Children will repeatedly come across the same order for (say) verb + adverb (WALK SLOWLY, HOLD IT CAREFULLY, SHUT IT QUIETLY). Counter-evidence such as SOFTLY FALLS THE LIGHT OF DAY is rare. Evidence of word order is thus both easily available and reliable, so English children will pay particular attention to the order of words. In another language, such as Turkish, the ends of words may get extra scrutiny. According to this view, then, the various operating principles compete with one another, and the structure of the language determines which ones will win out over others.

In short, children are enormously good at sussing out how their own language works. But perhaps we need more than the vague notion of competing strategies. Let us try to be more precise.

ADVANCING AND RETREATING

How do children advance? And how do they retreat? Being endowed with processing mechanisms which involve certain outline expectations about language does not tell us exactly how a child acquires any particular construction. Nor does it tell us how children manage to abandon their mistakes. Let us consider these matters.

A construction does not pop up suddenly, like a chicken out of an egg. There may be quite a gap between its *emergence* (first appearance) and its *acquisition* (reliable use). A typical profile of a developing structure was outlined earlier, when we discussed Sally's past tenses (Chapter 6). Judging from Sally's behaviour, children learn the first examples of a construction by rote, without fully analysing them. In this way, a structure gets a firm hold in a few places. The child then tentatively experiments by extending it to new examples. If she gets reinforcement for these experiments, the construction is likely to proliferate, affecting more and more vocabulary items. As an end result, a rule is acquired.

This general pattern of 'lexical diffusion' (Chapter 6) occurs in more complex constructions also, such as sentences which contain the sequence TO + verb (Bloom *et al.* 1984):

> FELIX TRIED TO REACH THE APPLE.
> I WANT THAT DOG TO STAY OUTSIDE.

The earliest examples of this construction occurred without any overt appearance of TO, as in:

> I WANNA PEE-PEE.
> I WANNA TAKE KITTY.

where the child had no realization that TO is a separate item. When a distinct TO did appear, children behaved as if it was fastened to the end of the previous verb, each of which was one of a small group of newly acquired verbs, such as TRY TO, LIKE TO, SUPPOSED TO, as in:

> I LIKE TO   SEE GRANDMA.
> I TRY TO   STAY CLEAN.

Gradually, they added in more and more verbs. They also re-analysed their old WANNA sequences, and produced utterances such as:

> I WANT TO   HOLD THE KITTY.

Finally, they began to acquire sentences in which a noun occurred between the first verb and TO:

> I'LL HELP YOU TO FIND THE BUTTONS.
> I WANT THIS DOLL TO STAY HERE.

They therefore realized that TO was more closely associated with the second verb.

As the move from WANNA to WANT TO suggests, verbs may be the key to understanding how children move forwards. Let us consider this.

VERBS AS MAYPOLES

Verbs are the maypole around which a sentence revolves. This may seem odd, since verbs vary so much. If an adult describes, say, an egg being dropped, he or she will use the word EGG, but the verb will vary from person to person: 'Mildred *dropped* the egg', 'The egg *slipped* through her fingers', 'The egg *smashed* on the ground', 'The egg *broke*', and so on. In one experiment, adults who were shown a videoclip agreed on the verb less than 10 per cent of the time (Gleitman and Gillette 1995).

But on reflection, verbs are not so strange. They describe straightforward events or linked ones. To 'boil potatoes' covers several different actions, but all are causally related. No verb means 'Simultaneously, John yawned and the cat fell off the roof.' No verb SUBNOUGATE exists for 'To eat the bottom caramels in a candy box and carefully replace the top level, hoping no one will notice' (Pinker 1989: 196).

Verb structure ties in with the verb's meaning. Take the sentences PENELOPE SNEEZED and PETE KICKED THE CAT. English speakers know that only Penelope is involved in the action in the first, and that Pete is doing something to something else in the second. And children pay careful attention to the words round the verb, as shown by Kelli, a blind child (Landau and Gleitman 1985).

Kelli couldn't see, but she learned to speak with only a marginal delay, compared with sighted children. She, like other children, focused on verbs and the words accompanying them. For example, she distinguished LOOK and SEE by paying attention to the different ways in which her mother used these words:

> *LOOK*, HERE'S HOW YOU WIND UP THE CLOCK.
> YOU *LOOK* LIKE A KANGAROO.
> *SEE* IF YOU CAN PUT THE SLIPPER ON.
> LET'S *SEE* IF GRANNY'S HOME.

These structural differences were important – though some of the clues also related to meaning. Kelli's mother tended to use LOOK when an object was near at hand:

> LET'S *LOOK* AT THIS (where LOOK meant 'feel').

and SEE when it was further away:

COME AND *SEE* THE KITTY.

As Kelli shows, syntax and meaning are intertwined in a way that is not always easy to tease out. The realization that verbs are the key to children's speech has led to considerable further work, and the way youngsters acquire them is slowly becoming clearer (Tomasello 1992, 2003, Tomasello and Brooks 1998). Michael Tomasello noted that his daughter Travis was young when she learned a wide array of verbs and relational words – 162 before her second birthday. Change of state verbs came early, for example, FALL-DOWN when she fell in a pool, and so did activity verbs, as with TRAVIS LICK-IT, as she licked a popsicle (iced lolly). Each of these verb uses seemed to be independent of others. Travis's earliest three or more word sentences, produced between the ages of 18–21 months, were almost all structured by verbs, and they typically involved building on word combinations that were already in use, such as FALL-DOWN WEEZER which she announced as she dropped the cat, whose name was Weezer, and WEEZER LICK-IT ARMS, as Weezer licked her arms.

In these early stages, Travis showed very few signs of having broad, general grammatical rules. Mostly, she worked on a verb-by-verb basis, with specific people performing the verb's actions, somewhat like the 'limited scope formulae' identified by Martin Braine (Chapter 6). Tomasello has labelled his verb findings the 'Verb Island hypothesis', which stresses the idea that the known verbs are isolated islands of knowledge, not yet linked up into broader rules.

BACKTRACKING

According to the view outlined above, children listen carefully to what people say, and add on verbs one by one. But youngsters do more than this: they sometimes generalize their knowledge to new verbs. The puzzle of why children do not go ahead and produce enormously overgeneralized grammars 'constitutes one of the most intriguing and difficult challenges for all students of language acquisition' (Bowerman 1988: 73). Researchers are still trying to discover how children acquire subtle verb distinctions, both in English and other languages, especially in cases where a verb behaves in an unpredictable way. A child needs to notice that you can say either:

MARION BAKED A CAKE FOR PETER.

or:

MARION BAKED PETER A CAKE.

But this double possibility isn't always available. You can say:

DONALD OPENED THE DOOR FOR PAMELA.

but not:

*DONALD OPENED PAMELA THE DOOR.

The recipient has to be able to possess the object in order to come in front of it. The problem is clear, but the answer is not: 'The essential challenge thus becomes that of developing a theory that allows just the appropriate degree of productivity . . . avoiding the opposing pitfalls of overgeneralization on the one hand and undergeneralization on the other' (Baker 1992). Similarly, you can say:

KEITH GAVE HELEN A BUNCH OF ROSES.

or:

KEITH GAVE A BUNCH OF ROSES TO HELEN.

You could also say:

KEITH GAVE HELEN A HEADACHE.

but not:

*KEITH GAVE A HEADACHE TO HELEN.

You can only give something to someone if a change of location is involved. Apparently, children notice these subtle meaning distinctions and tie them in with the syntax (Pinker 1989) – though how they do this is still unclear.

Yet overgeneralizations are less frequent than is sometimes assumed. They appear common because people tend to notice odd sentences such as:

MOMMY, OPEN HADWEN THE DOOR (Mazurkewich and White 1984).

But how do children retreat from these erroneous forms? It's not yet clear. Perhaps they are just experimenting, so do not have these wrong rules truly fixed in their minds. Or perhaps at this stage children are ultra-sensitive to constructions they are working on (Chapter 4).

In this chapter, then, we have tried to see exactly how children extract grammar from the data they hear around them. Chomsky appears to be wrong when he suggests that children are born with detailed linguistic knowledge which is triggered by only minimal exposure to language. In place of a Content Cuthbert, a child whose mind contains chunks of information about language, we should substitute a Process Peggy, a child whose mind is set up with puzzle-solving equipment.

Process Peggy seems to be geared specifically to language. Her achievements cannot be explained solely by her daily needs, her general cognitive ability, or her parents' speech, though these undoubtedly help her as she struggles to solve linguistic puzzles.

We now have some general idea of the kinds of linguistic expectations which Process Peggy brings to language, and how she advances as she acquires each new construction though we are less clear about how she backtracks, when she discovers she has made a mistake. The exact proportion of specific language mechanisms to other aspects of intelligence is also unclear. It may be that the two are so inextricably mixed, that perhaps we never shall succeed in fully untangling them. This is another question for the future.

We have now completed our discussion of language acquisition. But one point remains quite open. What kind of internal grammar does someone who has completed the acquisition of language have? In other words what does the internalized grammar of an adult look like? This is the next question to be considered. But before that, we have a brief excursus in which we discuss the following topic: how did Chomsky conceive the idea of a transformational grammar in the first place? And why has he, and most other linguists, changed his mind so much in recent years?

8

CELESTIAL UNINTELLIGIBILITY
Why do linguists propose such bizarre grammars?

'If any one of them can explain it,' said Alice, 'I'll give him sixpence. I don't believe there's an atom of meaning in it.'

'If there's no meaning in it,' said the King, 'that saves a world of trouble, you know, as we needn't try to find any. And yet I don't know,' he went on, 'I seem to see some meaning after all.'

Lewis Carroll, *Alice in Wonderland*

Linguists are sometimes accused of being 'too abstract' and 'removed from reality'. For example, one reviewer has condemned 'that celestial unintelligibility which is the element where the true student of linguistics normally floats and dances' (Philip Toynbee, *The Observer*). Yet almost all linguists, not just psycholinguists, are trying to find out about a speaker's mental 'grammar' – the internalized set of rules which enables someone to speak and understand their language. As Chomsky noted:

The linguist constructing a grammar of his language is in effect proposing a hypothesis concerning this internalized system.

(Chomsky 1972a: 26)

So the question which naturally arises is this: if linguists are really trying to form theories about an internalized system, why did Chomsky hit on something as complex and abstract as transformational grammar? Surely there are other types of grammar which do not seem as odd? Some of the reasons for setting up a transformational grammar were mentioned in Chapter 1. But the question will be considered again from a different angle here, including some of the reasons why Chomsky has shifted his ideas so radically. Indeed, to some people Chomsky has played a 'Duke of York' trick on us all, as in the old nursery rhyme:

> The grand old Duke of York,
> He had ten thousand men,
> He marched them up to the top of the hill,
> Then he marched them down again.

Why did Chomsky march us to the top of the transformational hill, then march us all down again? And post-Chomsky, where is everybody trying to go now? Let's start at the beginning.

JUPITER'S STICK INSECTS

Suppose . . . a spaceship full of English speakers had landed on Jupiter. They found the planet inhabited by a race of green stick insects who communicated by sitting down and wiggling their stick-like toes. The English speakers learned the Jupiter toe-wiggle language easily. It was a sign language like Washoe's in which signs stood for words, with no obvious structure. So communication was not a serious problem. But the Emperor of Jupiter became highly envious of these foreigners who were able to walk about and communicate at the same time. They did not have to stop, sit down, and wiggle their toes. He decided to learn English.

At first, he assumed the task was easy. He ordered his servants to record all the sentences uttered by the English speakers, together with their meanings. Each morning he locked himself into his study and memorized the sentences recorded on the previous day. He carried out this routine unswervingly for about a year, dutifully learning every single sentence spoken by the foreigners. As he was an inhabitant of Jupiter, he had no natural ability for understanding the way a language worked. So he did not detect any patterns in the words, he simply memorized them. Eventually, he decided he knew enough to start testing his knowledge in conversation with the Englishmen.

But the result was a disaster. He didn't seem to have learnt the sentences he needed to use. When he wanted to ask the Englishmen if they liked sea-urchin soup, the nearest sentence he could remember having learnt was 'This is funny-tasting soup. What kind is it?' When it rained, and he wanted to know if rain was likely to harm the foreigners, the most relevant sentence was 'It's raining, can we buy gumboots and umbrellas here?'

He began to have doubts about the task he had set himself of memorizing all English sentences. Would it ever come to an end? He understood that each sentence was composed of units called words, such as JAM, SIX, HELP, BUBBLE which kept recurring. But although he now recognized many of the words which cropped up, they kept appearing in new combinations, so the number of new sentences did not seem to be decreasing. Worse still, some of the sentences were extremely long. He recalled one in which an English speaker had been discussing a greedy boy: 'Alexander ate ten sausages, four jam tarts, two bananas, a Swiss roll, seven meringues, fourteen oranges, eight pieces of toast, fourteen apples, two ice-creams, three trifles and then he was sick.' The Emperor wondered despairingly what would have happened to the sentence if Alexander hadn't been sick. Would it have gone on for ever? Another sentence worried him, which an English speaker had read out of a magazine. It was a summary of previous episodes in a serial story: 'Virginia, who is employed as a governess at an old castle in Cornwall, falls in love with her employer's son Charles who is himself in love with a local beauty queen called Linda who has eyes only for the fisherman's nephew Philip who is obsessed with his half-sister Phyllis who loves the handsome young farmer Tom who cares only for his pigs.' Presumably the writer ran out of characters to describe, the Emperor reasoned. Otherwise, the sentence could have gone on even further.

The Emperor had therefore deduced for himself two fundamental facts about language. There are a finite number of elements which can be combined in a mathematically enormous number of ways. And it is in principle impossible to memorize every sentence because there is no linguistic bound on the length of a sentence. Innumerable 'sub'-sentences can be joined on to the original one, a process known as conjoining:

ALEXANDER ATE 10 SAUSAGES	+
(ALEXANDER ATE) 4 JAM TARTS	+
(ALEXANDER ATE) 2 BANANAS	+
(ALEXANDER ATE) A SWISS ROLL	+

Alternatively, sub-sentences can be inserted or embedded inside the original one:

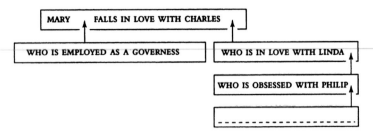

This property of language is known as *recursiveness* from the Latin to 'run through again' – you can repeatedly apply the same rule to one sentence, a process which could (in theory) go on for ever. Of course, in practice you would fall asleep, or get bored or get a sore throat. But these are not linguistic reasons for stopping. This means that no definite set of utterances can ever be assembled for any language.

The Emperor of Jupiter eventually concluded that memorization of all English sentences was impossible. He realized it was the *patterns* behind the utterances which mattered.

How should he discover what these were? One way would be to make a list of all the English words he had collected, and to note whereabouts in the sentence each one occurred. He started to do this. But he hit on problems almost immediately. He had a feeling that some of his sentences had mistakes in them, but he was not sure which ones. Was 'I hic have hic o dear hic hiccups' a well-formed English sentence or not? And what about 'I mean that what I wanted I think to say was this'?

His other problem was that he found gaps in the patterns, and he didn't know which ones were accidental, and which not. For example, he found four sentences containing the word ELEPHANT:

THE ELEPHANT CARRIED TEN PEOPLE.
THE ELEPHANT SWALLOWED TEN BUNS.
THE ELEPHANT WEIGHED TEN TONS.
TEN PEOPLE WERE CARRIED BY THE ELEPHANT.

But he did not find:

TEN BUNS WERE SWALLOWED BY THE ELEPHANT.
TEN TONS WERE WEIGHED BY THE ELEPHANT.

Why not? Were these gaps accidental? Or were the sentences ungrammatical? The Emperor did not know, and grew very depressed. He had discovered another important fact about language: collections of utterances must be treated with caution. They are full of false starts and slips of the tongue. And they constitute only a small subset of all possible utterances. In linguistic terms, a speaker's *performance* or *E-language* (externalized language) is likely to be a random sample bespattered with errors, and does not necessarily provide a very good guide to his or her *competence* or *I-language* (internalized language), the internal set of rules which underlie them.

The Emperor of Jupiter realized that he needed the help of the foreigners themselves. He arrested the spaceship captain, a man called Noam, and told him that he would free him as soon as he had written down the rules of English. Noam plainly knew them, since he could talk.

Noam was astounded. He pleaded with the Emperor, pointing out that speaking a language was an ability like walking which involved knowing *how* to do something. Such knowledge was not necessarily conscious. He tried to explain that philosophers on earth made a distinction between two kinds of knowing: knowing *that* and knowing *how*. Noam knew *that* Jupiter was a planet, and factual knowledge of this type was conscious knowledge. On the other hand, he knew *how* to talk and *how* to walk, though he had no idea how to convey this knowledge to others, since he carried out the actions required without being aware of how he actually managed to do them.

But the Emperor was adamant. Noam would not be freed until he had written down an explicit set of rules, parallel to the system internalized in his head.

Noam pondered. Where could he begin? After much thought he made a list of all the English words he could think of, then fed them into a computer with the instructions that it could combine them in any way whatsoever. First it was to print out all the words one by one, then all possible combinations of two words, then three words, then four words, and so on. The computer began churning out the words as programmed, and spewed out (in the four-word cycle) sequences such as:

    DOG INTO INTO OF
    UP UP UP UP
    GOLDFISH MAY EAT CATS
    THE ELEPHANT LOVED BUNS
    DOWN OVER FROM THE
    SKYLARKS KISS SNAILS BADLY.

Sooner or later, Noam reasoned, the computer would produce every English sentence.

Noam announced to the Emperor that the computer was programmed with rules which made it potentially capable of producing all possible sentences of English. The Emperor was suspicious that the task had been completed so quickly. And when he checked with the other foreigners, his fears were confirmed. The others pointed out that although Noam's computer program could in theory generate *all* English sentences, it certainly did not generate *only* the sentences of English. Since the Emperor was looking for a device which paralleled a human's internalized grammar, Noam's programme must be rejected, because humans did not accept sentences such as:

DOG INTO INTO OF.

It was also unlikely that they would accept:

GOLDFISH MAY EAT CATS.

or:

SKYLARKS KISS SNAILS BADLY.

But there was nothing really wrong with these grammatically: these were accidental facts about the diet of goldfish and the amatory preferences of skylarks which need not be included in the grammar.

So Noam went away again and thought hard. It dawned on him that all sentences were straightforward word 'strings': they were composed of words strung together, one after the other. And the order in which they occurred was partially predictable. For example, THE had to be followed either by an adjective such as GOOD, LITTLE or by a noun such as FLOWER, CHEESE, or occasionally an adverb such as CAREFULLY as in:

THE CAREFULLY NURTURED CHILD SCRIBBLED OBSCENE GRAFFITI ON THE WALLS.

Perhaps, he pondered, one's head contained a network of associations such that each word was in some way attached to the words which could follow it in a sentence. He started to devise a grammar which started with one word, which triggered off a choice between several others, which in turn moved to another choice, until the sentence was complete:

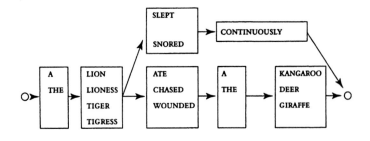

This simple device could account for quite a number of different sentences:

A LION ATE A KANGAROO.
THE TIGRESS CHASED THE GIRAFFE.

and so on. If he continued to elaborate it, perhaps it could eventually include all possible sentences of English.

He presented it to the Emperor, who in turn showed it to the other Englishmen. They pointed out a fatal flaw. Such a device could not possibly account for a speaker's internalized rules for English, because English (and all other languages) has sentences in which nonadjacent words are dependent on one another. For example, you can have a sentence:

THE LIONESS HURT HERSELF.

If each word triggered off the next only, then you would not be able to link the word following HURT with LIONESS, you would be just as likely to have

*THE LIONESS HURT HIMSELF.

Similarly, a sentence starting with EITHER, as in

EITHER BILL STOPS SINGING OR YOU FIND ME EAR-PLUGS.

would not fit into this system, since there would be no means of triggering the OR. Furthermore, in this left-to-right model, all the words had equal status, and were linked to one another like beads on a necklace. But in language, speakers treat 'chunks' of words as belonging together:

THE LITTLE RED HEN/WALKED SLOWLY/ALONG THE PATH/SCRATCHING FOR WORMS.

Any grammar which claimed to mirror a speaker's internalized rules must recognize this fact.

Noam, therefore, realized that an adequate grammar must fulfil at the very least two requirements. First, it must account for *all* and *only* the sentences of English. In linguistic terminology, it must be *observationally adequate*. Second, it must do so in a way which coincides with the intuitions of a native speaker. Such a grammar is spoken of as being *descriptively adequate*.

Noam decided, as a third attempt, to concentrate on a system which would capture the fact that sentences are split up into chunks of words which go together. He decided that a multi-layered, 'downward branching' system was the answer. At the top of the page he wrote the letter S to represent 'sentence'. Then he drew two branches forking from it, representing the shortest possible English sentence (not counting commands).

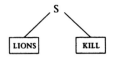

Then each branch was expanded into a longer phrase which could optionally replace it:

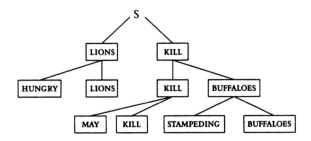

This tree diagram clearly captured the *hierarchical* structure of language, the fact that whole phrases can be the structural equivalent of one word. It diagrammed the fact that HUNGRY LIONS functions as a single unit in a way that KILL STAMPEDING does not.

The Emperor of Jupiter was delighted. For the first time he began to have an inkling of the way language worked. 'I want some soup . . . some seaweed soup . . . some hot seaweed soup . . . some steaming hot seaweed soup,' he murmured to himself, realizing the importance of Noam's new system.

The other Englishmen praised the system, but grudgingly. They admitted that the tree diagram worked well for sentences such as:

HUNGRY LIONS MAY KILL STAMPEDING BUFFALOES.

But they had one major objection. Did Noam realize just how many trees might be required for the whole language? And did he realize that sentences which speakers felt to be closely related would have quite different trees? For example:

HUNGRY LIONS MAY KILL STAMPEDING BUFFALOES.

would have a tree quite different from:

STAMPEDING BUFFALOES MAY BE KILLED BY HUNGRY LIONS.

And a sentence such as:

TO CHOP DOWN LAMP POSTS IS A DREADFUL CRIME.

would have a different tree from:

IT IS A DREADFUL CRIME TO CHOP DOWN LAMP POSTS.

Worse still, had Noam noticed that sentences which were felt to be quite different by the speakers of the language had the same trees?

THE BOY WAS LOATH TO WASH.

had exactly the same tree as:

THE BOY WAS DIFFICULT TO WASH.

Surely Noam could devise a system in which sentences felt by speakers to be similar could be linked up, and dissimilar ones separated?

After much contemplation, Noam realized he could economize on the number of trees needed, and he could also capture the intuitions of speakers that certain sentences were similar if he regarded similar sentences as belonging to the same basic tree! Actives and passives for example, could be related to an underlying tree:

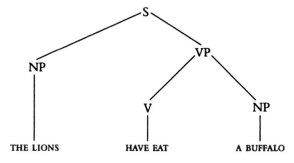

Then this 'deep structure' tree could be 'transformed' by operations known as transformations into different surface structures. It provided the basis for both 'the lions have eaten a buffalo' and 'a buffalo has been eaten by the lions'.

Using the same principle, Noam realized that he could explain the similarity of

TO CHOP DOWN LAMP POSTS IS A DREADFUL CRIME
IT IS A DREADFUL CRIME TO CHOP DOWN LAMP POSTS.

Conversely, the difference between

THE BOY WAS LOATH TO WASH.
THE BOY WAS DIFFICULT TO WASH.

could be explained by suggesting that the sentences are connected to different deep structure strings.

The Emperor of Jupiter was delighted with Noam's latest attempt, and the other Englishmen agreed that Noam seemed to have hit on a very good solution. He appeared to have devised a clear, economical system which was able to account for *all* and *only* the sentences of English, and which also captured the intuitions of the speakers about the way their language worked. A further important bonus was that the system could possibly be used for French, Chinese, Turkish, Arawak or any other language in the strange human world.

However, the Emperor was still somewhat puzzled. Had Noam explained to him how to actually *produce* English sentences? Or had he merely drawn him a map of the way in which related sentences were stored in an Englishman's head? Noam was rather vague when asked about this. He said that although the map idea seemed nearer the truth, the map nevertheless had important implications for the way in which sentences were produced and recognized. The Emperor was extremely puzzled by this statement. However, he decided that Noam had done some splendid work, and so should be set free and rewarded handsomely. Meanwhile, the Emperor made a mental note that when he had some more spare time, he would have to contemplate more thoroughly the question of how Noam's proposals related to the way humans produced and recognized sentences.

Let us summarize what the Emperor of Jupiter had discovered about the nature of human language and the type of 'grammar' which can account for it. First, he discovered that it is in principle impossible to memorize every sentence of a language, because there is no linguistic limit on the length of a sentence.

Second, he found that any collection of utterances must be treated with the utmost care. It contains slips of the tongue, and represents only a random sample of all possible utterances. For this reason it is important to focus attention on a speaker's underlying system of rules, his 'competence' rather than on an arbitrary collection of his utterances, or his 'performance'. Third, the

Emperor realized that a good grammar of a language will not only be observationally adequate – one which can account for all the possible sentences of a language. It will also be descriptively adequate – that is, it will reflect the intuitions of the native speaker about his language. This meant that a simple, left-to-right model of language, in which each word was triggered by the one before it, was unworkable. It was observationally inadequate because it did not allow for non-adjacent words to be dependent on one another. And it was descriptively inadequate because it wrongly treated all words as being of equal value and linked together like beads on a string, when in practice language is hierarchically structured with 'chunks' of words going together.

Fourth, the Emperor of Jupiter noted that a hierarchically structured, top-to-bottom model of language was a reasonable proposal – but it did not link up sentences which were felt by the speakers to be closely related, such as:

TO CHOP DOWN LAMP POSTS IS A DREADFUL CRIME.

and:

IT IS A DREADFUL CRIME TO CHOP DOWN LAMP POSTS.

On the other hand it wrongly linked up sentences such as:

THE BOY WAS LOATH TO WASH.

and

THE BOY WAS DIFFICULT TO WASH.

which seemed to be quite different. So finally, he became convinced that the most satisfactory system was a transformational model of language, in which sentences felt to be similar share the same deep structure. He came to believe that all sentences had both a hidden, deep structure and an obvious surface structure which might look quite different, and he accepted that these two levels were linked by processes known as transformations.

However, the Emperor remained puzzled about how this model of an internalized grammar might tie in with the way humans produce and comprehend sentences. He felt that Noam had been quite unclear on the topic.

Several of the things discovered by the mythical Emperor of Jupiter are points made by Noam Chomsky in his early, slim, but extremely influential work, Syntactic Structures (1957). In this, he explains why a left-to-right or 'finite-state' model of language is deficient, and also why a top-to-bottom or 'phrase structure' model is inadequate. He then justifies the need for a transformational grammar. He elaborated this basic model in his 'classic' work *Aspects of the Theory of Syntax* (1965). Within 20 years, however, his views had radically changed. Let us see how this alteration might be justified to the Emperor of Jupiter.

RETURN TO JUPITER

Many years later, after he had orbited the universe several times, and been acclaimed as one of the pioneers of his century, Noam decided to return to Jupiter. He wanted to see how the Emperor was coping with his old transformational system. More importantly, he wanted to explain his new ideas on language.

Noam found the Emperor full of complaints. After Noam's departure from Jupiter, the Emperor had continued to work on Noam's system. He had been helped by some of Noam's spaceship colleagues who had stayed behind on Jupiter to do some research on the climate. But things just hadn't worked out as he had hoped.

The Emperor had two types of grumble. There were general grumbles about the whole system, and specific grumbles about particular transformations.

His main complaint was that the system just didn't work properly. He had hoped that by now he would have found a set of rules which could account for all the possible sentences of English, and no others. But in spite of working long hours, there were dozens of sentences which he'd heard Noam's colleagues speak, for which he hadn't been able to specify the full set of rules. And the very best set of rules he'd come up with still included numerous sentences which apparently weren't English.

Furthermore, he had considerable doubts about his transformational rules. As long as he got the right outcome, it didn't seem to matter very much how he got there. Almost anything could be transformed into anything! There seemed to be too much latitude. Surely the whole thing ought to be tightened up a bit?

Noam agreed with these general points. The Emperor had discovered for himself the same problems as Noam had noticed. It seemed almost impossible to find a definitive set of rules which could specify what was, and what was not, a permissible sentence of English. The second, and more serious problem, was the enormous 'power' of the system: transformations appeared to be able to do almost anything. There were not enough constraints keeping them in check. A system which can do anything, as if with the wave of a magic wand, is not very informative.

Noam explained that he had been working very hard on the question of constraints. It was far more important, he had decided, to specify the general bounds within which human language worked, than to spend hours and hours fiddling with the exact rules which would account for any one particular language.

Encouraged by this, the Emperor started on his detailed complaints, which were mostly about transformations. First, he grumbled, some transformations were quite arbitrary, because they were linked to particular lexical items. You simply had to know which words were involved. For example, you could say:

FRED GAVE A GIRAFFE TO THE ZOO.
FRED DONATED A GIRAFFE TO THE ZOO.

Then, a transformation supposedly specified that with GIVE, you could also say:

FRED GAVE THE ZOO A GIRAFFE.

But this transformation did not work with DONATE. You could not say:

*FRED DONATED THE ZOO A GIRAFFE.

Wasn't this odd? he asked.

Noam agreed that any transformation which was restricted to particular lexical items was not a proper transformation. Instead, it was part of the dictionary or 'lexicon' which existed in any speaker's mind. In his more recent system, he had moved information about the structures which could follow GIVE and DONATE into this dictionary.

The Emperor continued grumbling. Some transformations seemed to him pointless. Why did a sentence such as:

FENELLA THOUGHT THAT SHE WAS ILL.

have a deep structure which included the word FENELLA twice, saying in effect:

FENELLA THOUGHT THAT FENELLA WAS ILL?

Wasn't this rather pointless? Couldn't one leave SHE in the deep structure, and add a note saying SHE referred to FENELLA?

Noam agreed that a transformation which changed FENELLA into SHE was quite unnecessary, and that the matter could be dealt with in the way the Emperor suggested. In any case, the linking up of a pronoun SHE to other words should be dealt with by the semantic component, not by a transformation.

The Emperor continued moaning. Why were there so many different transformations which all had more or less the same effect? Consider:

IT SEEMED THAT THE DUCHESS WAS DRUNK.
IT WAS DIFFICULT TO PLEASE THE DUCHESS.

These two sentences were fairly like their deep structures, compared to two others, which involved bringing THE DUCHESS to the front:

THE DUCHESS SEEMED TO BE DRUNK.
THE DUCHESS WAS DIFFICULT TO PLEASE.

Yet each of these two sentences involved a different transformation! Supposedly, they had to be different, because the deep structures were different. Wasn't this unnecessary proliferation of transformations?

Noam agreed with this criticism. It was foolish to have different transformations which performed the same manoeuvre. In his recent system, they had been combined.

The Emperor in his moans and groans had outlined many of the problems which eventually surrounded old-style transformations. They were too powerful, there were too many of them, they were too disparate. Gradually, they were reduced in number. Some were handed over to other components of the grammar, others were combined. In the end, only one transformation survived. This moved items about, though within strict limits.

The Emperor was amazed! Fancy having a transformational grammar with hardly any transformations! How on Jupiter did such a system work?

Noam started waving his arms about in excitement as he propounded his new system. He was on the verge of specifying a genetic blueprint for language, he announced. There were a number of fixed principles, which worked for all languages. There were also others which allowed a limited amount of variation. If you specified these properly, you hardly needed any rules at all!

The Emperor looked doubtful. Perhaps Noam had contracted space-sickness, which had sent him mad. How could one do without rules?

Noam tried to explain. Suppose you were designing a human being, he suggested. You had to give him or her a head. That would be a fixed principle. But the colour of the skin could vary in certain specified ways. As for doing away with rules, one might have a general principle saying: 'Limbs come in pairs.' Then one need not have separate rules which said: 'Humans have two arms' and 'Humans have two legs.' This sort of a system was applicable to language, he was convinced.

The Emperor was suspicious. Surely language was much too complicated to be dealt with in this simple way?

Not at all, argued Noam. On the contrary, language possibly consisted of a number of rather simple components. Each of the components worked in accordance with some quite straightforward principles, and they only appeared complex because of the way they interacted with principles from other components.

The Emperor seemed puzzled. So Noam used another analogy. 'Think of a human mouth,' he suggested. 'There's a mobile tongue which pushes food about. There are salivary glands which moisten it. And there are fixed teeth which grind it down. Each of these components is quite simple. Yet when they are working together the interaction is quite complex, and the effect powerful!' (Matthei and Roeper 1983).

The Emperor was partially persuaded. He begged Noam to hand over his genetic blueprint for language. But Noam stalled. He hadn't yet worked out how many components were involved, he admitted, nor what the basic principles were. He was fairly confident only that 'economy' or simplicity played a major role. Matters would be clearer in a hundred or so years' time, he predicted.

The Emperor felt quite frustrated. And he was even more puzzled as to how Noam's new system might link up with how humans understand and produce speech.

In this fictitious account, we have outlined several of the problems which caused disillusionment with transformations as they were formulated in the 'classic' (1965) version of transformational grammar. And we have put forward the general aims expressed by Chomsky first of all in *Lectures on Government and Binding* (1981), but expressed most clearly in *Knowledge of Language: Its Nature, Origin and Use* (1986) and later in the *The Minimalist Program* (1995b). Chomsky became more concerned with specifying the nature of the human language system than with formulating a complete picture of any one language. He believed that a 'principles and parameters' approach (with *parameter* referring to a factor which can be set variably) would largely do away with rules. And he became convinced that the overall system is modular, in that it is composed of a set of modules (components) which are simple in themselves, but become complex when they interact with other modules.

But this left many, including the fictional Emperor of Jupiter, deeply disappointed, as will be outlined below.

THE EMPEROR'S DISILLUSION

The Emperor of Jupiter felt let down. But was he angry with Noam, or angry with himself? He wasn't sure. He had, he felt, spent far too many years chasing moonbeams, exciting, glistening ideas that always just eluded him. Maybe he should have realized long ago that Noam and his earthling mates were born with abilities which were not available to people from Jupiter, just as Noam didn't take easily to the toe-wiggling that came so easily to the Jupiter inhabitants.

But what exactly was it that the earthlings could do? What underpinned their ability to talk to each other? Even before they started chatting, they seemed to have some hidden understanding of others. It wasn't just that they had formulaic ways of greeting each other, and (mostly) took it in turns to talk. Astonishingly, they seemed to be able to look into the other person's mind, and to guess (correctly) whether he or she needed to be helped or left alone. This type of mind-reading seemed truly amazing! And, judging from talking to Noam's crew, it was an ability which earthling babies developed early on in their lives. They not only had an enviable facility for combining sounds into words, and words into longer sequences, but they were also able to find the words they wanted remarkably fast, even though there seemed to be tens of thousands of them!

Eventually, the Emperor of Jupiter decided that he was profoundly grateful to Noam, because without Noam's inspiration he and his fellow Jupiterians might never have realized how interesting, and how important, human language was. But the time had now come to move on to other areas of interest. In particular, he wanted to think about the relationship between a grammar and the way that grammar is used in actual speech. Noam had been most unclear on this point.

To conclude, the Emperor of Jupiter felt, as eventually did earthbound linguists, that Noam Chomsky had usefully highlighted the importance of language, and drawn attention to some of its key properties. But he had not explained clearly the link between the grammar of a language, and the way that grammar could be used in actual speech.

This will be the topic of the next chapter.

9

THE WHITE ELEPHANT PROBLEM

Do we need a grammar
in order to speak?

'I have answered three questions, and that is enough,'
Said his father; 'don't give yourself airs!
Do you think I can listen all day to such stuff?
Be off, or I'll kick you downstairs!'
                        Lewis Carroll, *Old Father William*

Chomsky, for around half a century, tried to 'capture' a speaker's abstract knowledge of language. But it remained unclear how knowledge related to usage. According to Chomsky, the two were rather distant, since he denied that linguistic knowledge is directly related to the way we understand and produce utterances. This leads to a crucial and rather startling question: can a grammar actually be *irrelevant* to the problem of understanding and producing speech?

If we had put this question to a hardcore linguist, at a time when Chomsky's views were dominant, he would probably have answered: 'Of course language knowledge and language usage are not totally separate, they just have to be studied separately, because the relationship between them is indirect.'

If we persisted, and said, 'What exactly do you mean by an indirect relationship?' he would probably have said: 'Look, please stop bothering me with silly questions. The relationship between language usage and language knowledge is not my concern. Let me put you straight. All normal people seem to have a tacit knowledge of their language. If that knowledge is there, it is my duty as a linguist to describe it. But it is not my job to tell you how that knowledge is used. I leave that to the psychologists.'

This, to a psycholinguist, seemed an extremely unhappy state of affairs. She is just as much interested in language usage as language knowledge. In fact, she finds it quite odd that anybody is able to concentrate on one rather than the other of these factors, since they seem to her to go together rather closely. Consequently, in this chapter, we shall be briefly examining both Chomsky's views and attempts made by psycholinguists to assess the relationship between a linguist's grammar and the way someone produces and comprehends sentences.

LINGUISTIC KNOWLEDGE

Chomsky (1965) claimed that the grammar he proposed 'expresses the speaker-hearer's knowledge of the language'. This knowledge was latent or 'tacit', and 'may well not be immediately available to the user of the language' (Chomsky 1965: 21).

The notion of tacit or latent knowledge is a rather vague one, and may cover more than Chomsky intended. It seems to cover two types of knowledge. On the one hand, it consists of knowing *how* to produce and comprehend utterances. This involves using a rule system, but it does not necessarily involve any awareness of the rules – just as a spider can spin a web successfully without any awareness of the principles it is following. On the other hand, knowledge of a language also covers the ability to make various kinds of judgements about the language. The speaker not only knows the rules, but in addition, knows something about that knowledge. For example, speakers can quickly distinguish between well-formed and deviant sentences. An English-speaker would unhesitatingly accept:

HANK MUCH PREFERS CAVIARE TO SARDINES.

but would quickly reject:

*HANK CAVIARE TO SARDINES MUCH PREFERS.

In addition, mature speakers of a language can recognize sentence relatedness. They 'know' that a sentence:

FADING FLOWERS LOOK SAD.

is closely related to:

FLOWERS WHICH ARE FADING LOOK SAD.

and that:

IT ASTONISHED US THAT BUZZ SWALLOWED THE OCTOPUS WHOLE.

is related to:

THAT BUZZ SWALLOWED THE OCTOPUS WHOLE ASTONISHED US.

Moreover, they can distinguish between sentences which look superficially alike but in fact are quite different, as in:

EATING APPLES CAN BE GOOD FOR YOU.

(Is it good to eat a type of apple called an eating apple, or is any type of apple good to eat?), or:

SHOOTING STARS CAN BE FRIGHTENING.
SHOOTING BUFFALOES CAN BE FRIGHTENING.

(How do you know who is doing the shooting?)

There seems to be no doubt whatsoever that a 'classic' (1965) transformational grammar encapsulated this second type of knowledge, the speaker's awareness of language structure. People do have intuitions or knowledge of the type specified above, and a transformational grammar did seem to describe this.

However, it is by no means clear how a 'classic' transformational grammar or the later 'minimalist program' related to the first type of knowledge – the knowledge of how to actually use language. Chomsky claimed that a speaker's internal grammar has an important bearing on the production and comprehension of utterances, but he made it quite clear that this grammar 'does not, in itself, prescribe the character or functioning of a perceptual model or a model of speech production' (Chomsky 1965: 9). And at one point he even labelled as 'absurd' any attempt to link the grammar directly to processes of production and comprehension (Chomsky 1967: 399).

This viewpoint persisted in his later work, where he denied that knowledge had anything to do with ability to use a language: 'Ability is one thing, knowledge something quite different' (Chomsky 1986: 12), commenting that 'we should follow normal usage in distinguishing clearly between knowledge and ability to use that knowledge'. And as we have seen, the type of knowledge outlined in his later theories is considerably more abstract and deep-seated than that involved in a 'classic' transformational grammar.

In short, Chomsky is interested primarily in 'the system of knowledge that underlies the use and understanding of language' rather than in 'actual or potential behaviour' (Chomsky 1986: 24).

Let us put the matter in another way. Anyone who knows a language can do three things:

1	Produce sentences.	LANGUAGE
2	Comprehend sentences.	USAGE
3	Store linguistic knowledge.	LANGUAGE KNOWLEDGE

We are saying that Chomsky's proposals seem undoubtedly to cover (3), but appear to be separate from, or only indirectly related to (1) and (2).

LANGUAGE USAGE		LANGUAGE KNOWLEDGE

This is a rather puzzling state of affairs. Is it possible for linguistic knowledge to be completely separate from language usage? This is the topic of the rest of the chapter. We shall start by looking at the earliest psycholinguistic experiments on the topic, which were carried out in the early 1960s.

THE YEARS OF ILLUSION

When Chomsky's ideas spread across into the field of psychology in the early 1960s they made an immediate impact. Psychologists at once started to test the relevance of a transformational grammar to the way we process sentences. Predictably, their first instinct was to test whether there was a direct relationship between the two.

At this time, two different but similar viewpoints were put forward. The first was a strong and fairly implausible theory, sometimes known as the 'correspondence hypothesis', and the second was a weaker and (slightly) more plausible idea known as the 'derivational theory of complexity' or DTC for short.

Supporters of the correspondence hypothesis postulated a close correspondence between the form of a transformational grammar, and the operations employed by someone when they produce or comprehend speech. Supposedly 'the sequence of rules used in the grammatical derivation of a sentence . . . corresponds step by step to the sequence of psychological processes that are executed when a person processes the sentence' (Hayes 1970: 5). This was soon found to be unlikely.

Supporters of DTC put forward a weaker hypothesis. They suggested that the more complex the transformational derivation of a sentence – that is, the more transformations were involved – the more difficult it would be to produce or comprehend. They did not, however, assume a one-to-one correspondence between the speaker's mental processes and grammatical operations.

A number of now famous experiments were devised to test these claims. Perhaps the best-known was a sentence-matching experiment by George Miller of Harvard University (Miller 1962; Miller and McKean 1964).

Miller reasoned that if the number of transformations significantly affected processing difficulty, then this difficulty should be measurable in terms of time. In other words, the more transformations a sentence had, the longer it should take to cope with. For example, a passive sentence such as:

THE OLD WOMAN WAS WARNED BY JOE.

should be harder to handle than a simple active affirmative declarative (or SAAD for short) such as:

JOE WARNED THE OLD WOMAN.

since the passive sentence required an additional transformation. However, this passive should be easier to handle than a passive negative such as:

THE OLD WOMAN WASN'T WARNED BY JOE.

which required one more transformation still.

In order to test this hypothesis, Miller gave his subjects two columns of jumbled sentences, and asked them to find pairs which went together. The sentences to be paired differed from one another in a specified way. For example, in one section of the experiment actives and passives were jumbled, so that a passive such as:

THE SMALL BOY WAS LIKED BY JANE.

had to be matched with its 'partner':

JANE LIKED THE SMALL BOY.

And:

JOE WARNED THE OLD WOMAN.

had to be paired with:

THE OLD WOMAN WAS WARNED BY JOE.

Miller assumed that the subjects had to strip the sentences of their transformations in order to match them up. The more they differed from each other, the longer the matching would take, he predicted.

Miller carried out this experiment twice, the second time with strict electronic time-controls (a so-called 'tachistoscopic' method). His results delighted him. Just as he had hoped, it took nearly twice as long to match sentences which differed by two transformations as it took to match sentences which differed by only one transformation. When he added the time needed to match actives with passives (approximately 1.65 seconds) to the time taken to pair affirmatives with negatives(approximately 1.40 seconds), the total added up to almost the same as that required for matching active with passive negative sentences (approximately 3.12 seconds).

Active ◀ 1.65 ▶ Passive	
JOE WARNED THE OLD WOMAN	THE OLD WOMAN WAS WARNED BY JOE
Affirmative ◀ 1.40 ▶ Negative	
JOE WARNED THE OLD WOMAN	JOE DIDN'T WARN THE OLD WOMAN
Active ◀ 3.12 ▶ Passive Negative	
JOE WARNED THE OLD WOMAN	THE OLD WOMAN WASN'T WARNED BY JOE

Miller seemed to have proved that transformations were 'psychologically real', since each transformation took up a measurable processing time.

But this period of illusion was shortlived. A time of disappointment and disillusion followed. Fodor and Garrett (1966) gave a crushing paper at the Edinburgh University conference on psycholinguistics in March 1966, in which they clearly showed the emptiness of the 'correspondence hypothesis' and DTC. They gave detailed theoretical reasons why hearers do not 'unwind' transformations when they comprehend speech. For example, the correspondence hypothesis entailed the consequence that people do not begin to decode what they are hearing until a sentence was complete. It assumed that, after waiting until they had heard all of it, hearers then undressed the sentence transformation by transformation. But this was clearly wrong, it would take much too long. In fact, it can be shown that hearers start processing what they hear as soon as a speaker begins talking.

In addition, Fodor and Garrett pointed out flaws in the experiments carried out by Miller and others. The transformations, such as passive and negative, on which their results crucially depended, were atypical. Negatives changed the meaning, and passives moved the actor away from its normal place at the beginning of an English sentence. Passives and negatives are also longer than SAADs, so it was not surprising that they took longer to match and were more difficult to memorize. The difficulty of these sentences need not have anything to do with transformational complexity. Fodor and Garrett pointed out that some other transformations made no difference to processing difficulty. There was no detectable difference in the time taken to comprehend:

JOHN PHONES UP THE GIRL.

and

JOHN PHONES THE GIRL UP.

If the correspondence hypothesis or DTC was correct, the second should be more difficult, according to the 'classic' version of transformational grammar, because a 'particle separation' transformation had been applied, separating PHONES and UP. Worse still for the theory were sentences such as:

BILL RUNS FASTER THAN JOHN RUNS.
BILL RUNS FASTER THAN JOHN.

The second sentence had one more transformation than the first, because the word RUNS had been deleted. In theory it should be more difficult to comprehend, but in practice it was easier.

Fodor and Garrett followed their 1966 conference paper with another article in 1967 where they pointed out more problem constructions (Fodor and Garrett 1967). For example, DTC counter-intuitively treated 'truncated' passives such as:

THE BOY WAS HIT.

as more complex than full passives such as:

THE BOY WAS HIT BY SOMEONE.

After this, researcher after researcher came up with similar difficulties. According to DTC:

THERE'S A DRAGON IN THE STREET.

should have been more difficult to process than:

A DRAGON IS IN THE STREET.

Yet the opposite is true (Watt 1970). And so on.

Both the correspondence hypothesis and DTC had to be abandoned. Transformational grammar in its 'classic' form was not a model of the production and comprehension of speech, and derivational complexity as measured in terms of transformations did not correlate with processing complexity. Clearly, Chomsky was right when he denied that there was a direct relationship between language knowledge, as encapsulated in a 1965 version of transformational grammar, and language usage.

THE DEEP STRUCTURE HYPOTHESIS

By the mid-1960s, the majority of psycholinguists had realized quite clearly that transformations as then formulated had no direct relevance to the way a person produces and understands a sentence. However, the irrelevance of transformations did not mean that other aspects of transformational grammar were also irrelevant. So in the late 1960s another hypothesis was put forward – the suggestion that when people process sentences, they mentally set up a Chomsky-like deep structure. In other words, when someone produces, comprehends or recalls a sentence, 'the speaker-hearer's internal representation of grammatical relations is mediated by structures that are isomorphic to those that the grammatical formalism employs' (Fodor et al. 1974: 262). Some 'click' experiments were superficially encouraging (Bever, et al.. 1969).

The aim of the 'click' experiments was to test whether a person recovers a Chomsky-like deep structure (1965 version) when she decodes. The experimenters took pairs of sentences which had similar surface structures, but different deep structures. For example:

THE CORRUPT POLICE CAN'T BEAR CRIMINALS TO CONFESS QUICKLY.
THE CORRUPT POLICE CAN'T FORCE CRIMINALS TO CONFESS QUICKLY.

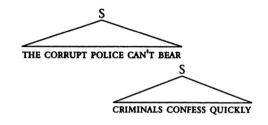

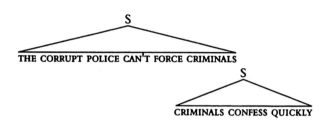

In the first sentence, the word *criminals* occurred once only in the deep structure, but in the second sentence it occurred twice according to a 'classic' transformational model. If anyone doubts that these sentences have a different deep structure, try turning them round into the passive, and the difference becomes clear: the first sentence immediately becomes quite ungrammatical, though there is nothing wrong with the second:

> *CRIMINALS CANNOT BE BORNE BY THE POLICE TO CONFESS QUICKLY.

> CRIMINALS CANNOT BE FORCED BY THE POLICE TO CONFESS QUICKLY.

In the experiment, the subjects were asked to wear headphones. Then the sentences were played into one ear, and a 'click' which occurred during the word CRIMINALS was played into the other. Subjects were asked to report whereabouts in the sentence they heard the click. In the first sentence, subjects tended to hear the click *before* the word CRIMINALS, where a Chomskyan deep structure suggests a structural break:

⬅

THE CORRUPT POLICE CAN'T BEAR/CRIMINALS TO CONFESS QUICKLY.

But in the second sentence, the click stayed still, as if the hearers could not decide where the structural break occurred. They behaved as if CRIMINALS straddled the gap between the two sections of the sentence. Since CRIMINALS occurred twice in the deep structure, with the structural break between the two occurrences, this was an encouraging result:

THE CORRUPT POLICE CAN'T FORCE CRIMINALS/CRIMINALS TO CONFESS QUICKLY.

This suggested that people might recover a 'classic' deep structure when they decoded a sentence.

But one swallow does not make a summer, and one experiment could not maintain the validity of deep structure. Both the design and interpretation of this particular experiment have been challenged. The results might have been due to the unusual experimental situation, or they could have been connected with meaning rather than with an underlying deep structure syntax (Fillenbaum 1971; Johnson-Laird 1974). The use of clicks and the 'muddled history of clickology' (Johnson-Laird 1974: 138) was, and still is a source of considerable controversy.

To summarize, a few early experiments were *consistent* with the suggestion that people recover a Chomsky-like deep structure when they recalled or understood sentences. But they were consistent with other hypotheses also. All that we could be sure about was that underlying every sentence was a set of internal relations which may well not be obvious on the surface. As Bever noted (1970: 286):

> The fact that every sentence has an internal and external structure is maintained by all linguistic theories – although the theories may differ as to the role the internal structure plays within the linguistic description. Thus talking involves actively mapping internal structures on to external sequences, and understanding others involves mapping external sequences on to internal structures.

In other words, it is very unlikely that we recover a Chomskyan (1965) deep structure when we understand sentences, though no one ever totally disproved this possibility.

The key point is, science proceeds by *disproving* hypotheses, not by proving them. Suppose you were interested in flowers. You might formulate a hypothesis, 'All roses are white, red, pink, orange or yellow.' There would be absolutely no point at all in collecting hundreds, thousands or even millions of white, red, pink, orange and yellow roses. You would merely be collecting additional evidence consistent with your hypothesis. If you were genuinely interested in making a botanical advance, you would send people in all directions hunting for black, blue, mauve or green roses. Your hypothesis would stand until somebody found a blue rose. Then, in theory, you should be delighted that botany had made progress, and found out about blue roses. Naturally, when you formulate a hypothesis it has to be one which is capable of disproof. A hypothesis such as 'Henry VIII would have disliked spaceships' cannot be disproved, and consequently is useless. A hypothesis such as 'The planet Neptune is made of chalk' would have been useless in the year AD 100, when there was no hope of getting to Neptune – but it is a perfectly legitimate, if implausible, one in the twenty-first century when planet probes and space travel are becoming routine.

This leads us back to Chomsky. Some people have claimed that because deep structures could not be disproved, they were useless as a scientific hypothesis. It is true that, at the moment, it is difficult to see how they might have been tested. But psycholinguistic experimentation takes steps forward all the time. Perhaps with the development of further new techniques, ways will be found of definitively disproving theories about the 'inner structure' of a language. At the moment, as one psycholinguist noted 'Presently available evidence on almost any psycholinguistic point is so scanty as to blunt any claim that this or that hypothesis has truly been disconfirmed' (Watt 1970: 138). The same is true today.

To sum up, the suggestion that people utilize a Chomskyan deep structure (1965 version) when they comprehend or produce sentences seems increasingly unlikely, but the hypothesis has not been truly disconfirmed. So was this work all wasted? Probably not. At the very least, it has enabled us to think more clearly about language and what it involves.

THE LINGUISTIC ARCHIVE

We have now come to the conclusion that 1965-style transformations are irrelevant to sentence processing, and that deep structure is quite unlikely to be relevant. But some steps forward have been made.

We are coming round to the view that a classic (1965) transformational grammar represents metaphorically a kind of archive which sits in the brain ready for consultation, but is possibly only partially consulted in the course of a conversation. Perhaps it could be likened to other types of knowledge, such as the knowledge that four times three is the same as six times two. This information is mentally stored, but is not necessarily directly used when checking to see if the milk bill is correct.

The information is probably represented in the brain in a rather different way from that suggested in a 1965-style transformational grammar. But such a grammar might provide a useful way of encapsulating speakers' latent knowledge of their language.

We are not assuming a clean break between language knowledge and language usage. In practice the two overlap to a quite considerable extent, and the extent of the overlap varies from sentence to sentence.

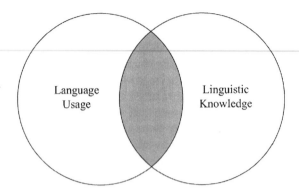

Let us take a simple example:

AUNT AGATHA WAS RUN OVER LAST THURSDAY.

A short passive of this type is generally simpler and quicker to comprehend than a full passive such as:

AUNT AGATHA WAS RUN DOWN BY SOMEONE (OR SOMETHING) LAST THURSDAY.

It therefore seems quite unnecessary to suppose that, in order to understand the sentence, hearers have to recover a Chomsky-like deep structure which includes the agent SOMEONE (or SOMETHING):

SOMEONE (OR SOMETHING) RAN OVER AUNT AGATHA LAST THURSDAY.

Instead, they may not pay attention to the agent, they may be too busy thinking about Aunt Agatha. However, if they did spend rather longer pondering about the sentence, they could recover not only the agent SOMEONE (or SOMETHING) which the 'classic' deep structure suggests, but much more information in addition (Watt 1970). They could suggest that Aunt Agatha was run over by SOMETHING, rather than SOMEONE, and that this something was probably a MOVING VEHICLE. They obtained all this information from their knowledge of the lexical item RUN OVER – but it is optional whether they use it or not when they comprehend the sentence.

And RUN OVER is not an isolated example. Another verb from which a person could also extract a considerable amount of information if necessary is GORE (Watt 1970). In the sentence:

CHARLIE WAS GORED.

the hearer can assume that the gorer was male and bovine. In other words, a bull. This information is *potentially* recoverable, though it *need* not be recovered.

In short, someone who knows a language has an enormous amount of knowledge which she *could* use when she understands or produces a sentence, but she does not have to. Or rather, she usually has to use some of it, but often only a rather small proportion.

Another example is the sentence:

DROWNING HEFFALUMPS CAN CAUSE A TERRIBLE COMMOTION.

Here, the hearer might well subconsciously have to query, 'Are we dealing with heffalumps which are drowning, or someone who is drowning heffalumps?' And he might even put his query into words.

This again suggests that a 'classic' transformational grammar represented a linguistic archive whose contents are available for use when a person processes a sentence. In principle, someone could, if he wanted to, recover all the knowledge stored in connection with a sentence when he understands or produces it. This may be what Chomsky meant when he wrote that:

> the generative grammar represents the information concerning sentence structure that is available, in principle, to one who has acquired a language. It indicates how, ideally . . . he would understand a sentence.
>
> (Chomsky 1963: 326)

The word 'ideally' may mean perfect understanding of the sentence as far as is possible within the limits of grammatical and lexical knowledge. Of course, in practice, no one has the time or the need to unravel every sentence in this way. Most people make a quick decision about the sentences they hear, and do not consider all the ramifications. In Bever's words, they rely on 'perceptual strategies' or short cuts, rather than on full utilization of 'epistemological structures' or beliefs about language structure (Bever 1970: 281).

But it would be a mistake to assume that 'epistemological structures' are an optional extra. A person who could not detect ambiguities, who could not make judgements of grammaticality and who could not link up related sentences would only 'know' their language in a very limited way. There is no clear-cut line between knowing *how* to utter and comprehend sentences, and knowing *that* these sentences are grammatical and how they are related to other sentences. Humans do not behave like spiders, who can weave webs without any conscious knowledge about their skill. Humans need knowledge about their language in order to function properly as articulate mammals. As far as language is concerned, the distinction between knowing *how* (as in knowing how to walk) and knowing *that* (as in knowing that the world is round) is a fuzzy one, because the two types of knowledge overlap.

Let us summarize what we have just said. We have concluded that a transformational grammar, in its classic form, incorporates mainly 'archival knowledge' or 'epistemological structures' – a set of beliefs or intuitions about one's language which may not necessarily be recoverable at a conscious level. These beliefs are not merely optional extras, they are an essential part of anyone's ability to speak and understand a language.

How are these 'epistemological structures' acquired? Do children learn how to use language, then later build up full knowledge about it? Or do the two learning processes go on simultaneously? This question was studied by three psychologists from the University of Pennsylvania (Gleitman et al. 1972). They concluded that the process of learning how to speak was intertwined with that of acquiring beliefs about one's language. Both types of knowledge progress simultaneously, though the latter develops rather more slowly. Even 2-year-olds have *some* notion of grammaticality, though this is rather shaky. And children's judgements about their language remain shaky even when they can speak fluently. But between the ages of 5 and 8 children start to have intuitions about their language that parallel those of an adult. Let us illustrate these points.

Even quite young children have *some* beliefs about their language, as shown by 2-year-old Allison, who judged the sequence:

*BALL ME THE THROW.

to be 'silly', and corrected it to:

THROW ME THE BALL.

Similarly, 2-year-old Sarah amended:

*SONG ME A SING.

to:

SING ME A SONG.

However, Sarah's judgements were not consistently reliable, since she found:

WASH THE DISHES.

an odd sentence, and corrected it to:

WASH THE DISHES(!)

It was easier to elicit responses from the older children, and the results were more clear-cut. For example, when seven children between the ages of 5 and 8 were asked whether the sentence:

I AM KNOWING YOUR SISTER.

sounded 'sensible' or 'silly', the 5- and 6-year-olds found nothing wrong with it, but the 7- and 8-year-olds disapproved of it, though they could not always say why it was odd. The following is the response given by 7-year-old Claire:

R (Researcher):   How about this one: I AM KNOWING YOUR SISTER.
C (Claire):   No. I KNOW YOUR SISTER.
R: Why not I AM KNOWING YOUR SISTER? You can say I
                  AM EATING YOUR DINNER.
C: It's different! (shouting) You say different sentences in
                  different ways. Otherwise it doesn't make sense!

But for other sentences, Claire not only gave adult judgements concerning grammaticality, she also gave an adult-type reason:

R: How about this one: BOY IS AT THE DOOR.
C: If his name is BOY. You should – the kid is named John, see? JOHN
     IS AT THE DOOR or A BOY IS AT THE DOOR.

The researchers noted:

The ability to reflect upon language dramatically increases with age. The older children were better not only in noting deviance but also in explaining where the deviance lies.

(Gleitman et al. 1972: 160)

Spontaneous repairs – cases in which a child corrects himself or herself without prompting – provide another way of looking at children's awareness of language structure (Karmiloff-Smith 1986). Younger children often provide unnecessary repairs, as in:

YOU PUT THE CHURCH – THE TINY LITTLE CHURCH INTO THE TIN.

Since only one church was involved, this alteration by a 4-year-old was not essential. Slightly older children tend to correct themselves if their original speech could lead to misunderstanding:

LEND ME THE BALL – THE GREEN BALL.

This repair by a 5-year-old was important, because there were several different coloured balls around. However, the most sophisticated repairs are those which are inessential for getting across the right message, yet show a deep understanding of the linguistic system:

AND THEN FORTUNATELY THE GIRL – A GIRL OFFERS THE DOG A BONE.

Since there was only one girl in the story, this 6-year-old need not have changed *the* to *a*. But since no girl had yet appeared in the story, the change reflected a realization that it would have been correct to use *the* only if a girl had previously been mentioned.

Repairs, then, reflect a deepening awareness of the linguistic system. First, children can correctly use constructions, but cannot repair their mistakes. At a later stage, they begin to use repairs, sometimes sophisticated ones. Finally, they are able to explain various linguistic points.

PSYCHOLINGUISTICS WITHOUT LINGUISTICS?

We can now summarize the conclusions reached in this chapter. We have been examining the relationship between language knowledge (as 'captured' by the classic version of transformational grammar) and the way in which we handle sentences. In the first section we noted that transformations were irrelevant to the way in which we produce and comprehend language. In the second section, we saw that the hypothesis that we recover a classic Chomsky-like deep structure when we comprehend a sentence was unlikely. In the final section we concluded that a 1965 transformational grammar represented a person's linguistic archive – a store of knowledge about language that is only partially utilized in the course of conversations. This archive develops simultaneously with, though rather more slowly than, the ability to speak and comprehend sentences.

Chomsky's latest ideas, however, have not been discussed. This is largely because they have not been tested by psychologists, for two reasons. First, many of them turned away from transformational grammar in disappointment. As one noted: 'By the mid 1970s there remained no unequivocal evidence that transformational grammars provided a model of either the rules or representations that listeners and speakers use during comprehension. As a result, psycholinguistics largely severed its ties with linguistics' (Tanenhaus 1988: 11). Second, Chomsky's more recent ideas are mostly too imprecise and abstract to test.

Does this mean that psycholinguists can safely ignore abstract linguists such as Chomsky in the future? Should they turn to other linguistic theories, or give up linguistics altogether?

In order to answer this point, let us briefly consider the relationship of language knowledge to usage in Chomsky's changing systems. Perhaps a cooking analogy might make this clearer, since it can illustrate the various levels of knowledge that might be involved.

Take chocolate mousse. Even a child might make a perfect mousse by following instructions, without any understanding of what she was doing, or what a mousse should look like. In language, this is equivalent to a young child who can talk, but has as yet little awareness of linguistic structure. Chomsky, as we have seen, has never regarded this 'how to do it' level as being his concern.

The next level involves a notion of what a proper mousse should look like, as well as a growing understanding of how a chocolate mousse relates in its composition to other mousses, such as salmon mousse or lemon mousse. In language, this is the level at which a person can reliably judge what is, and what is not a well-formed sentence. It is also the level at which sentences such as IT IS HARD TO HANDLE FLAMINGOS and FLAMINGOS ARE HARD TO HANDLE can be judged to be paraphrases of one another. This is the type of knowledge encapsulated in the classic (1965) version of a transformational grammar.

But there is a final, more basic level. This is the discovery that only a few fundamental principles underlie the whole of cooking. For example, trapping gas particles within food is the way to make it large in volume and light, a process found in mousse and buns. Or heating causes liquid to evaporate, and the remaining molecules to cling together, as in fried eggs or fudge. These principles are so general, and apply to such a wide range of foods, that they are unlikely to become apparent to the average cook, although she may underlyingly 'know' them, as she prepares food. In relation to language, this basic level is the one Chomsky and his followers finally aimed at: a few simple principles which would show how the whole thing works

Such a grandiose aim, if achieved, would be of great importance to psycholinguists. At the moment, it is unclear how one might test Chomsky's fluctuating and somewhat vague proposals (as we have already noted). He himself has likened linguistic theories to those put forward by physicists to account for why the sun's light gets converted into heat (Chomsky 1978: 202). Scientists cannot send a probe into the sun, so they have to make the best guess they can from the light emitted at the sun's outermost layers. Linguists cannot as yet reliably identify grammar in the brain, so similar guesses have to be made.

Such theory-building is a valid enterprise. Speculation has led to great steps forward in some areas of science. It would therefore be foolish of psycholinguists to ignore it. Meanwhile, it makes sense for them to push ahead, finding out independently how humans understand and produce speech. These are the topics of the next two chapters.

10

THE CASE OF THE MISSING FINGERPRINT
How do we understand speech?

'It seems very pretty,' Alice said, 'but it's rather hard to understand.' You see, she didn't like to confess, even to herself, that she couldn't make it out at all. 'Somehow it seems to fill my head with ideas – only I don't know exactly what they are!'

Lewis Carroll, *Through the Looking Glass*

'Sentence comprehension is like riding a bicycle – a feat far easier performed than described' (Cutler 1976: 134). This feat is the topic of this chapter.

First, however, we should consider whether there might be a link between speech comprehension and production. It would be simpler for psycholinguists if they were directly related. However, there is no reason to assume this is so, any more than we should presume that the same muscles are used in sucking and blowing. We must therefore allow for four possibilities:

1 Comprehension and production are totally different.
2 Comprehension is production in reverse.
3 Comprehension is the same as production: that is, comprehenders reconstruct the message for themselves in the same way as they would construct it if they were speakers.
4 Comprehension and production are partially the same and partially different.

This range of options means that we must deal with comprehension and production separately. We shall begin with speech understanding, because this has been more intensively studied.

HEARING WHAT WE EXPECT TO HEAR

At the beginning of the twentieth century, psycholinguists assumed that the process of understanding speech was a simple one. The hearer was envisaged, metaphorically, as a secretary taking down a dictation. She mentally wrote down the sounds she heard one by one, then read off the words formed by them. Or, taking another metaphor, the hearer was envisaged as a detective solving a crime by matching fingerprints to known criminals. All the detective had to do was match a fingerprint found on the scene of the crime against one on his files, and see who it belonged to. Just as no two people's fingerprints are the same, so each sound was regarded as having a unique acoustic pattern.

Unfortunately, this simple picture turns out to be wrong. A series of experiments conducted by phoneticians and psycholinguists disproved the 'passive secretary' or 'fingerprints' approach. There are a number of problems.

First of all, it is clear that hearers cannot 'take down' or 'match' sounds one by one. Apart from anything else, the speed of utterance makes this an impossible task. If we assume an average of four sounds per English word, and a speed of five words a second, we are expecting the ear and brain to cope with around twenty sounds a second. But humans cannot process this number of separate signals in that time – it is just too many (Liberman *et al.* 1967).

A second reason why the 'passive secretary' or 'fingerprint' approach does not work is that there is no fixed acoustic representation of, say, a T, parallel to the fixed typewriter symbol T. The acoustic traces left by sounds are quite unlike the fingerprints left by criminals. In actual speech, each sound varies considerably depending on what comes before and after it. The T in TOP differs from the T in STOP or the T in BOTTLE. In addition, a sound varies from speaker to speaker to a quite surprising extent. So direct matching of each sound is impossible.

A third, related problem is that sounds are acoustically on a continuum: B gradually shades into D which in turn shades into G. There is no definite borderline between acoustically similar sounds, just as it is not always possible to distinguish between a flower vase and a mug, or a bush and a tree (Liberman *et al.* 1967).

These findings indicate that there is no sure way in which a human can 'fingerprint' a sound or match it to a single mental symbol, because the acoustic patterns of sounds are not fixed and distinct. And even if they were, people would not have time to identify each one positively. The information extracted from the sound waves forms 'no more than a rough guide to the sense of the message, a kind of scaffolding upon which the listener constructs or reconstructs the sentences' (Fry 1970: 31).

In interpreting speech sounds, hearers are like detectives who find that solving a crime is not a simple case of matching fingerprints to criminals. Instead, they find a situation where 'a given type of clue might have been left by any of a number of criminals or where a given criminal might have left any of a number of different types of clue' (Fodor *et al*. 1974: 301). What they are faced with is 'more like the array of disparate data from which Sherlock Holmes deduces the identity of the criminal.' In such cases, the detectives' background information must come into play.

In other words, deciphering the sounds of speech is an *active* not a passive process. Hearers have to compute *actively* the possible phonetic message by using their background knowledge of the language. This is perhaps not so astonishing. We have plenty of other evidence for the active nature of this process. We all know how difficult it is to hear the exact sounds of a foreign word. This is because we are so busy imposing on it what we expect to hear, in terms of our own language habits, that we fail to notice certain novel features.

IDENTIFYING WORDS

Listeners try first of all to identify words. They are 'constrained by the sounds of language, on the one hand, and by the desire to make sense of what they hear on the other' (Bond 1999: xvii). Consequently, we can find out quite a lot by looking both at English word structure, and at mishearings or 'slips of the ear'. English words contain some useful clues about their beginnings and endings. For example, T at the beginning of a word has a puff of breath (aspiration) after it, and –ING often comes at the end of a word. As a result, when someone mishears a word, it is typically a whole word: 85 per cent of mishearings involved single words in one study (Browman 1980). And this has been confirmed by later studies, as with RACING for RAISING in the sentence: 'He's in the turkey-raising businesss', GRANDMA for GRAMMAR in the phrase 'Grammar Workshop', and CHAMELEON heard as COMEDIAN (Bond 1999).

As soon as a hearer comes across the beginning of a word, he or she starts making preliminary guesses as to what it might be. It would take far too long to check out each guess one by one, and numerous words are considered at the same time: 'There is now considerable evidence that, during spoken-word recognition, listeners evaluate multiple lexical hypotheses in parallel' (McQueen 2005: 230).

Exactly how this is done is disputed. One suggestion is that as soon as the beginning of a word is detected, the hearer immediately flashes up onto his or her mental screen a whole army of words with a similar beginning. The hearer hears maybe 'HAVE YOU SEEN MY P . . .?' At this point her mind conjures up a whole list of words which start in a similar way, maybe 'PACK, PAD, PADLOCK, PAN, PANDA, PANSY'. This idea is known as the 'cohort' model. Words beginning with the same sounds were envisaged as lining up like soldiers in a cohort, a division of the Roman army (Marslen-Wilson and Tyler 1980). The hearer then eliminates those that do not fit in with the sound or meaning of the rest of the sentence. But the cohort model, in its original form, did not allow for the fact that even if a hearer missed the first sound, it was still possible to make a plausible guess about the word being heard. If someone heard BLEASANT then the degree of overlap with PLEASANT, and the lack of any word BLEASANT, together with the context, allowed the hearer to make a good guess. So the model was amended to allow for more than just the initial sound, even though it was widely recognized that initial sounds, if heard properly, are very important for word identification.

But this widening of the information accessed meant that the revised cohort model was similar to another, more powerful type of framework, known as 'spreading activation' or 'interactive activation' models, which can be envisaged as working somewhat like electric circuitry, in which the current flows backwards and forwards, rushing between the initial sounds heard, and the words aroused. The sounds will activate multiple meanings, then the other meanings triggered will arouse further sounds. BLEASANT would eventually fade away, but PLEASANT might trigger, say, PHEASANT, PLEASURE, and others. Those which fitted in with other aspects of the sentence, the meaning and the syntax, would get more and more activated, and those which seemed unlikely would fade away. These network models, in which everything is (ultimately) connected to everything else, are sometimes referred to by the general label 'connectionism' (McClelland and Elman 1986).

Inevitably, controversy exists as to how such models work, and several variants have been proposed. A model that is currently being assessed is labelled 'Shortlist' (Norris 1994, 2005), which proposes that 'a lexical lookup process ... identifies all the words that correspond to sequences of phonemes in the input. So, for example, the input CATALOG would match the words CAT, CATTLE, A, LOG, and CATALOG.' (Norris 2005: 336). Here, CATALOG would emerge as the winner, as shown in the following diagram.

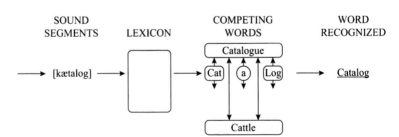

Hearers are not aware of these multiple word choices, just as they are unaware that when they hear an ambiguous word (such as BANK which could be a financial institution or the edge of a river) they mentally consider more than one meaning. This somewhat suprising discovery was made well over a quarter of a century ago, when psycholinguists were first seriously interested in ambiguity. They discovered that hearers consider multiple meanings, though often subconsciously. When subjects were asked to check for the presence of a given sound in a sentence ('Press a button if you come to a word starting with B'), a procedure known as 'phoneme monitoring', an ambiguous word slowed them down even when they claimed not to have noticed the ambiguity (Foss 1970). For example, they responded more slowly to the B in a sentence such as:

THE SEAMEN STARTED TO DRILL BEFORE THEY WERE ORDERED TO DO SO.

(drill holes or take part in a life-boat drill?), than in:

THE SEAMEN STARTED TO MARCH BEFORE THEY WERE ORDERED TO DO SO.

Furthermore, even irrelevant meanings are apparently considered. In one now famous experiment (Swinney 1979), passages containing homonyms (words with more than one meaning) were read out to subjects. For example:

THE MAN FOUND SEVERAL SPIDERS, ROACHES AND OTHER BUGS IN THE CORNER OF THE ROOM.

Here BUGS clearly referred to insects, though in another context, BUGS could be electronic listening devices. Just after the ambiguous word, the experimenter flashed a sequence of letters up on to a screen, and asked if they formed a word or not (a so-called 'lexical decision task'). He found that subjects responded fastest to words which were related to either meaning of the ambiguous word. They said 'Yes' faster to ANT and SPY than they did to SEW. And this was not just due to some accidental experimental effect, because other psycholinguists came to the same conclusion (e.g. Tanenhaus et al. 1979; Seidenberg et al. 1982; Kinoshita 1986).

More surprising still, perhaps, subjects reacted similarly even with a homonym such as ROSE which involves two different parts of speech, a noun (the flower) and a verb (past tense of RISE). They were played four sentences, which included the words:

> THEY BOUGHT A ROSE.
> THEY BOUGHT A SHIRT.
> THEY ALL ROSE.
> THEY ALL STOOD.

The subjects responded fastest to a lexical decision about the word FLOWER following either type of ROSE, both the noun and the verb (Seidenberg et al. 1982).

This may be a 'veiled controlled process', in that it is neither automatic, nor consciously carried out. 'Veiled controlled processes are opaque to consciousness, faster than conscious controlled processes, and they make fewer demands on limited processing resources' (Tanenhaus et al. 1985: 368).

Much more is going on than we consciously realize. Any human is like a powerful computer in that the limited amount of information appearing on his or her mental screen at any one time gives no indication of the multiple processes which have whizzed through in the computer's inner workings. And these human processes are happening in parallel, rather than one after the other, and are more impressive even than those found in the world's most powerful computers. Computers which can deal with the multiple computations routinely carried out by humans are still a future dream.

But exactly how much parallel processing is going on in humans? Verbs are a particular area of controversy. Do humans activate in parallel all structures that can occur with them? Let us consider this matter.

VERSATILE VERBS

'They've a temper some of them – particularly verbs, they're the proudest – adjectives you can do anything with, but not verbs.' This comment by Humpty Dumpty to Alice in Lewis Carroll's Through the Looking Glass reflects a feeling shared by many psycholinguists that verbs are more complicated than other parts of speech. They may provide the 'key' to the sentence by imposing a structure on it.

The effect of verbs has been a major issue for around half a century. Fodor et al. (1968) suggested that when someone hears a sentence, they pay particular attention to the verb. The moment they hear it, they look up the entry for this verb in a mental dictionary. The dictionary will contain a list of the possible constructions associated with that verb. For example:

KICK	+	NP	HE KICKED THE BALL
EXPECT	+	NP	HE EXPECTED A LETTER
	+	TO	HE EXPECTED TO ARRIVE AT SIX O'CLOCK
	+	THAT	HE EXPECTED THAT HE WOULD BE LATE.

If these psychologists are correct in their claim, then sentences containing verbs which give no choice of construction should be easier to process than those which contain 'versatile verbs' – verbs associated with multiple constructions. In the case of a verb such as KICK, the hearer only has a simple lexical entry to check. But in the case of a verb such as EXPECT, they mentally activate each of the possible constructions before picking on the correct one. This suggestion was known as the 'verbal complexity hypothesis'.

Several psycholinguists tried to test this theory, including Fodor, Garrett and Bever themselves. In one experiment, they gave undergraduates pairs of sentences which were identical except for the verb. A single-construction verb was placed in one sentence (e.g. MAIL), and a multiple-construction verb in the other (e.g. EXPECT):

> THE LETTER WHICH THE SECRETARY MAILED WAS LATE.
> THE LETTER WHICH THE SECRETARY EXPECTED WAS LATE.

They jumbled up the words in each, and then asked the students to unscramble them. They found what they had hoped to find – that it was much easier to sort out the single-construction verb sentences. But this experiment has been criticized. The problem is that it did not test comprehension directly: it assessed the difficulty of a task which occurred *after* the sentence had been originally processed.

Later researchers checked on the difficulty of versatile verbs via a lexical decision task – asking subjects to decide whether a sequence of letters such as DOG or GLIT flashed up on a screen is a word or not. Supposedly, reaction times to this task will be slower if the letter sequence is presented just after subjects have heard a versatile verb. One group of researchers who tried this did not find the predicted effect (Clifton et al. 1984). They concluded that hearers had no extra difficulty provided that the verb was followed by its preferred construction. For example, I THINK THAT ... (e.g. I THINK THAT MAVIS IS A FOOL) would cause less trouble than I THINK AS ... (e.g. I THINK AS I WALK TO WORK). In other words, hearers may activate in advance one favoured construction for a given verb, but there is no need for them to activate mentally all possible constructions associated with it. If only one favoured construction is activated per verb, then 'versatile verbs' are no more difficult to deal with than non-versatile ones, except when an odd or unexpected option is chosen.

This conclusion is supported by the work of some other researchers (e.g. Ford et al. 1982). Consider the sentence:

> THE PERSON WHO COOKS DUCKS OUT OF WASHING THE DISHES.

At first, we expect the word DUCKS to be the object of the word COOKS. But since we need a main verb, we are forced to revise our interpretation to:

THE PERSON [WHO COOKS] DUCKS OUT OF WASHING THE DISHES.

Our knowledge of the verb COOKS led us astray, since it is often, though not necessarily, followed by the thing which is cooked.

However, another group of researchers *did* find that a versatile verb caused problems, though in a somewhat unexpected way. The number of different constructions following a verb did not matter particularly. Instead, difficulties arose with verbs where it was not immediately obvious who did what to whom (Shapiro *et al.* 1987). Consider the sentence:

SHELDON SENT DEBBIE THE LETTER.

This type of sentence took up extra processing time because people were not at first sure whether Debbie or something else was being sent.

On balance, versatile verbs do not cause the problems they were once expected to cause. Listeners may be mentally prepared for a variety of constructions, but this does not seem to delay processing, unless there is some additional difficulty, such as an unusual construction, or problems in deciding who did what to whom. Perhaps a hearer is like a car-driver, driving behind a bus. She has certain expectations about what the bus in front is likely to do. It can go straight on, turn left or turn right, and she is ready to respond appropriately to any of these. But she might be taken by surprise if the bus reversed. Similarly, perhaps versatile verbs are a problem only if they spring a surprise on the hearer.

INFORMED GUESSES

A key question which puzzled researchers for a number of years is whether listeners take a 'top-down' or 'bottom-up' approach when they process sentences. That is, do they impose their expectations on what they are hearing, and get puzzled if these expectations are not fulfilled? This is a top-down approach. On the other hand, do they listen to the words said to them, and then try to assemble them in some type of order? This is a bottom-up approach. As we learn more about the way human speech comprehension works, it now seems that both viewpoints combine together. But some of the earlier work on the subject explored a top-down approach, and this can still explain a lot about how humans understand chunks of words.

When someone hears a sentence, she often latches on to outline clues, and 'jumps to conclusions' about what she is hearing. An analogy might make this clearer. Suppose someone found a large foot sticking out from under her bed one night. She would be likely to shriek 'There's a man under my bed', because past experience has led her to believe that large feet are usually attached to male human beings. Instead of just reporting the actual situation 'There is a foot sticking out from under the bed', she has jumped to the conclusion that this foot belongs to a man, and this man is lying under the bed.

The evidence suggests that we make similar 'informed guesses' about the material we hear. One of the first people to work on listeners' expectations was Tom Bever, a psychologist at Columbia University, New York. The next few pages are based to a large extent on suggestions made by him.

Hearers approach the sentences of English with at least four basic assumptions, according to a key paper by Bever, published over a quarter of a century ago (1970). Guided by their expectations, they devise rules of thumb or 'strategies' for dealing with what they hear. Let us briefly consider these assumptions and linked strategies. Although we shall be labelling them 'first', 'second', 'third' and 'fourth', this is not meant to refer to the order in which they are used, since all four may be working simultaneously.

Assumption 1 'Every sentence consists of one or more sentoids or sentence-like chunks, and each sentoid normally includes a noun-phrase followed by a verb, optionally followed by another noun-phrase.' That is, every sentence will either be a simple one such as:

DO YOU LIKE CURRY?
TADPOLES TURN INTO FROGS.
DON'T TOUCH THAT WIRE.

or it will be a 'complex' one containing more than one sentence-like structure or sentoid. For example, the sentence:

IT IS NOT SURPRISING THAT THE FACT THAT PETER SINGS IN HIS BATH UPSETS THE LANDLADY.

contains three sentoids:

IT IS NOT SURPRISING
THAT THE FACT UPSETS THE LANDLADY
THAT PETER SINGS IN HIS BATH.

Within a sentence, each sentoid normally contains either a noun phrase–verb sequence such as:

THE LARGE GORILLA GROWLED.

or a noun phrase–verb–noun phrase sequence such as:

COWS CHEW THE CUD.

The strategy or working principle which follows from assumption 1 seems to be: 'Divide each sentence up into sentoids by looking for noun phrase–verb (–noun phrase) sequences.' This is sometimes referred to as the *canonical sentoid* strategy, since noun phrase–verb–noun phrase is the 'canonical' or standard form of an English sentence. It is clear that we need such a strategy when we distinguish sentoids, since there are often no acoustic clues to help us divide a sentence up (Chapter 1).

A clear confirmation of this strategy comes when people are presented with a sentence such as:

LLOYD KICKED THE BALL KICKED IT.

which was said in a football commentary. Most people deny that it is possible, claiming it must be:

LLOYD KICKED THE BALL THEN KICKED IT AGAIN.

But it is a well-formed English sentence, as shown by the similar one:

LLOYD THROWN THE BALL KICKED IT.

People just cannot think of the interpretation 'to whom the ball was kicked', the canonical sentoid strategy is too strong. And similar examples abound in the literature, perhaps the most famous being:

THE HORSE RACED PAST THE BARN FELL.

A common comment about this one is: 'I can't understand it because I don't know the word BARNFELL.' The alternative interpretation of RACED as 'which was raced' is rarely considered.

Further confirmation of this strategy comes from so-called 'centre embeddings' – sentences which have a Chinese box-like structure, one lying inside the other. The following is a double centre embedding – one sentence is inside another which is inside yet another.

THE MAN THE GIRL THE BOY MET BELIEVED LAUGHED.

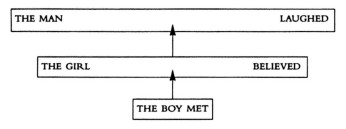

(The man laughed: the girl believed the man; the boy met the girl.)

Blumenthal (1966) tested to see what happened when sentences of this type were memorized. He noted that subjects tended to recall them as noun–verb sequences:

THE MAN, THE GIRL AND THE BOY MET, BELIEVED AND LAUGHED.

Their immediate reaction to being presented with such an unusual sentence was to utilize the canonical sentoid strategy even though it was, strictly speaking, irrelevant. In a later experiment, Bever found to his surprise that subjects imposed an NP–V–NP sequence on sentences of this type *even after practice*. He comments, 'the NVN sequence is so compelling that it may be described as a "linguistic illusion" which training cannot readily overcome' (Bever 1970: 295).

The canonical sentoid strategy seems to start young. Bever noted that by around the age of 2, children are already looking out for noun–verb sequences – though they tend to assume that the first noun goes with the first verb, and interpret:

THE DOG THAT JUMPED FELL.

as:

THE DOG JUMPED.

Assumption 2 'In a noun phrase–verb–noun phrase sequence, the first noun is usually the actor and the second the object.' That is, an English sentence normally has the word order actor–action–object with the person doing the action coming first as in:

GIRAFFES EAT LEAVES.
DIOGENES BOUGHT A BARREL.

The strategy which stems from assumption 2, seems to be as follows: 'Interpret an NP–V–NP sequence as actor – action – object unless you have strong indications to the contrary.'

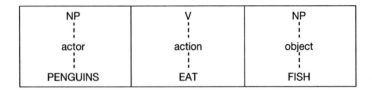

NP	V	NP
actor	action	object
PENGUINS	EAT	FISH

A number of experiments have shown that sentences which do not have the actor first take longer to comprehend if there are no semantic clues. The best known of these may be Slobin's 'picture verification' experiment (1966b). He showed subjects pictures, and also read them out a sentence. Then he timed how long it took them to say whether the two matched. He found that passives such as:

THE CAT WAS CHASED BY THE DOG.

took longer to verify than the corresponding active:

THE DOG CHASED THE CAT.

Another picture verification experiment showed that actor–action–object structures are comprehended more quickly than other structures which would fit the NP–V–NP sequence (Mehler and Carey 1968):

THEY	ARE KIDNAPPING	BABIES
actor	action	object

was verified more quickly than:

THEY	ARE	NOURISHING LUNCHES
subject	copula	complement

Assumption 3 'When a complex sentence is composed of a main clause and one or more subordinate clauses, the main clause usually comes first.' That is, it is more usual to find a sentence such as:

NERO FIDDLED [WHILE ROME BURNED].

than:

[WHILE ROME BURNED] NERO FIDDLED.

Similarly:

PETRONELLA EXPECTED [THAT PERICLES WOULD SCRUB THE FLOOR].

is considerably more likely than:

*[THAT PERICLES WOULD SCRUB THE FLOOR] PETRONELLA EXPECTED.

The strategy which follows from assumption 3 seems to be 'Interpret the first clause as the main clause unless you have clear indications to the contrary.' The existence of this strategy accounts for the correct interpretation of:

IT WAS OBVIOUS HE WAS DRUNK FROM THE WAY HE STAGGERED ACROSS THE ROAD.

Here, the subordinate clause is not marked in any way, but the hearer automatically assumes that it comes after the main clause. This strategy also partly accounts for the difficulty of:

THE ELEPHANT SQUEEZED INTO A TELEPHONE BOOTH COLLAPSED.

Until coming across the unexpected word COLLAPSED at the end of the sentence the hearer probably assumes that THE ELEPHANT SQUEEZED . . . was the beginning of the main clause.

Assumption 4 'Sentences usually make sense.' That is, people generally say things that are sensible. They utter sequences such as:

HAVE YOU DONE THE WASHING UP?
THE TRAIN GOES AT EIGHT O'CLOCK.

rather than:

HAPPINESS SHOOTS LLAMAS.
THE HONEY SPREAD MOTHER WITH A KNIFE.

The strategy attached to this assumption is the most powerful of all – though from the linguistic point of view, it is the least satisfactory because it is so vague. It says: 'Use your knowledge of the world to pick the most likely interpretation of the sentence you are hearing.' In certain circumstances this can override all other strategies, and reverse well-attested aspects of language behaviour. For example, under normal circumstances people find it much easier to remember sentences that are superficially grammatical than random strings of words. It is considerably easier to learn the apparently grammatical:

THE YIGS WUR VUMLY RIXING HUM IN JEGEST MIV.

than the shorter string:

THE YIG WUR VUM RIX HUM IN JEG MIV. (Epstein 1961)

But this well-attested result can be *reversed* if the subjects are presented with semantically strange grammatical sentences and ungrammatical strings of words which appear to make sense. Subjects remember more words from strings such as:

NEIGHBOURS SLEEPING NOISY WAKE PARTIES
DETER DRIVERS ACCIDENTS FATAL CARELESS

than they do from sentences such as:

RAPID BOUQUETS DETER SUDDEN NEIGHBOURS.
PINK ACCIDENTS CAUSE SLEEPING STORMS. (Marks and Miller 1964)

So far, then, we have listed a number of assumptions which hearers have about English, and suggested a number of linked 'perceptual strategies':

1   Divide each sentence up into sentoids by looking for NP–V(–NP) sequences ('canonical sentoid strategy').
2   Interpret an NP–V–NP sequence as actor–action–object.
3   Interpret the first clause as the main clause.
4   Use your knowledge of the world to pick the most likely interpretation.

Even quite odd sentences seem easy to understand if they fit in with the 'strategies' listed above:

THE KANGAROO SQUEEZED THE ORANGE AND THE KOOKABURRA
ATE THE PIPS.

But sentences which do not fulfil the hearer's expectations are more difficult to comprehend. Each of the following goes against one of the four basic
strategies. The sentences can be understood reasonably easily, but they need
marginally more attention from the hearer:

AFTER RUSHING ACROSS THE FIELD THE BULL TOSSED HARRY.
THE VAN WAS HIT BY THE BUS, AND THE CAR WAS RAMMED BY A TAXI.
THE POSTMAN BIT THE DOG, AND THE BABY SCRATCHED THE CAT.

When a sentence goes against more than one strategy the effect is rather
worse:

THE SHARK PUSHED THROUGH THE SEAWEED WAS ATTACKED BY A
TADPOLE.

The sentence is neither ungrammatical, nor incomprehensible. It just seems
clumsy and strange, and would possibly cause a hearer to say: 'I'm sorry, I
didn't get that. Could you repeat it?'
It is an interesting fact that speakers tend to avoid sentences which go
against perceptual strategies to too great an extent. People just do not *say*
things such as:

THE POODLE WALKED RAPIDLY UP THE MOUNTAIN COLLAPSED.
JOAN GAVE JUNE A PRESENT ON SATURDAY AND JANE ON SUNDAY.

Strictly speaking, these sentences are not ungrammatical, just odd and unac-
ceptable. Compare the syntactically similar sentences:

THE RAG DOLL WASHED IN THE WASHING MACHINE FELL TO PIECES.
MAX GAVE HIS DOG A BATH YESTERDAY AND HIS CAT LAST WEEK.

However, since the 'sensible' sentences above are interpretable only because
the speaker is able to use the imprecise strategy 4 ('Use your knowledge of
the world to pick the most likely interpretation'), sentences of this type may
be in the process of being eliminated from the English language – since
perceptual needs can often influence linguistic rules. To quote Bever: 'The
syntax of a language is partly moulded by grammatical responses to behavioural constraints' (1970: 321).
Obviously, the four strategies noted so far are not the only ones we use
when we comprehend sentences. Bever's paper triggered a search for others,

particularly ones which might apply to a wider range of languages than his first three (e.g. Kimball 1973; Gruber *et al.* 1978). Let us therefore outline two which might have a broader application, and partially encapsulate the 'canonical sentoid' strategy (Frazier and Rayner 1982, 1988).

The first of these says: 'Assume you are dealing with a simple structure, unless you have evidence to the contrary.' This has been called the 'Principle of Minimal Attachment', because each word is attached to the existing structure with the minimum amount of extra elaboration. On hearing the word PARADED in a sentence such as:

THE LION PARADED THROUGH THE TOWN ESCAPED.

it is far simpler to set up a simple NP–VP structure, than one which involves the added complexity of an extra sentence inserted after THE LION.

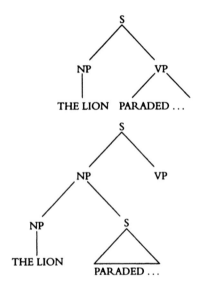

The second says: 'Try and associate any new item with the phrase currently being processed.' This has been called the 'Principle of Late Closure', because the previous phrase is held open, waiting for new additions, until there is strong evidence that it is complete. In a sentence such as:

FIONA DISCOVERED ON MONDAY THE PENGUIN HAD HURT ITS FOOT.

it is more natural to assume that ON MONDAY goes with the previous verb DISCOVERED, even though it would be equally plausible from the meaning point of view to assume that Monday was the day on which the penguin injured itself.

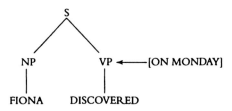

Both these strategies would explain why:

THE MAN THE GIRL THE BOY MET BELIEVED LAUGHED

was so readily interpreted as 'The man, the boy, and the girl, all met, believed and laughed' (p. 216). This interpretation involves a much simpler structure than the 'correct' centre-embedded version, and tacking each new person introduced onto the previous one fits in with Late Closure.

As we have seen, the notion of strategies works well. There is plenty of proof that we impose our expectations on to what we hear, so at first sight there is no more to be said. All we need to do, it might seem, is to continue adding to our list of strategies until we have enough to cover the whole of language, and then try to divide them up into strategies that relate only to a single language, such as English; strategies that apply to a whole group of languages, such as those which have the basic word order subject–verb–object; and third, strategies that are universal.

However, when we consider the situation in detail, the notion of strategies raises some problems. Above all, language is enormously complex. Hardly any sentences are as straightforward as:

MARY LIKES STRAWBERRIES.

or even:

SEBASTIAN DISCOVERED THAT THE GORILLA HAD ESCAPED.

Many of them are considerably more complicated. For example, anyone who listens to a serious discussion is likely to hear sequences such as the following, in which a doctor is giving his opinion on a controversial illness (ME 'myalgic encephalomyelitis'):

I was very sceptical initially, I have to say, for a while it seemed to be y'know this decade's thing, and went along the same sort of lines as Total Allergy

Syndrome, and things like that, which ultimately became pretty well discred-
ited as diagnoses and so I think initially, I think it was seen as this year's
trendy illness to have.

(Wetherell *et al.* 2001: 156)

How many strategies are involved in a sentence like this? Obviously, many
more than the few we have discussed. Perhaps twenty? Or a hundred? And
supposing there are a hundred, what order do people apply them in? When
faced with the problem of organizing dozens of strategies into a coherent
model of comprehension some psycholinguists have argued first, that the task
is impossible. Second, that the whole notion of strategy is meaningless in
relation to these longer sentences. Strategies become vague devices of
immense power which provide very little concrete information about
sentence processing. As one psycholinguist commented: 'One wonders what
couldn't be accomplished with an armful of strategies' (Gough 1971: 269).

The notion of strategies therefore solves some problems, but raises others.
Strategies cannot be totally replaced, but they need to be held in check and
supplemented by more precise procedures. Let us go on to consider how
researchers have tried to instill more orderliness into models of comprehension.

WORD-BY-WORD

As a reaction against the chaos of strategies, a number of researchers turned
towards the neatness and orderly behaviour of computers. Perhaps they could
program a computer so that it would be an 'automatic parser', that is, a
machine which could unaided identify the syntactic role of each word, and
show how they all fit together. Such machines move from one end of the
sentence to the other, dealing with each group of words in turn, checking
them against an internal grammar which contains information about the
structure of English sentences. This is sometimes called a 'left-to-right' model,
or in more fashionable terminology, an 'incremental parser', since the parser
moves onwards by adding extra information word by word, in so far as this
is possible.

Of course, when faced with a simple sentence such as:

PETRONELLA SAW A GHOST.

there is hardly any difference between a model which says 'Assume you are
dealing with an NP–V–NP structure' (strategy model), and one which says
'Work your way through the sentence word-by-word looking first for a noun
phrase, then for a verb, then another noun phrase' (left-to-right model). But
the difference becomes apparent when we look at how to deal with questions.

Suppose we have a sentence which begins with the words:

WHICH ELEPHANT . . .?

This sentence could end in a number of different ways. We could say:

WHICH ELEPHANT CAN DANCE THE POLKA?
WHICH ELEPHANT SHALL I BUY?
WHICH ELEPHANT SHALL I GIVE BUNS TO?

In the first sentence, the elephant is the subject of the verb, the one who is dancing the polka; in the second, the elephant is the object, the thing being bought; in the third, it is the indirect object, the animal to whom something is being given.

A dedicated strategy model would suggest that hearers start guessing immediately about the role of the word elephant, based on their expectations of the role elephants usually play in sentences. A left-to-right model, on the other hand, suggests that if hearers encounter a group of words which does not immediately fit into the straightforward NP–V–NP pattern, they do not make any rash guesses, they wait and see. They mentally store the words WHICH ELEPHANT in their memory until they have heard enough of the rest of the sentence to enable them to interpret it reliably. For example, in the case of WHICH ELEPHANT SHALL I BUY? they would wait until after the word BUY, since they know that the verb BUY usually has an object, the thing which is bought. They then mentally insert the stored phrase WHICH ELEPHANT into the gap where the object is usually found:

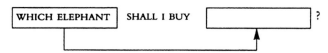

Similarly, in the sentence WHICH ELEPHANT SHALL I GIVE THESE BUNS TO? the hearers would store the words WHICH ELEPHANT until after the word TO. They would know that the word TO must normally be accompanied by a noun, so they would insert the stored phrase into the gap after TO:

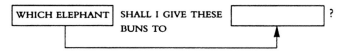

But this type of decision making may be unnecessary. Early work on comprehension suggested that psycholinguists needed to make decisions about whether strategies or gap-filling models were preferable. Later work has led to the realization that the human language processor is likely to be more powerful, and more commonsensical than was once assumed (e.g. Townsend and Bever 2001). And far more may be happening simultaneously than we previously realized. As a hearer works through a sentence, he or she may encounter temporary ambiguity quite often, but is often able to make a provisional decision, while still keeping other possibilities in mind. One interpretation is 'foregrounded', though others are kept in the background, ready to be moved forward if necessary. Hearers probably avoid making a definitive decision, if they are at all uncertain: having to go back and make a totally new analysis would be time-consuming and inefficient.

A solution which involves two layers of processing has also been proposed (Frazier and Clifton 1996). Primary parsing principles could first cut up any sentence into broad chunks. The 'canonical sentoid' strategy is possibly one of these, so are the more recently proposed principles which overlap with it, the Principles of Minimal Attachment and Late Closure (p. 200–1). These primary decisions may be followed by a second set of decisions, which look at smaller chunks and take individual lexical items into account.

Let us now assess the comprehension process. Left-to-right models may be right in assuming that speakers work through sentences in a principled way. But such models also present problems. A critical weakness is that they cannot cope with ill-formed, but comprehensible sentences, such as:

I HAVE MUCH PROBLEM IN MAKING TO WORK YOUR TELEPHONE.

They therefore need to be integrated with strategy models which can make guesses about imperfect utterances. A further possibility is that humans make a provisional decision, but keep likely alternatives in their mind, so that they can switch over to these if necessary. This compromise solution may be the correct one. The human mind is capable of much more simultaneous computation than was once assumed.

FURTHER DIFFICULTIES

So far, the factors we have discussed which affect comprehension have been mainly linguistic ones. But understanding speech may use abilities which relate to other aspects of human behaviour. In the next few pages we will discuss some aspects of sentence processing which involve other specific linguistic abilities, though we must bear in mind that it is not always easy to separate linguistic factors out from general cognitive ones, and researchers frequently disagree about which is which. Broadly speaking, a hearer is likely to find a sentence hard to comprehend if it goes beyond certain 'psychological' limits.

Let us begin by considering the amount of material which can be processed at any one time. Clearly, there is a limit on this. We know from numerous other areas of human behaviour that there is only a certain amount that human beings can cope with simultaneously, whether they are trying to remember things or are solving a problem. So a sentence that is long or involved will be difficult. Take length. It is often hard on a journey to follow the route directions of a passerby. People tend to say things like: 'Take the third turning on the left past the fourth pub just before the supermarket next door to the church.' Apart from anything else, this sentence is just too long to be retained in the memory. Before the speaker gets to the end, the hearer is likely to have forgotten the first part.

However, length alone is not particularly important. What matters is the interaction of length with structure. Early research suggested that listeners prefer to deal with the speech they hear sentoid by sentoid. As soon as one sentoid has been decoded, hearers possibly forget the syntax, and remove the gist of what has been said to another memory space (Fodor *et al.* 1974: 339). The hearer 'wipes the slate clean', and starts afresh.

Subsequent research suggested that this view is somewhat over-simplified (e.g Flores d'Arcais 1988). Sentoids are cleared away only if their contents appear to be no longer needed. Speakers are able to retain sentoids in their memory to a greater or lesser extent, if they sense that this will help future processing.

But the overall conclusion is clear. Humans have limited immediate memory space and processing ability. Therefore they clear away sections of speech as soon as they have dealt with them, preferably sentoid by sentoid. This would explain not only why unusually long sentoids are difficult (as in the direction-finding example given earlier), but also, perhaps, why sentences which cannot easily be divided into sentoids are a problem. For example:

THIS IS THE BUS THAT THE CAR THAT THE PROFESSOR THAT THE GIRL KISSED DROVE HIT.

is more difficult than:

THIS IS THE GIRL THAT KISSED THE PROFESSOR THAT DROVE THE CAR THAT HIT THE BUS.

even though the second sentence has exactly the same number of words and almost the same meaning. Part of the trouble with the first is that you have to carry almost all of it unanalysed in your head. You have to wait until the end of the verb HIT that goes with CAR before you can divide it into sentoids:

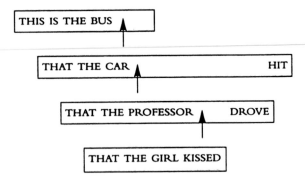

However, in dealing with sentences which cannot easily be divided into sentoids like the one above, it is not only the memory load, but also the difficulty of processing three sentoids simultaneously which cause problems. Three are not impossible (as some people have suggested, e.g. Kimball 1973) because we can, after some thought, compose sentences such as:

THE NEWBORN CROCODILE [WHICH THE KEEPER [YOU WERE TALKING TO THIS AFTERNOON] LOOKS AFTER] IS BEING MOVED TO ANOTHER ZOO.

But in general it is unusual to find more than two sentoids being coped with easily, and two are more difficult than one. It is a fact about human nature that a person can deal only with a limited number of things at one time.

This leads us on to another difficulty, which overlaps with the simultaneous processing problem – that of interruptions. An interrupted structure is only slightly more difficult to process than an uninterrupted one, providing there are clear indications that you are dealing with an interruption. For example, the following sentence has a seventeen-word interruption:

THE GIRL [WHOM CUTHBERT KISSED SO ENTHUSIASTICALLY AT THE PARTY LAST NIGHT WHEN HE THOUGHT NO ONE WAS LOOKING] IS MY SISTER.

It is not particularly difficult to understand because the hearer knows (from the opening sequence THE GIRL WHOM . . .) that he is still waiting for the main verb. However, if there are no indications that an interruption is in progress, the sentence immediately increases in difficulty and oddness:

CUTHBERT PHONED THE GIRL [WHOM HE KISSED SO ENTHUSIASTICALLY AT THE PARTY LAST NIGHT WHEN HE THOUGHT NO ONE WAS LOOKING] UP.

Here UP goes with PHONED, but the hearer has already 'closed off' that branch on his mental tree. He has not left it 'open' and ready for additional material:

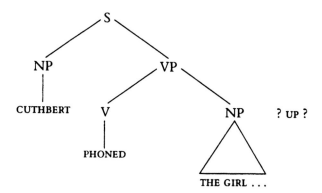

A fourth general difficulty concerns compression of information. Humans need thinking space to let information 'sink in', and they comprehend best if they are presented only with a small amount of new information at one time. This is why Longfellow's poem *The Song of Hiawatha* is so easy to follow. Each line repeats some information from the previous one, so there is only a small amount of new material in each one:

> By the shores of Gitche Gumee,
> By the shining Big-Sea-Water,
> Stood the wigwam of Nokomis,
> Daughter of the Moon, Nokomis.
> Dark behind it rose the forest,
> Rose the black and gloomy pine-trees,
> Rose the firs with cones upon them;
> Bright before it beat the water,
> Beat the clear and sunny water,
> Beat the shining Big-Sea-Water.

This slow dropping of information contrasts strikingly with the over-compressed:

> THIS IS THE BUS THAT THE CAR THAT THE PROFESSOR THAT THE GIRL KISSED DROVE HIT.

A further difficulty involves the repetition of items and structures. It is difficult to process a sentence which contains the same word twice, or more than one instance of the same type of structure, especially if the similar constructions are one inside the other. Take the sentence:

THIS IS THE BUS [THAT THE VAN [THAT THE CAR HIT] HIT].

This sentence with the repeated word HIT is more difficult than:

THIS IS THE BUS [THAT THE VAN [THAT THE CAR HIT] COLLIDED WITH].

And the sentence above, which has a so-called relative clause inside another relative clause, is more difficult than a relative clause inside a different type of clause:

I EXPECT [THAT THE BUS [WHICH HIT THE VAN] IS DAMAGED].

In fact, it is so difficult to process one type of clause inside another similar one, that at least one linguist has suggested excluding such sentences from a grammar altogether. But this is not a workable suggestion, because it would also exclude perfectly good sentences such as:

THE OCTOPUS [WHICH THE FISHERMAN [YOU WERE TALKING TO] HAD CAUGHT] LOOKED QUITE REVOLTING.

This is a relative clause inside another relative clause.

Another difficulty, which seems to be partly a general psychological one, and partly a linguistic one, is the difficulty of backward processing (Grosu 1974). In English we normally move forwards when we process sentences. For example, it is easy to comprehend:

MARY, PETER AND PRISCILLA PLAY THE FLUTE, THE PIANO AND THE GUITAR RESPECTIVELY.

In this, the order of the people and the instruments they play moves from left to right:

1	2	3		1	2	3
MARY	PETER	PRISCILLA	–	FLUTE	PIANO	GUITAR.

It is considerably more difficult to understand:

MARY, PETER AND PRISCILLA PLAY THE GUITAR, THE PIANO AND THE FLUTE REVERSELY.

Here, the instruments are given backwards, and you have to reverse the order in which they occur before you can sort out who is playing what:

1	2	3		3	2	1
MARY	PETER	PRISCILLA	–	FLUTE	PIANO	GUITAR.

The same kind of reversal occurs in the sentence:

THE CAR THAT THE PROFESSOR THAT THE GIRL KISSED DROVE CRASHED.

1	2	3		3	2	1
CAR	PROFESSOR	GIRL	–	KISSED	DROVE	CRASHED.

Backward processing (and compression) may also be why it is difficult to understand:

MY AUNT'S EMPLOYER'S SON'S UMBRELLA'S COLOUR IS YELLOW.

compared with the left-to-right uncompressed sentence:

THE COLOUR OF THE UMBRELLA OF THE SON OF THE EMPLOYER OF MY AUNT IS YELLOW.

though alternative explanations are possible (Yngve 1961/1972; Miller and Chomsky 1963; Frazier and Rayner 1988).

Another partly linguistic, partly psychological factor which increases comprehension difficulty is the omission of surface 'markers'. These are items which help to identify the various constructions. The fewer clues available for recognizing a structure, the more difficult it will be to identify. This is true whether we are dealing with a sentence in a language, or a partly hidden object in front of our eyes. Just as a picture of a face which lacks a nose may take longer to recognize than one with eyes, nose and mouth all complete, so a sentence with a word seemingly missing will take longer to comprehend (Fodor *et al.* 1968; Hakes 1971; Fodor *et al.* 1974). For example:

THE CROW THE FOX FLATTERED LOST ITS CHEESE.

is more difficult than:

THE CROW WHICH THE FOX FLATTERED LOST ITS CHEESE.

210 THE ARTICULATE MAMMAL

In the second sentence WHICH is retained, enabling speakers to note more quickly that they are dealing with a relative clause. Similarly:

SEBASTIAN NOTICED THE BURGLAR HAD LEFT FOOTPRINTS.

takes longer to comprehend than:

SEBASTIAN NOTICED THAT THE BURGLAR HAD LEFT FOOTPRINTS.

Here, the word THAT gives an immediate indication to the hearer that he is dealing with a so-called 'complement structure'.

Yet another factor which straddles the gap between psychological and linguistic difficulties is the presence of a negative. In general, negative sentences take longer to comprehend than affirmative ones. However, within negative sentences there are some strange discrepancies which relate to the hearer's expectations about his world. For example, it is easier and quicker to negate an expected fact than an unexpected one: it takes less time to comprehend the sentence:

THE TRAIN WAS NOT LATE THIS MORNING

if you had *expected* the train to be late. If the train was normally on time, the same sentence would take longer to process. Similarly:

A WHALE IS NOT A FISH and A SPIDER IS NOT AN INSECT.

are simpler, and take less time to understand, than:

A WHALE IS NOT A BIRD and A SPIDER IS NOT A MAMMAL.

because hearers had *expected* the whale to be a fish and the spider an insect (Wason 1965).

Let us now summarize this section. We have listed a number of general factors which can make a sentence more difficult to understand. We noted that short-term memory space is limited, that there seems to be a constraint on the number of sentoids that can be processed simultaneously, that unmarked interruptions are difficult to deal with, and so is a sentence which contains too much compressed information. We saw that repetition of items and structures causes problems, and so does backward processing. The deletion of surface clues slows down syntax recognition, and negatives delay sentence processing.

THE STORY SO FAR

A great deal of work still needs to be done before we fully understand what is happening when we comprehend speech. But, as we have seen, there are a number of ways in which we can usefully approach the problem. First, we can explore the lexicon, looking in particular at how words are identified, at the treatment of ambiguous words, and at the role of verbs. Second, we can build up a list of basic assumptions that hearers make about their language, and note the strategies which they utilize when they understand sentences. Third, we can explore both the step-by-step stages and the multiple actions which are taking place as a human tries to interpret what they hear. Fourth, we can assess the general psychological difficulties which affect speech processing. A final step, still in the future, is to integrate all these various strands into a coherent model of speech comprehension.

A further issue is how general background information is combined with the linguistic facets of a sentence. The tricky and voluminous question of how humans represent the world they live in has not been examined in this book.

Resolving these problems might seem impossible, considering the conflicting views of psycholinguists. But certain facts are becoming clear. Above all, the human mind is an amazingly powerful machine, capable of multiple parallel processing. The major question for the future is how it manages to amalgamate everything together into a manageable whole, instead of getting lost in the umpteen possibilities which are inherent in the data.

Let us now turn to the topic of speech production. As we shall see, this presents us with even more problems than comprehension.

11

THE CHESHIRE CAT'S GRIN
How do we plan and produce speech?

'I wish you wouldn't keep appearing and vanishing so suddenly,' said Alice. 'You make one quite giddy.'

'All right,' said the Cat; and this time it vanished quite slowly, beginning with the end of the tail, and ending with the grin, which remained some time after the rest of it had gone.

'Well! I've often seen a cat without a grin,' thought Alice; 'but a grin without a cat! It's the most curious thing I ever saw in all my life!'

Lewis Carroll, *Alice in Wonderland*

It is tantalizingly difficult to observe how anyone actually plans and produces speech. When somebody utters a sentence, we have very little idea how long it actually took to plan it, and what processes were involved. It is equally hard to devise experiments to test what is going on. There are relatively few reported in psycholinguistic journals, compared with the thousands available on speech comprehension. Consequently, we shall be very tentative over any conclusions we draw. As Fodor *et al.* commented over a quarter-century ago: 'Practically anything that one can say about speech production must be considered speculative, even by the standards current in psycholinguistics' (1974: 434). Almost the same is true in the twenty-first century: 'There has been less research on language production than on language comprehension ... The investigation of production is perceived to be more difficult than the investigation of comprehension' (Harley 2001: 349).

Clues to what is happening are infuriatingly elusive. In fact, there seems to be only one situation in which we can actually catch a speaker as he mentally prepares an utterance, and that is when someone is trying to recall a forgotten name. The name is often on 'the tip of their tongue', but they cannot quite remember it. Their mind is not completely blank as far as the word is concerned. A teasing and seemingly uncatchable wraith of it remains. He is left with a 'kind of disembodied presence, a grin without the Cheshire Cat' (Brown 1970: 234). This 'tip of the tongue' phenomenon will be discussed on pp. 225–6.

'Repairs' – situations when speakers correct themselves – are sometimes proposed as an extra source of information, as in:

FERDINAND CRASHED THE CAR ON MONDAY, SORRY, ON TUESDAY.

But in repairs there is a relatively long time-lag between making a mistake and correcting it (Blackmer and Mitton 1991). Mostly, speakers behave as if they are listening to another speaker: 'Controlling one's own speech is like attending to somebody else's talk' (Levelt 1983: 96–7). So repairs do not shed as much light as we might hope on the original planning process.

We therefore have to rely on indirect evidence. This is of two main types. First of all, we can look at the pauses in spontaneous speech. The object of this is to try to detect pause patterns – gaps in utterances – which may give clues about when speech is planned. Second, we can examine speech errors, both the slips of the tongue found in the conversation of normal people (e.g. HAP-SLAPPY for 'slap-happy', CANTANKEROUS for 'contentious'), as well as the more severe disturbances of aphasics – people whose speech is impaired due to some type of brain damage (e.g. TARIB for 'rabbit', RABBIT for 'apple'). Breakdown of the normal patterns may give us vital information about the way we plan and produce what we say, especially as: 'Natural speech is full of mismatches between intention and output.' (Harley 2006).

PAUSES

It may seem rather paradoxical to investigate speech by studying non-speech. But the idea is not as irrelevant as it appears at first sight. Around 40 to 50 per cent of an average spontaneous utterance consists of silence, although to hearers the proportion does not seem as high because they are too busy listening to what is being said.

The pauses in speech are of two main types: *breathing* pauses and *hesitation* pauses, sometimes with *er* ... *um* vocalizations, known as *filled pauses*. The first type are relatively easy to cope with. There are relatively few of them, partly because we slow down our rate of breathing when we speak, and they account for only about 5 per cent of the gaps in speech. They tend to come at grammatical boundaries, although they do not necessarily do so (Henderson *et al.* 1965).

Hesitation pauses are more promising. There are more of them and they do not have any obvious physical purpose comparable to that of filling one's lungs with air. Normally they account for one-third to one-half of the time taken up in talking. Speech in which such pausing does not occur is some-times referred to as 'inferior' speech (Jackson 1932). Either it has been rehearsed beforehand, or the speaker is merely stringing together a number of standard phrases she habitually repeats, as when the mother of the 7-year-old who threw a stone through my window rattled off at top speed, 'I do apologize, he's never done anything like that before, I can't think what came over him, he's such a good quiet little boy usually, I'm quite flabbergasted.' Unfortunately, we tend to over-value fluent, glib speakers who may not be thinking what they are saying, and often condemn a hesitant or stammering speaker who may be thinking very hard.

Hesitation pauses are rather difficult to measure, because a long-drawn-out word such as WE . . . ELL, IN FA . . . ACT may be substituted for a pause. This type of measurement problem may account for the huge differences of view found among psycholinguists who have done research on this topic. The basic argument is about *where* exactly the pauses occur. One researcher claims that hesitations occur mainly after the first word in the clause or sentoid (Boomer 1965). But other psycholinguists, whose experiments seem equally convincing, have found pauses mainly before important lexical items (Goldman-Eisler 1964; Butterworth 1980). It seems impossible, from just reading about their experiments, to judge who is right.

But in spite of this seemingly radical disagreement we can glean one important piece of information. *All* researchers agree that speakers do not normally pause between clauses, they pause *inside* them. This means that there is overlapping in the planning and production of clauses. That is, instead of a simple sequence:

Plan clause A	*Utter* clause A	*Plan* clause B	*Utter* clause B

we must set up a more complicated model:

Plan clause A	*Plan* clause B	
	Utter clause A	*Utter* clause B

In other words, it is quite clear that we do not cope with speech one clause at a time. We begin to plan the next clause while still uttering the present one.

Armed with this vital piece of information, we can now attempt to elaborate the picture by looking at the evidence from speech errors.

SPEECH ERRORS: THE NATURE OF THE EVIDENCE

Linguists are interested in speech errors because they hope that language in a broken-down state may be more revealing than language which is working perfectly. It is possible that speech is like an ordinary household electrical system, which is composed of several relatively independent circuits. We cannot discover very much about these circuits when all the lamps and sockets are working perfectly. But if a mouse gnaws through a cable in the kitchen and fuses one circuit, then we can immediately discover which lamps and sockets are linked together under normal working conditions. In the same way, it might be possible to find selective impairment of different aspects of speech.

The errors we shall be dealing with are, first, slips of the tongue and, second, the speech of aphasics – people with some more serious type of speech disturbance. Let us consider the nature of this evidence.

Everybody's tongue slips now and again, most often when the tongue's owner is tired, a bit drunk or rather nervous. So errors of this type are common enough to be called normal. However, if you mention the topic of slips of the tongue to a group of people at least one of them is likely to smirk knowingly and say 'Ah yes, tongue slips are sexual in origin, aren't they?' This fairly popular misconception has arisen because Sigmund Freud, the great Viennese psychologist, wrote a paper suggesting that words sometimes slipped out from a person's subconscious thoughts, which in his view were often concerned with sex. For example, he quotes the case of a woman who said her cottage was situated ON THE HILL-THIGH (BERGLENDE) instead of 'on the hillside' (Berglehne), after she had been trying to recall a childhood incident in which 'part of her body had been grasped by a prying and lascivious hand' (Freud 1901). In fact, this type of example occurs only in a relatively small number of tongue slips (Ellis 1980). It is true, possibly, that a percentage of girls have the embarrassing experience of sinking rapturously into, say, Archibald's arms while inadvertently murmuring 'Darling Algernon'. It is also perhaps true that anyone talking about a sex-linked subject may get embarrassed and stumble over his words, like the anthropology professor, who, red to the ears with confusion, talked about a PLENIS-BEEDING CEREMONY (penis-bleeding ceremony) in Papua New Guinea. But otherwise there seems little to support the sexual origin myth. Perhaps one might add that people tend to notice and remember sexual slips more than any other type. During the anthropology lecture mentioned above, almost everybody heard and memorized the PLENIS-BEEDING example. But few people afterwards, when questioned, had heard the lecturer say, YAM'S BOOK ON YOUNG-GROWING (Young's book on yam-growing). So laying aside the sex myth, we may say that slips of the tongue tell us more about the way a person plans and produces speech than about his or her sexual fantasies.

Aphasia is rather different from slips of the tongue, in that it is far from 'normal'. The name *aphasia* comes from a Greek word which means literally 'without speech', though is widely used in both the UK and USA to mean 'impaired speech' (the more accurate term *dysphasia* is now rarely found).

Aphasia covers an enormous range of speech problems. At one end of the range we find people who can only say a single word such as O DEAR, O DEAR, O DEAR, or more usually, a swear word such as DAMN, DAMN, DAMN. One unproved theory is that people who have had a severe stroke sometimes find their speech 'petrified' into the word they were uttering as the stroke occurred. At the other end of the scale are people with only occasional word-finding difficulties – it is not always clear where true aphasia ends and normal slips of the tongue begin. The fact that one merges into the other means that we can examine both types of error together in our search for clues about the planning and production of speech.

The typology of aphasia (attempts to classify aphasia into different kinds of disturbance) is a confused and controversial topic, and is beyond the scope of this book. Here we shall look at examples of name-finding difficulties, which is perhaps the most widespread of all aphasic symptoms. It affects some patients more than others, but it is usually present to some degree in most types of speech disturbance. A vivid description of this problem occurs in Kingsley Amis's novel *Ending Up* (1974). The fictional aphasic is a retired university teacher, Professor George Zeyer, who had a stroke 5 months previously:

> 'Well, anyway, to start with he must have a, a, thing, you know, you go about in it, it's got, er, they turn round. A very expensive one, you can be sure. You drive it, or someone else does in his case. Probably gold, gold on the outside. Like that other chap. A bar – no. And probably a gold, er, going to sleep on it. And the same in his . . . When he washes himself. If he ever does, of course. And eating off a gold – eating off it, you know. Not to speak of a private, um, uses it whenever he wants to go anywhere special, to one of those other places down there to see his pals. Engine. No. With a fellow to fly it for him. A plate. No, but you know what I mean. And the point is it's all because of us. Without us he'd be nothing, would he? But for us he'd still be living in his, ooh, made out of . . . with a black woman bringing him, off the – growing there, you know. And the swine's supposed to be some sort of hero. Father of his people and all that. A plane, a private plane, that's it.'
>
> It was not that George was out of his mind, merely that his stroke had afflicted him, not only with hemiplegia, but also with that condition in which the sufferer finds it difficult to remember nouns, common terms, the names

of familiar objects. George was otherwise fluent and accurate and responded normally to other's speech. His fluency was especially notable; he was very good at not pausing at moments when a sympathetic hearer could have supplied the elusive word. Doctors, including Dr Mainwaring, had stated that the defect might clear up altogether in time, or might stay as it was, and that there was nothing to be done about it.

Of course, not every aphasic is as fluent as George. And sometimes a patient is in the disquieting situation of thinking she has found the right word – only to discover to her dismay, when she utters it, that it is the wrong one. A description of this unnerving experience occurs in Nabokov's *Pale Fire*:

> She still could speak. She paused and groped and found
> What seemed at first a serviceable sound,
> But from adjacent cells imposters took
> The place of words she needed, and her look
> Spelt imploration as she sought in vain
> To reason with the monsters in her brain.

Perhaps the following two extracts will give a clearer picture of the problem. They are taken from tape-recordings of a severely aphasic patient in her seventies who had had a stroke 2 months earlier.

The patient (P) has been uttering the word RHUBARB, apparently because she is worried about her garden which is going to rack and ruin while she is in hospital. The therapist (T) tries to comfort her then says:

T: NOW THEN, WHAT'S THIS A PICTURE OF? (showing a picture of an apple)
P: RA-RA-RABBIT.
T: NO, NOT A RABBIT. IT'S A KIND OF FRUIT.
P: FRUIT.
T: WHAT KIND OF FRUIT IS IT?
P: O THIS IS A LOVELY RABBIT.
T: NOT A RABBIT, NO. IT'S AN APPLE.
P: APPLE, YES.
T: CAN YOU NAME ANY OTHER PIECES OF FRUIT? WHAT OTHER KINDS OF FRUIT WOULD YOU HAVE IN A DISH WITH AN APPLE?
P: BEGINNING WITH AN A?
T: NO, NOT NECESSARILY.
P: O WELL, RHUBARB.
T: PERHAPS, YES.
P: OR RHUBARB.

In the second extract, the same type of phenomenon occurs, but in a different context.

> *T:* WHAT'S THIS BOY DOING? (showing a picture of a boy swimming)
> *P:* O HE'S IN THE SEA.
> *T:* YES.
> *P:* DRIVING . . . DRIVING. IT'S NOT VERY DEEP. HE'S DRIVING WITH HIS FEET, HIS LEGS. DRIVING. WELL DRIVING, ER DIVING.
> *T:* IN FACT HE'S . . .
> *P:* SWIMMING.
> *T:* GOOD, WHAT ABOUT THIS ONE? (showing a picture of a boy climbing over a wall)
> *P:* DRIVING, ON A . . . ON A WALL.
> *T:* HE'S WHAT?
> *P:* DR . . . DRIVING, HE'S CLIMBING ON A WALL.

Some of the mistakes in these passages represent an extension of the selection problems seen in ordinary slips of the tongue. That is, some of the same kinds of mistakes occur as in normal speech, but they occur more often. But there is often one major difference: aphasics tend to *perseverate*, they perpetually repeat the same words, again and again, as in the first dialogue above where the patient kept repeating the word RHUBARB. Or, to take another example from the same patient, she was shown a picture of an apple. After some prompting, she said the word APPLE. She was then shown a picture of a blue ball. When asked what it was, she replied without hesitation APPLE. The therapist pointed out that she was confusing the new object with the previous one. 'Of course, how stupid of me', replied the patient. 'This one's an APPLE. No, no, I didn't mean that, I mean APPLE!'

Meanwhile, repetitions are relatively unusual among normal people, because they mostly have a very effective 'wipe the slate clean' mechanism. As soon as they have uttered a word, the phonetic form no longer remains to clutter up the mind. But aphasics, often to their frustration and despair, keep repeating sounds and words from the sentence before.

TYPES OF TONGUE SLIP

Broadly speaking, we may categorize the speech errors of normal speakers into two basic types. First, we have those in which a wrong item is chosen, where something has gone wrong with the *selection* process. For example:

> DID YOU REMEMBER TO BUY SOME TOOTHACHE? (Did you remember to buy some toothpaste?)

Such errors are perhaps more accurately labelled 'slips of the brain'.

Second, we find errors in which the correct choice of word has been made, but the utterance has been faultily assembled as in:

SOMEONE'S BEEN WRITENING THREAT LETTERS (Someone's been writing threatening letters).

Let us look at these two categories, *selection errors* and *assemblage errors* more carefully, and attempt to subdivide them.

Errors in which wrong items have been chosen are most commonly whole word errors. There are three main types: *semantic errors* (or similar meaning errors), *malapropisms* (or similar sound errors) and *blends*.

So-called *semantic* or *similar meaning* errors are fairly common. In fact, they are so usual that they often pass unnoticed. We are talking about naming errors in which the speaker gets the general 'semantic field' right, but uses the wrong word, as in:

DO YOU HAVE ANY ARTICHOKES? I'M SORRY, I MEAN AUBERGINES.

This kind of mistake often affects pairs of words. People say LEFT when they mean 'right', UP when they mean 'down', and EARLY instead of 'late', as in:

IT'S SIX O'CLOCK. WON'T THAT BE TOO EARLY TO BUY BREAD?

Mistakes like this occur repeatedly in the speech of some aphasics, and in its extreme form the general condition is sometimes rather pompously labelled 'conceptual agrammatism' (Goodglass 1968). Such patients confuse words like YESTERDAY, TODAY and TOMORROW. They seem able to find names connected with the general area they are talking about, but unable to pinpoint particular words within it, so that a 'garden roller' could be called a LAWN MOWER, a 'spade' may be called a FORK, and a 'rake' may be called a HOE. A mistake like this occurred in one of the aphasic passages quoted above, when the patient said DIVING instead of 'swimming'.

The second type of word selection error, so-called *malapropisms* occur when a person confuses a word with another, similar sounding one. The name comes from Mrs Malaprop, a character in Richard Sheridan's play *The Rivals*, who continually confused words which sounded alike, as in:

SHE'S AS HEADSTRONG AS AN ALLEGORY ON THE BANKS OF THE NILE (She's as headstrong as an alligator on the banks of the Nile).
A NICE DERANGEMENT OF EPITAPHS (A nice arrangement of epithets).

Not only in Sheridan's play, but in real life also, the results are sometimes hilarious, as when an angry woman demanded:

WHAT ARE YOU INCINERATING? (insinuating)

Equally funny was a man's statement that he had NUBILE TOES meaning 'mobile' ones – though it is of course impossible to tell sometimes, as in this case, whether he was genuinely confused about the meaning of NUBILE.

So far, we have mentioned selection errors connected with meaning, and selection errors connected with the sound of the word. But it would be a mistake to assume that we can easily place mistakes into one or the other category. Often the two overlap. Although children's mistakes are usually purely phonetic ones, as in:

MUSSOLINI PUDDING (semolina pudding)
NAUGHTY STORY CAR PARK (multi-storey car park),

the majority of adult ones have some type of semantic as well as phonetic link as when a lady lecturer claimed that:

YOU KEEP NEWBORN CHICKS WARM IN AN INCINERATOR (You keep newborn chicks warm in an incubator).

In addition to the phonetic similarity, both words are connected with the idea of heat. Another example is the statement:

YOU GO UNDER A RUNWAY BRIDGE (You go under a railway bridge).

Here, in addition to the similar sounds, both words describe a track for a means of transport. Yet another example is the error:

COMPENSATION PRIZE (consolation prize).

However, the semantic connection does not always have to be between the two words that are being confused. Sometimes the intruding idea comes in from the surrounding context, as in the statement:

LEARNING TO SPEAK IS NOT THE SAME THING AS LEARNING TO TALK (Learning to speak is not the same thing as learning to walk).

Another example of this type of confusion was uttered by a nervous male involved in a discussion on BBC's *Woman's Hour* about a cat who never seemed to sleep, because it was perpetually chasing mice. He said:

HOW MANY SHEEP DOES THE CAT HAVE IN ITS HOUSE THEN? I'M
SORRY, I MEAN MICE, NOT SHEEP.

The speaker correctly remembered that he was talking about an animal of
some kind, but the animal had somehow become contaminated by the sound
of the word SLEEP, resulting in SHEEP! He may also have been influenced by
the fact that humans reputedly count sheep jumping over fences in order to
get to sleep.

The third type of selection error, so-called *blends*, are an extension and variation of semantic errors. They are fairly rare, and occur when two words are
'blended' together to form one new one. For example:

NOT IN THE SLEAST

is a mixture of 'slightest and least'. And:

PLEASE EXPLAND THAT

is a mixture of 'explain and expand'. A rather more bizarre example of a blend
occurs in the first passage of aphasic speech quoted on p. 217. The patient had
been talking about RHUBARB, and was trying to think of the word APPLE.
What came out was a mixture of the two, RABBIT! Such mixes are also known
as *contaminations* since the two words involved 'contaminate' one another. Often,
if the speaker is quite well, both the items chosen are equally appropriate. The
speaker seems to have accidentally picked two together – or rather failed to
choose between two equally appropriate words in time. She has not so much
picked the wrong word, as not decided which of the right ones she needed.

Sometimes two items are intentionally blended together in order to create
a new word. Lewis Carroll makes Humpty Dumpty explain in *Alice Through the
Looking Glass* that SLITHY means 'lithe and slimy', commenting, 'You see, it's
like a portmanteau – there are two meanings packed up into one word' –
though Lewis Carroll's made-up words may not be as intentional as they
appear. Apparently, he suffered from severe migraine attacks, and many of his
strange neologisms are uncannily like the kind of temporary aphasia produced
by some migraine sufferers (Livesley 1972). Perhaps better examples of
intentional blends are SMOG from 'smoke and fog', and BRUNCH from
'breakfast and lunch'. Occasional parallels of this type can be spotted between
slips of the tongue and language change (Aitchison 2001).

Let us now turn to *assemblage errors* – errors in which the correct word choice
has been made, but the items chosen have been faultily assembled. There are
three main types: transpositions, anticipations and repetitions, which may
affect words, syllables or sounds.

Transpositions are not, on the whole, very common (Cohen 1966; Nooteboom 1969). Whole words can switch places, as in:

> DON'T BUY A CAR WITH ITS TAIL IN THE ENGINE (Don't buy a car with its engine in the tail).
>
> I CAN'T HELP THE CAT IF IT'S DELUDED (I can't help it if the cat's deluded).

and so can syllables:

> I'D LIKE A VIENEL SCHNITZER (I'd like a Viener schnitzel).

But perhaps the best known are the sound transpositions known as spoonerisms. These are named after a real-life person, the Reverend William A. Spooner, who was Dean and Warden of New College, Oxford, around the turn of the century. Reputedly, he often transposed the initial sounds of words, resulting in preposterous sentences, such as:

> THE CAT POPPED ON ITS DRAWERS (The cat dropped on its paws).
>
> YOU HAVE HISSED ALL MY MYSTERY LECTURES (You have missed all my history lectures).
>
> YOU HAVE TASTED THE WHOLE WORM (You have wasted the whole term).

However, there is something distinctly odd about these old spoonerisms. One suspects that the utterances of the Reverend Spooner were carefully prepared for posterity, probably by his students. The odd features are that they always make sense, they affect only initial sounds, and there is no discernible phonetic reason for the transposed sounds. In real life, spoonerisms do not usually make sense, as in:

> TILVER SILLER (silver tiller).

They can affect non-initial sounds, as in:

> A COP OF CUFFEE (a cup of coffee).

And they frequently occur between phonetically similar sounds, as

> LEAK WINK (weak link).

Anticipations, particularly sound anticipations, are the most widespread type of assemblage error. Here, a speaker anticipates what he is going to say by bringing in an item too early. It is not always possible to distinguish between anticipations and potential transpositions if the speaker stops himself half-way through, after realizing his error. This may partially account for the high recorded proportion of anticipations compared with transpositions. For example, the following could be a prematurely cut off transposition:

I WANT YOU TO TELL MILLICENT . . . I MEAN, I WANT YOU TO TELL MARY WHAT MILLICENT SAID.

But the following sound anticipations are clearly just simple anticipations. A participant in a television discussion referred, much to his embarrassment, to:

THE WORST GERMAN CHANCELLOR (The West German Chancellor).

Here he had anticipated the vowel in GERMAN. The same thing happened to the man who, interrupting over-eagerly, begged to make:

AN IMPOITANT POINT (an important point).

Repetitions (or *perseverations*) are rather rarer than anticipations, though commoner than transpositions. We find repeated words, as in:

A: ISN'T IT COLD? MORE LIKE A SUNDAY IN FEBRUARY.
B: IT'S NOT TOO BAD – MORE LIKE A FEBRUARY IN MARCH I'D SAY (It's not too bad – more like a Sunday in March).

An example of a repeated sound occurred when someone referred to:

THE BOOK BY CHOMSKY AND CHALLE (Chomsky and Halle).

perhaps an indication of the mesmerizing effect of Chomsky on a number of linguists!

We have now outlined the main types of selection and assemblage errors:

Selection Errors	Assemblage Errors
Semantic errors	Transpositions
Malapropisms	Anticipations
Blends	Repetitions

The most slippable units, incidentally, are words and phonemes (significant sounds), after these come morphemes (meaningful chunks of word) (Bock 1991).

What (if anything) can we learn from this seemingly strange array of errors? In fact, quite a lot. First, we can suggest what the units of planning are – in other words, the size of chunk we prepare in advance ready for utterance. Second, we can look at the process of word selection. Third, we can make hypotheses as to how words and syntax are planned and assembled.

THE UNIT OF PLANNING

The unit of planning appears to be what is sometimes called a tone group, or phonemic clause – a short stretch of speech spoken with a single intonation contour. For example:

WHAT TIME IS IT?

DEBORAH BOUGHT SOME SNAILS.

MAX TOOK A BATH.

Note, by the way, that a so-called phonemic clause (or tone group) must not be confused with a syntactic clause (or sentoid). The two quite often coincide, but do not necessarily do so. For example:

I WANT TO BUY SOME BUNS.

is a single phonemic clause, though is usually regarded as containing two underlying syntactic clauses. In this chapter the word clause refers to a phonemic clause, unless otherwise stated.

The main reason for confidently asserting that the tone group is the unit of planning is that slips of the tongue usually occur within a single tone group. For example:

WE'LL GO TO TAXI IN A CHOMSKY (We'll go to Chomsky in a taxi).

WE FORGED THIS CONGRESS . . . CONTRACT IN OUR OWN CONGRESSES (We forged this contract in our own congresses).

This strongly suggests that each tone group is planned and executed as a whole. If larger units were prepared, we would expect to find frequent contamination between clauses. As it is, such interference is rare, so much so that Boomer and Laver (1968) regard it as a tongue slip 'law' that 'The target and the origin of a tongue-slip are both located in the same tone-group' (with 'law' to be understood in a statistical rather than in an absolute sense).

On the rare occasions when this 'law' is broken, whole words can slip into the preceding clause. That is, words can cross clause boundaries, whereas sounds generally do not. For example:

WHEN YOU BUY THE LAUNDRY . . . (When you take the laundry, please buy me some cigarettes).

WHEN YOU TAKE THE ROSES OUT, ADMIRE . . . (When you take the garbage out, admire the roses).

EXTINGUISH YOUR SEATBELTS . . . (Extinguish your cigarettes and fasten your seatbelts).

Compare these with the following sound transpositions and anticipations, which all occur within the same clause:

SHE WROTE ME A YETTER . . . (letter yesterday).

TWAPTER CHELVE (chapter twelve).

A COP OF CUFFEE (a cup of coffee).

DOG WAS . . . (Doug was a doctor).

This phenomenon indicates that key words are thought out while the preceding clause is being uttered – whereas the detailed organization of a tone group is probably left till later.

WORD SELECTION

Moving on therefore to word selection, our most direct information comes from a famous 'tip of the tongue' (TOT) experiment (Brown and McNeill 1966). Less direct evidence comes from selection errors.

The TOT experiment was a simple one. The researchers assembled a group of students, and read them out definitions of relatively uncommon words. For example, when the 'target' word was SEXTANT, the students heard the definition: 'A navigational instrument used in measuring angular distances, especially the altitude of sun, moon and stars at sea.' Some of the students recognized the right word immediately. But others went into a TOT ('tip of the tongue') state. They felt they were on the verge of getting the word, but not quite there. In this state the researchers asked them to fill in a question-naire about their mental search. To their surprise, they found that the students could provide quite a lot of information about the elusive missing name. Sometimes the information was semantic, and sometimes it was phonetic. For example, in response to the definition of SEXTANT, several students provided the similar meaning words ASTROLABE, COMPASS and PROTRACTOR. Others remembered that it had two syllables and began with an S, and made guesses such as SECANT, SEXTON or SEXTET.

Semantically, this suggests that similar meaning words are linked together in the mind. We probably activate a number of them, before pinpointing one in particular. When errors occur, we have been insufficiently precise in locating the exact one needed – as with YESTERDAY instead of 'tomorrow,' SHIRT instead of 'blouse,' and (another example from the TOT experiment) BARGE, HOUSE-BOAT, JUNK instead of 'sampan'.

Phonetically, we find a similar picture. People seem to activate several similar-sounding words, before narrowing down the field to one. Malapropisms such as COMPETENCE for 'confidence' and NATIVE APE for 'naked ape' suggest that people look for words with certain outline characteristics, such as similar initial consonant and number of syllables before they finally select one. Adults give higher priority to the initial consonant than to the number of syllables, so that they often produce malapropisms such as CONDESCENDING for 'condensing', and SEGREGATED for 'serrated'. Children, on the other hand, seem to pay extra attention to the number of syllables, and produce comparatively more malapropisms with a wrong initial consonant, as in ICE CREAM TOILET for 'ice cream cornet' (cornet = cone), MISTAKE CAR for 'estate car', LEPRECHAUN for 'unicorn' (Aitchison and Straf 1981). The situation is not quite as straightforward as suggested above, because a number of other factors play a role in memory, such as the presence of a rhyming suffix, as in PERISCOPE for 'stethoscope', PORCUPINE for 'concubine'. And sometimes a word can get 'blocked' by a similar-sounding one: 'His name begins with an R. I know it's not Rupert, but that's the name I keep thinking of.' The target was Robert. As with all psycholinguistic phenomena, a large number of intertwined variables need to be considered (Aitchison 2003a).

The mechanism involved when words are selected is becoming clearer. We probably start with the 'idea of a word', then only later fit it to a phonetic form. This is shown by cases when we cannot remember a key word, even though it is clearly 'there' in some sense:

HE TOOK A LOT OF . . . WHAT'S THE WORD I WANT? ER . . . PERSUASION.

But in fluent speech, selecting the meaning and fitting on the sounds are processes which overlap. People probably begin to find possible phonetic forms while they are still finalizing their choice of word. This is shown by slips in which the word uttered has some meaning and some sound similarity to the target, as in HE WAS IN THE NEXT TRAIN COMPONENT (compartment).

A 'spreading activation' or 'interactive activation' model is a plausible explanation (Roelofs 1992; Aitchison 2003a). In this model, activation of similar words spreads out and diffuses in a chain reaction. If someone was trying to say MONDAY, all the days of the week would be strongly activated, which would in turn activate the months of the year, though less strongly. Each meaning would stimulate a sound pattern which in turn would rouse further sound patterns. So the 'idea' of MONDAY might trigger MONDAY, MAYDAY or MIDDAY, SATURDAY and SUNDAY would trigger each other, and so on. The task of the speaker is not only to select the word she wants, but to suppress the ones she does not require, though sometimes this process goes wrong:

IT'S AN EXOTIC PLANT, AN ASPIDISTRA NO, AN AMARYLLIS, ER, GLADIOLI, AH – CHAMELEON (CAMELLIA).

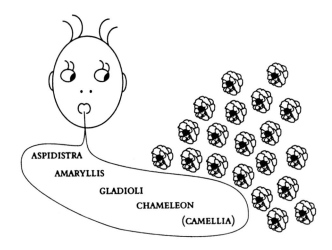

Such word-searches are normal. They usually take place fast and privately, but occasionally slowly and openly, as here. The speaker has activated various polysyllabic plant names, homed in on those with a stressed syllable before L, then at the last moment substituted an animal, CHAMELEON, for the shrub 'camellia'.

Aphasics in particular have problems over suppression. They let through a far wider range of inappropriate words than normal speakers, though there is usually some link with the target, as in DRIVING for 'swimming', caused by DRIVING for 'diving' and DIVING for 'swimming'. Sufferers from Alzheimer's disease have even greater problems (Astell and Harley 1996; Blanken 1998).

The general picture is clear. Words which are relevant both in sound and meaning get more and more excited. Finally, one wins out over the others – though a TOT state may occur if the word has been only partially activated (Harley and Bown 1998).

PLANNING AND ASSEMBLAGE

Let us now consider how the words and syntax are planned and assembled. We can divide this into two main stages: first, *outline planning*, which begins while the previous clause is being uttered. Second, *detailed planning*, which takes place while the clause is actually in progress. Outline planning means the choice of key words, syntax and intonation pattern, whereas detailed planning involves the fitting together of previously chosen words and syntax.

We know that outline planning includes the choice of intonation pattern, because errors which occur within the tone group (the unit of planning) do not normally disrupt the intonation pattern, as in:

TAKE THE FREEZES OUT OF THE STEAKER.

We are now faced with a tricky and once much disputed question: which comes first, the words or the syntactic pattern? Those who argued that the words come first pointed out quite simply that 'key' words determine the choice of syntax, and by 'key' words they mean above all nouns, verbs and sometimes adjectives. Clearly, verbs influence the choice of syntax more than the nouns – but the noun may, in some cases, influence the choice of verb.

Those who suggest that the syntax comes first note that when a speaker makes a word selection error, she almost always picks a wrong word belonging to the same word class as the target word. That is, nouns are confused with other nouns, verbs with other verbs, and adjectives with other adjectives. Even aphasic speech, which is often quite garbled, tends to follow this pattern (though exceptions do occur). People say UP instead of 'down', JELLY instead of 'blancmange', TRANSLATION instead of 'transformation'. But there is no reason for parts of speech to cling together like this. Why shouldn't verbs and nouns get confused? The fictional Mrs Malaprop gets her word classes confused much of the time, which is why many of her malapropisms are implausible. She says things such as:

YOU WILL PROMISE TO FORGET THIS FELLOW – TO ILLITERATE HIM, I SAY, QUITE FROM YOUR MEMORY (You will promise . . . to obliterate him . . . from your memory).

But in real life, it is extremely unusual to find adjective–verb confusions of the ILLITERATE for 'obliterate' type uttered by Mrs Malaprop. Even malapropisms uttered by children generally follow this similar word-class pattern:

YOU TAKE AN ANTELOPE IF YOU SWALLOW POISON (You take an antidote if you swallow poison).
I'M LEARNING TO PLAY THE ELBOW (I'm learning to play the oboe).

According to the 'syntax first' supporters, the most likely explanation for this phenomenon is that the syntax has already been chosen, and the words are then slotted in: 'Unless the syntactic structure is already constructed, word selection would not be constrained to proper word classes' (Fromkin 1973: 30).

How are we to solve this controversy between the 'words first' and 'syntax first' supporters? Who is right? Possibly both sides, to some extent, and the controversy seems fairly old-fashioned. We now know that the human brain is capable of complex parallel processing, so possibly, the speaker is thinking up both at the same time. On the one hand, it is unlikely that the key-word advocates are entirely correct. There is no evidence that we assemble *all* the key words, and then bind them together with joining words. On the other hand, it is quite impossible to plan the syntax with no idea of the lexical items which are going to be used. For example, the syntax of:

JOHN CLAIMED TO BE ABLE TO EAT A LIVE FROG.

must depend to some extent on the word CLAIM since other words with a similar meaning take a different construction. We cannot say:

*JOHN ASSERTED TO BE ABLE TO EAT A LIVE FROG.

or

*JOHN DECLARED TO BE ABLE TO EAT A LIVE FROG.

We possibly start by picking *one* key verb or noun, and then build the syntax around it. Later we slot other words into the remaining gaps.

If one key word triggers off the syntax, then we must assume that words in storage are clearly marked with their word class or part of speech (e.g. noun, verb) as well as with information about the constructions they can enter into. For example:

EAT	VERB
	NP–EAT–NP

We are, therefore, hypothesizing that when people plan utterances they mentally set up syntactic trees which are built around selected key words:

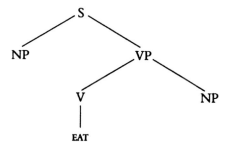

A key word can be used in planning before it has acquired its phonetic form. This is indicated by slips of the tongue such as:

WHEN IS IT GOING TO BE RECOVERED BY?

In this sentence the syntax was picked for 'mend', but the phonetic form activated was RECOVERED. The 'word idea' or *lemma* here is not just an intangible 'concept', but a definite and firmly packaged lexical item. The useful, and now widely used term *lemma* has been borrowed from lexicographers (dictionary writers) who have for a long time used it for a 'dictionary entry'. It includes both an understanding of what is being referred to and a firm word class label (verb), as well as (perhaps) information about the syntactic configurations it can enter into. Throughout this outline stage, sentence plans are flexible and can be altered (Ferreira 1996). Outline and detailed planning partly overlap.

By the detailed planning stage, at least some major lexical and syntactic choices have been firmly made. The items already chosen now have to be correctly assembled. Lexical items have to be put into their correct slots in the sentence. This has been wrongly carried out in:

IT'S BAD TO HAVE TOO MUCH BLOOD IN THE ALCOHOL STREAM (It's bad to have too much alcohol in the blood stream).

A FIFTY-POUND DOG OF BAG FOOD (A fifty-pound bag of dog food).

The slotting in of lexical items must also include fitting in negatives, since these can get disturbed, as in:

IT'S THE KIND OF FURNITURE I NEVER SAID I'D HAVE (It's the kind of furniture I said I'd never have).

I DISREGARD THIS AS PRECISE (I regard this as imprecise).

Another type of detailed planning involves adding on word endings in the appropriate place (Garrett 1988). This has been done incorrectly in:

SHE WASH UPPED THE DISHES (She washed up the dishes).

SHE COME BACKS TOMORROW (She comes back tomorrow).

HE BECAME MENTALIER UNHEALTHY (He became mentally unhealthier).

However, we can say rather more about the assemblage of words and endings than the vague comment that they are 'slotted together'. We noted in Chapter 3 that speakers seem to have an internal neural 'pacemaker' – a biological 'beat' which helps them to integrate and organize their utterances, and that this pacemaker may utilize the syllable as a basic unit. If we look more carefully, we find that syllables are organized into *feet* — a foot being a unit which includes a 'strong' or stressed syllable. And feet are organized into tone groups. In other words, we have a hierarchy of rhythmic units: tone groups made up of feet, and feet made up of syllables:

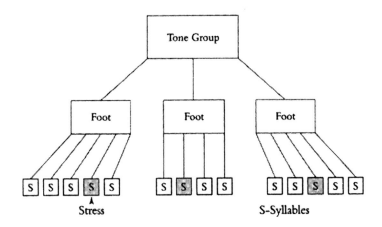

So within each tone group an utterance is planned foot by foot. This is indicated by the fact that transposed words are normally similarly stressed, and occupy similar places in their respective feet. For example:

HE FOUND A WÍFE FOR HIS JÓB (He found a job for his wife).

THE QUÁKE CAUSED EXTENSIVE VÁLLEY IN THE DÁMAGE (The quake caused extensive damage in the valley).

Within each foot, the stressed or 'tonic' word may be activated first, since tonic words are statistically more likely to be involved in tongue slips than unstressed ones (Boomer and Laver 1968). Moreover, the importance of the syllable as a 'psychologically real' unit is shown by the fact that tongue slips 'obey a structural law with regard to syllable place'. That is, the initial sound of a syllable will affect another initial sound, a final sound will affect another final, and vowels affect vowels, as in:

JAWFULLY LOINED (lawfully joined).

HASS OR GRASH (hash or grass).

BUD BEGS (bed bugs).

According to one theory, sound misplacements like those above occur because a 'scan-copying' mechanism has gone wrong (Shattuck-Hufnagel 1979). Supposedly, words already selected for utterance are kept chalked up on a mental blackboard, waiting to be used. A scanning device copies each word segment across into its correct place, then wipes it off the blackboard. In an error such as LOWING THE MORN (mowing the lawn) the L in LAWN was mistakenly copied across to the beginning of the wrong word, and wiped away. The remaining M was then copied on to the only available word-beginning. In a repetition error, such as CHEW CHEW (two) TABLETS, the speaker forgot to wipe CH off the board after copying it.

As in CHEW CHEW, misplaced segments end up forming real though inappropriate words more often than one would expect from chance (Motley 1985). HOLED AND SEALED (soled and heeled), BEEF NEEDLE (noodle) SOUP, MORE THAN YOUR WIFE'S (life's) WORTH are further examples of this tendency. This is possible evidence of the existence of a monitoring device which double-checks the final result to see if it is plausible. An over-hasty check has perhaps allowed these real words through.

The general picture of speech production is of practised behaviour performed in a great hurry, such a hurry that the speaker does not have time to check the details in full. Just as in the comprehension of speech, listeners employ perceptual strategies (short cuts which enable them to jump to conclusions about what they are hearing), so in the production of speech, production strategies are possibly utilized. A speaker does not have time to check each segment of the word in detail, but may make use of a monitoring device to stop the utterance of too many inappropriate words. If, however, a word happens to be superficially plausible, it is likely to pass the monitoring device and be uttered.

Let us recapitulate: at the outline planning stage, the key words, syntax, and intonation of the tone group as a whole are set up. At the detailed planning stage, words and endings are slotted in foot by foot, with the stressed word in each foot possibly activated first. Finally, the remaining unstressed syllables are assembled – though all these stages overlap partially. The next stage starts before the previous one is finished.

Where does all this leave us? We are gradually assembling information, and testing hypotheses. More importantly, psycholinguists have realized the need for a model which ties everything together. Such models are under continuous development, and these days computers are an essential tool. They allow one to specify components precisely, and to test their interactions. A promising model is one known as WEAVER, which is an acronym (word formed from initial letters) of 'Word-form Encoding by Activation and VERification' (Roelofs 1997, 2005). There are still gaps in our knowledge, and much of what we have said is hypothetical. We have realized that, for every clause uttered, a human speaker must be carrying out a number of complex overlapping tasks. The question of how all this is fitted together still needs further clarification. Perhaps, as an epilogue to the problems of speech planning and production, we can quote the words of a character in Oscar Wilde's play *The Importance of Being Earnest*, who commented that 'Truth is never pure, and rarely simple.'

12

BANKER'S CLERK OR HIPPOPOTAMUS?
The future

He thought he saw a Banker's Clerk
Descending from a bus:
He looked again, and found it was
A Hippopotamus.
Lewis Carroll, *Sylvie and Bruno*

Psycholinguistics is, as this book has shown, a field of study riddled with controversies. Frequently, apparently simple data can be interpreted in totally different ways. Psycholinguists often find themselves in the same situation as the Lewis Carroll character who is not sure whether he is looking at a banker's clerk or a hippopotamus.

In this general situation, it would be over-optimistic to predict the future with any confidence. However, certain lines of inquiry have emerged as important. Perhaps a useful way to summarize them is to outline briefly the conclusions we have reached so far, and show the issues which arise from them.

GENERAL CONCLUSIONS

Three psycholinguistic topics were singled out in the Introduction as particularly important: the acquisition question, the relationship of linguistic knowledge to language usage, and the comprehension and production of speech – and these areas were the principal concerns of this book.

In Chapter 1, the age-old nurture versus nature controversy was outlined. Is language a skill which humans learn, such as knitting? Or is it natural phenomenon, such as walking or sexual activity? Skinner's (1957) attempt to explain language as similar to the bar-pressing antics of rats was a dismal failure, as Chomsky showed. Chomsky proposed instead that the human species is pre-programmed for language. This claim was examined in the next few chapters.

In Chapter 2, human language and animal communication were compared. Some features of human language were found to be shared with some animal communication systems, but no animal system possessed them all. Attempts to teach sign and symbol systems to non-human apes were described: after a lot of effort, these apes could cope with some of the rudimentary character-istics of human language, but their achievements were far inferior to those of human children. Above all, intention reading and pattern finding seemed to be beyond the ability range of non-humans.

In Chapter 3, the hard biological evidence was discussed: the human brain, teeth, tongue and vocal cords have been adapted to the needs of speech. In addition, talking requires the synchronization of so many different opera-tions, humans seem to be 'set' to cope with this task.

In Chapter 4, Lenneberg's claim (1967) that language is biologically controlled behaviour was examined. Language fits into this category of behaviour: it emerges when the individual reaches a certain level of matura-tion, then develops at its own natural pace, following a predictable sequence of milestones. In modern terminology, the behaviour is innately guided. This makes the nature versus nurture debate unnecessary: nature triggers the behaviour, and lays down the framework, but careful nurturing is required for it to reach its full potential.

In Chapter 5, Chomsky's changing views on innateness were outlined. His ideas became increasingly abstract, and difficult to test. Consequently, some younger scholars have proposed that careful attention now needs to be paid to the actual step-by-step stages by which children acquire language.

Chapter 6 looked at children's early speech. Their output is not just a random amalgam of badly copied adult utterances. Instead, they are instinc-tively aware that language is 'rule-governed', in that it follows consistent patterns. However, in the early stages, the rules are not necessarily linguistic ones: children might just be applying their general intelligence.

In Chapter 7, three different views on child language were considered. First, Chomsky's proposal that children contain specific linguistic informa-tion which requires minimal exposure to activate was not borne out by the evidence. Second, the claim that children solve the puzzle of language by using their general intelligence, aided by helpful parents and a desire to satisfy their everyday needs, was not supported either: several individuals had been found who displayed a huge discrepancy between their linguistic and general cognitive abilities. Third, the suggestion that children make use of an inbuilt linguistic puzzle-solving device seemed nearest the truth, though the interaction between inherited principles, caretaker input, and changing mental organization is still unclear.

In Chapter 8, the reasons behind Chomsky's changing ideas about language were outlined: why he proposed a transformational grammar in his early work, and why he has now moved on to trying to specify deeper, more abstract linguistic knowledge.

In Chapter 9, we described attempts by psycholinguists in the 1960s and 1970s to test whether a transformational grammar was used in the comprehension and production of speech. We concluded that it represents a linguistic archive which is not directly used, but is available for consultation if necessary. This archive was of interest to anyone trying to understand language, but was not specifically linked to either comprehension or production.

Chapter 10 explored comprehension. The role of the lexicon, or mental dictionary, is crucial. Numerous possible candidate words are automatically activated as a sentence is heard, then unwanted ones are suppressed. Verbs, and the structure associated with them, are of particular importance. These linguistic factors interact with general psychological ones, such as memory limitations.

Chapter 11 looked at speech production. 'Slips of the tongue' provide useful clues. They indicate that each clause is partially planned while the previous one is being uttered. Some key words, outline syntax and the intonation pattern are possibly planned first, then the remaining words and endings are slotted into place.

FUTURE PROSPECTS

Let us now summarize our broad conclusions concerning the three topics we investigated, and look at future prospects.

The acquisition question

Language cannot be explained simply as an offshoot of general intelligence, even though humans obviously use general cognitive abilities when they speak. Equally, infants do not have fixed chunks of pre-information about language. Instead, they are naturally geared to processing linguistic data.

At each stage, children can handle only a certain amount: their mind is a natural filter, like a fishing net with a particular size mesh, which catches some fish, but lets others slip away. A child's mind therefore never gets overloaded. Once a certain amount of language is in place, this forms the basis for another trawl with another net, probably one with a slightly different-sized mesh. And so on and so on. Children move forward partly because each stage reached forms the basis for tackling the next. This general process is known as *epigenesis* (e.g. Carey and Gelman 1991). Psychologists and linguists need to combine in order to tease out the details of the epigenetic sequence associated with language.

But what about the perennial nature versus nurture problem with which this book started? Current research suggests that children classify the world in accordance with the categories within their own language to a far greater extent than had previously been realized. At one time, it was assumed that children had some basic inbuilt spatial concepts such as *up* versus *down*, *in* versus *out*, *front* versus *back*, and so on. But this is turning out to be unlikely. Instead, children quickly learn about the spatial categories adopted by their own language (e.g. Bowerman and Levinson 2001; Bowerman and Choi 2003; Gentner and Goldin-Meadow 2003). Research on languages such as Korean and Tzotzil (a Mayan language) has led to a renewed interest in language diversity, and is revealing the flexibility of young minds. Children's ability to cope with unpredictable variation is pre-ordained, but language-specific principles have to be learned from experience: 'One thing . . . is becoming clear: just as infants are geared from the beginning to discover umderlying phonological regularities in the speech stream, so too they are born to zero in on language-specific patterns in the organization of meaning' (Bowerman and Choi 2003: 418).

Renewed interest in acquisition has led to further exploration into the origin of language and general principles of linguistic evolution (e.g. Aitchison 1996/2000; Jackendoff 2002), as well as the similarities and differences between child language and language development in the species.

The relationship of language knowledge to language usage

Chomsky has always denied that his views have any direct connection to language usage, and as already pointed out, his latest work explores ever more abstract constraints on language, in the hope of enabling linguists to gain a better idea of the bounds within which language operates.

However, Chomsky is not the only linguist whose ideas are worth attention. Several more recent proposals about human grammars are currently being explored, and almost all of them propose a fairly close relationship between language knowledge and language usage. Michael Tomasello's usage-based theory was introduced in Chapter 5 (Tomasello 2003). Adele Goldberg (1995) was a major attempt to bridge the gap between verb structure and semantics. (Verb structures were discussed in Aitchison (2003a): this topic has therefore not been a major concern in the current book.) Culicover and Jackendoff have written a book titled *Simpler Syntax* (2005) which, they claim, 'leads to a vision of the language faculty that better facilitates the integration of linguistic theory with concerns of processing, acquisition and biological evolution' (2005: xiv).

Within psychology, connectionist approaches have revolutionized psycholinguistics, it is sometimes claimed (e.g. Harley 2001: 22). The physiological flavour of such models exerts a great appeal (Chapter 3), in that they use the brain as a metaphor for the mind: they manipulate units which are somewhat like neurons, and their interactions can be observed. Connectionist models do not 'wave their arms about'. Instead, they explicitly predict how humans are likely to behave, even though, so far, they have handled only small parts of language. How far they will succeed with bigger chunks and more complex constructions is of great interest.

However, the links between humans and machines is by no means straightforward (e.g. Zock 1997; Fitch 2005). Humans are not very logical, and have a limited working memory. They recognize complex patterns, and are good pattern matchers. But they are also intuitive and creative, and often jump to premature conclusions. They are good at solving some types of problems, and not others: if their self-interest is involved, their performance increases dramatically (Cosmides and Tooby 1995). The similarities and differences between humans and machines will undoubtedly continue to attract considerable attention.

Speech comprehension and production

Comprehending and producing speech are far more complex processes than was once assumed. Parallel processing is the norm, and the suppression of unwanted alternatives is as important as the selection of particular words and structures.

A major existing strand of research which will increasingly supplement experimental and naturalistic studies is brain monitoring as words are comprehended or uttered (Chapter 3).

An expanding body of work is exploring general cognitive development, looking at why and how humans have won out over other species. A paper, aptly called 'Why We're so Smart' (Gentner 2003) attempts to list the cognitive skills we possess, and the list is impressive. It includes an ability to reason analogically (Gentner *et al.* 2001), to think abstractly, to compare representations, to reason about different possible worlds, and so on, and so on. Current thinking suggests that language and thought interact productively: 'Language can act as a lens through which we see the world; it can provide us with tools through which we enlarge our capabilities; it can help us appreciate groupings in the world that we might not have otherwise grasped' (Gentner and Goldin-Meadow 2003: 12).

The growing interest in language and other aspects of cognition has led to a huge interest in the encoding of spatial information and how this interacts with language (e.g. Bloom *et al.* 1996; Levinson 2003).

However, psycholinguistics is like a railway, with numerous branching tracks. Many other topics have already attracted the attention of psycholinguists, and will in all likelihood continue to do so, as, for example, the origin of language (Aitchison 1996/2000), language change (Aitchison 2001) and the mental lexicon (Aitchison 2003a). A broad approach known as 'cognitive linguistics' is expanding (e.g. Ungerer and Schmid 1996; Taylor 2002;). Note also discourse analysis and language use (Chafe 1994; Brown 1995; Clark 1996) as well as capacities other than language, such as music (Jackendoff 1994.)

Half a century ago, psycholinguistics was a new, fringe discipline, like a small spring or a seedling compared to the more mature areas of linguistics and psychology. Now, it can be viewed as a wide river, which is gathering increasing momentum as other streams feed into it. Or we can perhaps envisage it as a flourishing tree, whose branches shoot out in all directions, and which is likely to get taller and stronger still. Exactly how the subject will develop is uncertain. Psycholinguistics is a field of study likely to spring surprises on researchers. A seemingly dead and forgotten area may suddenly spring into life. The words of the folklorist A.L. Lloyd are as applicable to psycholinguistics as they are to traditional music. Like the local song tradition, it has:

> proved robust enough to receive all kinds of new nourishment and to digest it satisfactorily. Only a moribund tradition is *dominated* by the past; a living tradition is constantly sprouting new leaves on old wood and sometimes quite suddenly the bush is ablaze with blossom of a novel shade.
>
> (Lloyd 1967: 71)

SUGGESTIONS FOR FURTHER READING

This section contains suggestions for further reading. I have kept these fairly sparse, since the books recommended all provide further references. Also, many other books and papers are mentioned in the text.

INTRODUCTION

This book does not require any background reading. Everything is (I hope) explained in the text. But for those who would like to acquaint themselves with linguistics, there are numerous elementary textbooks. The following are straightforward, fairly easy-to-read introductions: Akmajian *et al.* (2001); Aitchison (2003b); Fromkin *et al.* (2007).

Aitchison (1996/2000) explores the origin of language, but includes quite a lot of basic linguistic information; Aitchison (1997) deals with several key language topics; Clark *et al.* (1994) is a book of elementary readings, which cover a wide range.

Altmann (1997) is a shortish introduction written by a psychologist, and so is the more extensive introduction to psycholinguistics by Harley (2001). Jackendoff (2002) explores language within a broad cognitive and evolutionary framework.

Aitchison (2003c) provides a concise glossary of terms relating to language and the mind, and Field (2004) explores some of these terms in greater depth. Field (2005) is a workbook on topics relating to psycholinguistics.

CHAPTER 1

This chapter is based to a large extent on Chomsky's review of Skinner's book *Verbal Behavior* (Chomsky 1959). This article, now a linguistic 'classic', is still a useful starting point for understanding the direction taken by language acquisition studies in the 1960s and early 1970s. Note that Chomsky sometimes in his writings wrongly implied that Skinner typified the mainstream of psychological thought, a misleading fallacy (as Sampson 1975, explains).

The viewpoint that language is entirely dependent on general cognitive abilities gained popularity in the 1970s, when it was christened 'the cognitive revolution' by some of its supporters. This movement is well represented by Donaldson (1978), Sampson (1980), Bates *et al.* (1988) and MacWhinney and Bates (1989). More recently, the pendulum has swung back the other way, towards the viewpoint that humans are pre-wired for language, e.g. Pinker (1994), though mostly in an increasingly milder form, which accepts that language is a nature–nurture mix (e.g. Tomasello 2003).

CHAPTER 2

Animal and human communication is looked at in a wider, evolutionary perspective in Anderson (2004), Hauser (1996, 2000). In addition to the books referenced in the course of Chapter 2, the Web contains further information about several of the animals discussed, e.g. for Alex (grey parrot), see http://alexfoundation.org/alex.htm, for Washoe, Loulis, and other chimps, see www.friendsofwashoe.org/.

Wallman (1992) provides an overview of earlier ape-language projects, which includes other famous animals, such as Sarah (a chimp), Koko (a gorilla) and Chantek (an orang-utan) whose achievements have been omitted here due to lack of space.

The linguistic abilities of children and chimps are compared in Greenfield and Savage-Rumbaugh (1993) and Savage-Rumbaugh *et al.* (1993). For further discussion, see Rumbaugh and Washburn (2004), Savage-Rumbaugh *et al.* (1998) and Shanker *et al.* (1999).

CHAPTER 3

This chapter took its inspiration from Lenneberg's pioneering (1967) work, which is still worth reading, though certain sections are now out of date.

Springer and Deutsch (1998), Greenfield (1997) and Firlik (2006) are brief readable introductions to the brain as a whole. Cotterill (1998) ranges more widely.

Obler and Gjerlow (1999) is a user-friendly discussion of language in the brain, Hugdahl and Davidson (2003) and also Pulvermüller (2002) provide more detailed accounts. Deacon (1997) looks at brain evolution, and discusses differences between the brains of humans and other primates. Müller (1996) discusses linguistic specializations within the brain, and how they come about. Kempen (2000) discusses a recent controversy.

Techniques for studying the brain are outlined in Blumstein (1995), Posner and Raichle (1994) and Raichle (1994).

CHAPTER 4

The early part of this chapter is based on Lenneberg (1967), who is now regarded as an insightful pioneer.

The section on the stages of child language is based on Brown (1973) which contains a comprehensive summary of his own work with the 'Harvard children', Adam, Eve and Sarah, in the early stages of language acquisition. Lust and Foley (2004) also contains some key articles about these children. For further information on child language, see the reading suggestions for Chapter 6.

Scovel (1988) and Newport (1991) discuss the 'critical period' issue.

The Nicaraguan language project is reported in Kegl (1994), Senghas (1994) and Kegl et al. (1999).

CHAPTER 5

This chapter is based on Chomsky (1965) for his 'classical' transformational grammar, and Chomsky (1986) for his later views. His more recent ideas are taken from Chomsky (1995a, 1995b, 2000, 2002). McGilvray (2005) contains a variety of views in a book assessing Chomsky's legacy. Tomasello's views are from Tomasello (2003).

CHAPTER 6

Numerous books now exist on child language: O'Grady (2005) is a concise introduction, and Chiat (2000) outlines problems which may arise.

A number of useful books of readings are available. See Berko-Gleason (1993), Bloom (1994), Fletcher and MacWhinney (1995) and especially Lust and Foley (2004).

Boysson-Bardies (1999) explores the early stages of speech; Jusczyk (1997) looks at the capacity for speech perception; Vihman (1996) discusses the overlap of babbling with speech; Hirsch-Pasek and Golinkoff (1996) explore early language comprehension; Barrett (1985) analyses one-word utterances.

Brown (1973) and Braine (1976) are 'classics' on the beginnings of syntax; Bloom (1991) summarizes her earlier work with Kathryn, Eric and Gia.

O'Grady (1997) explores syntactic development in general.

Past tenses and learning network (connectionist) approaches to them are discussed in Pinker and Prince (1988), Marcus *et al.* (1992), Kim *et al.* (1994), Plunkett (1995) and Elman *et al.* (1996). Shirai and Andersen (1995) present an alternative account. Bybee (1995) compares various views.

Vocabulary learning is not dealt with in this book: Aitchison (2003a) outlines what is involved. More extensive coverage can be found in Anglin (1993), Clark (1993), Gleitman and Landau (1994) and Bloom (2000).

CHAPTER 7

The books of readings suggested for Chapter 6 also contain work relevant to this chapter.

Cognitive development in general and its relation to language is outlined in McShane (1991) and Gopnik *et al.* (1999).

Of the linguistic 'savants', Laura (Marta) is discussed in Yamada (1988, 1990), Christopher in Smith and Tsimpli (1995), and Kate in Dowker *et al.* (1996). Children with exceptional linguistic ability in general are dealt with in Boucher (1998) and Rondal (1994).

Child-directed speech is examined in Gallaway and Richards (1994), which views itself as a sequel to the widely read earlier work by Snow and Ferguson (1977). On language understanding, see Bishop (1997).

The 'bootstrapping' question is explored in Pinker (1989). Comments on his views and further work on the topic are found widely, e.g. Baker (1992), Braine (1992, 1994), Tomasello (1992) and Lieven and Pine (1995).

Slobin (1986a, 1986b, 1986c, 1992, 1997a, 1997b) documents the acquisition of a wide range of languages.

Methods of analysing children's language are discussed in Bennett-Kastor (1988) and McDaniel *et al.* (1996).

CHAPTER 8

This chapter is based on the same basic Chomsky writings as Chapter 5.

CHAPTER 9

Fodor, Bever and Garrett (1974) is now outdated, but provides a reliable account of much early work on the attempts by psycholinguists to test the plausibility of a transformational grammar. Watt (1970) was the first person to propose the archival nature of a classic transformational grammar.

CHAPTER 10

Altmann and Shillcock (1993) Berko-Gleason and Bernstein-Ratner (1998), McQueen (2004), and Miller and Eimas (1995) are books of readings which contain information on a range of comprehension issues. Altmann (1997), Harley (2001), Jackendoff (2002) and Pinker (1994) deal readably with some controversial topics.

Handel (1989) discusses how humans deal with sound in general. Nygaard and Pisoni (1995) give an outline of speech perception.

Tanenhaus and Trueswell (1995) provide a historical overview of the changing views on sentence comprehension over the last quarter century. Bever (1970) was the original 'classic' paper on perceptual strategies; Frazier and Clifton (1996) provide an updated view of syntactic strategies. Tanenhaus et al. (1993) discuss the integration of lexical and grammatical information.

Comprehending words is dealt with more fully in Aitchison (2003a). Further information on the lexicon is available in Bard and Shillcock (1993), Cutler (1995) and Marslen-Wilson (1989, 1993). Seidenberg (1995) examines visual word recognition.

The relationship between perception and production is explored in Cutler (2005).

CHAPTER 11

Levelt (1989) presents a wide-ranging overview of speech production. Bock (1995), Fowler (1995) and Harley (2001) also provide overviews.

Boomer and Laver (1968) was the 'classic' article that started serious work on 'slips of the tongue'. It is reprinted in Fromkin (1973) and Laver (1991). The slips of the tongue in this chapter are mainly from my own collection, supplemented by examples from Fromkin (1973, 1980) and Cutler (1982). Dell (1995) and Dell et al. (1993) discuss tongue slips and speech production within a connectionist framework.

On the lexicon, see Aitchison (2003a), Levelt (1993), Levelt et al. (1999), Marslen-Wilson (1989) and Miller (1991).

Gathercole and Baddeley (1993) explore the role of short term memory. Caplan (1987) looks at aphasia. Shenk (2001/2002) is a highly readable introduction to Alzheimer's disease.

CHAPTER 12

Altmann (1997) provides a non-technical introduction to connectionism. Rumelhart and McClelland (1986) and McClelland and Rumelhart (1986) are early 'classics' on the topic. See also McClelland (1988) for a brief overview of this approach.

References have been provided in the text for other future prospects in psycholinguistics.

References

Aitchison, J. (1996/2000) *The Seeds of Speech: Language Origin and Evolution*, Cambridge: Cambridge University Press. Canto edition with added Foreword, 2000.

Aitchison, J. (1997) *The Language Web: The Power and Problem of Words*, Cambridge: Cambridge University Press.

Aitchison, J. (2001) *Language Change: Progress or Decay?* 3rd edn, Cambridge: Cambridge University Press.

Aitchison, J. (2003a) *Words in the Mind: An Introduction to the Mental Lexicon*, 3rd edn, Oxford: Blackwell.

Aitchison, J. (2003b) *Linguistics*, 6th edn, London: Hodder & Stoughton (Teach Yourself).

Aitchison, J. (2003c) *A Glossary of Language and Mind*, Edinburgh: Edinburgh University Press.

Aitchison, J. (2007) *The Word Weavers: Newshounds and Wordsmiths*, Cambridge: Cambridge University Press.

Aitchison, J. and Straf, M. (1981) 'Lexical storage and retrieval: a developing skill?' *Linguistics* 19: 751–95. Also in Cutler (1982).

Akmajian, A., Demers, R.A., Farmer, A.K. and Harnish, R.M. (2001) *Linguistics: An Introduction to Language and Communication*, 5th edn, Cambridge, MA: MIT Press.

Altmann, G.T.M. (1997) *The Ascent of Babel: An Exploration of Language, Mind, and Understanding*, Oxford: Oxford University Press.

Altmann, G.T.M. and Shillcock, R. (eds) (1993) *Cognitive Models of Speech Processing*, Hove, Sussex: Lawrence Erlbaum.

Amis, Kingsley (1974) *Ending Up*, London: Jonathan Cape.

Anderson, S.R. (2004) *Doctor Dolittle's Delusion: Animals and the Uniqueness of Human Language*, New Haven, CT: Yale University Press.

Anglin, J.M. (1993) *Vocabulary Development: A Morphological Analysis*, Monographs of the Society for Research in Child Development 58.10, Chicago, IL: University of Chicago Press.

Astell, A.J. and Harley, T.A. (1996) 'Tip-of-the-tongue states and lexical access in dementia', *Brain and Language* 54: 196–215.

Au, W. (1993) *The Sonar of Dolphins*, Berlin: Springer Verlag.

Baker, C.L. (1992) 'Review of Pinker (1989)', *Language* 68: 402–13.

Bar-Adon, A. and Leopold, W.F. (eds) (1971) *Child Language: A Book of Readings*, Englewood Cliffs, NJ: Prentice-Hall.

Bard, E.G. and Shillcock, R.C. (1993) 'Competitor effects during lexical access: chasing Zipf's tail', in G.T.M. Altmann and R. Shillcock (eds) *Cognitive Models of Speech Processing*, Hove, Sussex: Lawrence Erlbaum.

Baron-Cohen, S. (1999) *Mindblindness: An Essay on Autism and Theory of Mind*, Cambridge, MA: MIT Press.

Barrett, M. (1985) *Children's Single-word Speech*, Chichester: Wiley.

Bates, E. (1993) 'Comprehension and production in early language development', in E.S. Savage-Rumbaugh *et al.* (eds) *Language Comprehension in Ape and Child*, Monographs of the Society for Research in Child Development 58.3–4, Chicago, IL: University of Chicago Press.

Bates, E. and MacWhinney, B. (1987) 'Competition, variation and language learning', in B. MacWhinney (ed.) *Mechanisms of Language Acquisition*, Hillsdale, NJ: Lawrence Erlbaum.

Bates, E., Bretherton, I. and Snyder, L. (1988) *From First Words to Grammar: Individual Differences and Dissociable Mechanisms*, Cambridge: Cambridge University Press.

Bellugi, U. (1971) 'Simplification in children's language', in R. Huxley and E. Ingram (eds) *Language Acquisition: Models and Methods*, New York: Academic Press.

Bellugi, U., Bihrle, A. and Corina, D. (1991) 'Linguistic and spatial development: dissociations between cognitive domains', in N.A. Krasnegor *et al. Biological and Behavioral Determinants of Language Development*, Hillsdale, NJ: Lawrence Erlbaum.

Bennett-Kastor, T. (1988) *Analyzing Children's Language: Methods and Theories*, Oxford: Blackwell.

Berko, J. (1958) 'The child's learning of English morphology', *Word* 14: 150–77. Also in Bar-Adon and Leopold (1971).

Berko-Gleason, J. (ed.) (1993) *The Development of Language*, 3rd edn, New York: Macmillan.

Berko-Gleason, J. and Bernstein-Ratner, N. (eds) (1998) *Psycholinguistics*, 2nd edn, Orlando, FL: Harcourt Brace.

Bernstein, B. (1972) 'Social class, language and socialisation', in P.P. Giglioli (ed.) *Language and Social Context*, Harmondsworth: Penguin.

Bever, T.G. (1970) 'The cognitive basis for linguistic structures', in J.R. Hayes (ed.) *Cognition and the Development of Language*, New York: Wiley.

Bever, T.G., Lackner, J.R. and Kirk, R. (1969) 'The underlying structure of sentences are the primary units of immediate speech processing', *Perception and Psychophysics* 5: 225–31.

Bishop, D.V.M. (1997) *Uncommon Understanding: Development and Disorders of Language Comprehension in Children*, Hove, Sussex: Psychology Press.

Blackmer, E.R. and Mitton, J.L. (1991) 'Theories of monitoring and the timing of repairs in spontaneous speech', *Cognition* 39: 173–94.

Blank, M., Gessner, M. and Esposito, A. (1979) 'Language without communication: a case study', *Journal of Child Language* 6: 329–52.

Blanken, G. (1998) 'Lexicalization in speech production: evidence from form-related word substitution errors in aphasia', *Cognitive Neuropsychology* 25: 321–60.

Bloch, B. and Trager, G. (1942) *Outline of Linguistic Analysis*, Baltimore, MD: Waverley Press.

Bloom, L. (1970) *Language Development: Form and Function in Emerging Grammars*, Cambridge, MA: MIT Press.

Bloom, L. (1973) *One Word at a Time*, The Hague: Mouton.

Bloom, L. (1991) *Language Development from Two to Three*, Cambridge: Cambridge University Press.

Bloom, L., Lightbown, P. and Hood, L. (1975) *Structure and Variation in Child Language*, Monographs of the Society for Research in Child Development 40.2, Chicago, IL: University of Chicago Press.

Bloom, L., Tackeff, J. and Lahey, M. (1984) 'Learning "to" in complement constructions', *Journal of Child Language* 11: 319–406.

Bloom, P. (ed.) (1994) *Language Acquisition: Core Readings*, Cambridge, MA: MIT Press.

Bloom, P. (2000) *How Children Learn the Meaning of Words*, Cambridge, MA: MIT Press.

Bloom, P., Peterson, M.A., Nadel, L. and Garrett, M.F. (eds) (1996) *Language and Space*, Cambridge, MA: MIT Press.

Blumenthal, A.L. (1966) 'Observations with self-embedded sentences', *Psychonomic Science* 6: 453–4.

Blumstein, S.E. (1995) 'The neurobiology of language', in J.L. Miller and P.D. Eimas (eds) *Speech, Language and Communication*, San Diego: Academic Press.

Bock, K. (1991) 'A sketchbook of production problems', *Journal of Psycholinguistic Research* 20: 141–60.

Bock, K. (1995) 'Sentence production: from mind to mouth', in J.L. Miller and P.D. Eimas (eds) *Speech, Language and Communication*, San Diego, CA: Academic Press.

Bond, Z.S. (1999) *Slips of the Ear: Errors in the Perception of Casual Conversation*, San Diego, CA: Academic Press

Boomer, D.S. (1965) 'Hesitation and grammatical encoding', *Language and Speech* 8: 148–58. Also in Oldfield and Marshall (1968).

Boomer, D.S. and Laver, J.D.M. (1968) 'Slips of the tongue', *British Journal of Disorders of Communication* 3: 1–12. Also in Fromkin (1973).

Boucher, J. (1998) 'The prerequisites for language acquisition: evidence from cases of anomalous language development', in P. Carruthers and J. Boucher (eds) *Language and Thought: Interdisciplinary Themes*, Cambridge: Cambridge University Press.

Bowerman, M. (1973) *Early Syntactic Development*, Cambridge: Cambridge University Press.

Bowerman, M. (1986) 'What shapes children's grammars?', in D.I. Slobin (ed.) *The Crosslinguistic Study of Language Acquisition*, vols 1–2, Hillsdale, NJ: Lawrence Erlbaum.

Bowerman, M. (1988) 'The "no negative evidence" problem: how do children avoid constructing an overly general grammar?', in J.A. Hawkins (ed.) *Explaining Language Universals*, Oxford: Blackwell.

Bowerman, M. and Levinson, S. (2001) *Language Acquisition and Conceptual Development*, Cambridge: Cambridge University Press.

Bowerman, M. and Choi, S. (2003) 'Space under construction: language-specific spatial categorization in first language acquisition', in D. Gentner and Goldin-Meadow (eds) *Language in Mind: Advances in the Study of Language and Thought*, Cambridge, MA: MIT Press.

Boysson-Bardies, B. de (1999) *How Language Comes to Children: From Birth to Two Years*, trans. by M. DeBevoise, Cambridge, MA: MIT Press.

Boysson-Bardies, B. de, Sagart, L. and Durand, C. (1984) 'Discernible differences in the babbling of infants according to target language', *Journal of Child Language* 11: 1–15.

Braine, M.D.S. (1963) 'The ontogeny of English phrase structure: the first phrase', *Language* 39: 1–14. Also in Bar-Adon and Leopold (1971); Ferguson and Slobin (1973).

Braine, M.D.S. (1971) 'The acquisition of language in infant and child', in C.E. Reed (ed.) *The Learning of Language*, New York: Appleton-Century-Crofts.

Braine, M.D.S. (1976) *Children's First Word Combinations*, Monographs of the Society for Research in Child Development 41.1, Chicago, IL: University of Chicago Press.

Braine, M.D.S. (1992) 'What kind of innate structure is needed to "boot-strap" into syntax?', *Cognition* 45: 77–100.

Braine, M.D.S. (1994) 'Is nativism sufficient?', *Journal of Child Language* 21: 9–31.

Browman, C.P. (1980) 'Perceptual processing: evidence from slips of the ear', in V. Fromkin (ed.) *Errors in Linguistic Performance: Slips of the Tongue, Ear, Pen and Hand*, New York: Academic Press.

Brown, G. (1995) *Speakers, Listeners and Communication: Explorations in Discourse Analysis*, Cambridge: Cambridge University Press.

Brown, R. (1958) *Words and Things*, New York: The Free Press.

Brown, R. (1970) *Psycholinguistics: Selected Papers*, New York: The Free Press.

Brown, R. (1973) *A First Language*, London: Allen & Unwin.

Brown, R. and Bellugi, U. (1964) 'Three processes in the child's acquisition of syntax', in E.H. Lenneberg (ed.) *New Directions in the Study of Language*, Cambridge, MA: MIT Press. Also in Brown (1970).

Brown, R. and Fraser, C. (1964) 'The acquisition of syntax', in U. Bellugi and R. Brown (eds) *The Acquisition of Language*, Monographs of the Society for Research in Child Development 29.1, Chicago, IL: University of Chicago Press.

Brown, R. and McNeill, D. (1966) 'The "Tip of the Tongue" phenomenon', *Journal of Verbal Learning and Verbal Behavior* 5: 325–37. Also in Brown (1970).

Brown, R., Cazden, C. and Bellugi, U. (1968) 'The child's grammar from I to III', in J.P. Hill (ed.) *Minnesota Symposium on Child Psychology*, vol. II, Minneapolis, MN: University of Minnesota Press. Shortened version in Brown (1970); Ferguson and Slobin (1973).

Buffery, A.W.H. (1978) 'Neuropsychological aspects of language development', in N. Waterson and C. Snow (eds) *The Development of Communication*, Chichester: John Wiley.

Butterworth, B. (1980) 'Evidence from pauses in speech', in B. Butterworth (ed.) *Language Production*, vol. 1, Speech and Talk, New York: Academic Press.

Bybee, J. (1995) 'Regular morphology and the lexicon', *Language and Cognitive Processes* 10: 425–55.

Byrne, R.H. and Whiten, A. (1992) 'Cognitive evolution in primates: evidence from tactical deception' *Man* 27: 609–27.

Caplan, D. (1987) *Neurolinguistics and Linguistic Aphasiology: An Introduction*, Cambridge: Cambridge University Press.

Caplan, D. (1988) 'The biological basis for language', in F.J. Newmeyer (ed.) *Linguistics: The Cambridge Survey*, vol. 3, Cambridge: Cambridge University Press.

Carey, S. and Gelman, R. (eds) (1991) *The Epigenesis of Mind: Essays on Biology and Cognition*, Hillsdale, NJ: Lawrence Erlbaum.

Cazden, C. (1972) *Child Language and Education*, New York: Holt, Rinehart & Winston.

Chafe, W. (1994) *Discourse, Consciousness and Time*, Chicago, IL: University of Chicago Press.

Chambers, J.K. (1995) *Sociolinguistic Theory*, Oxford: Blackwell.

Cheney, D.L. and Seyfarth, R.M. (1990) *How Monkeys See the World: Inside the Mind of another Species*. Chicago, IL: Chicago University Press.

Chiat, Shula (2000) *Understanding Children with Language Problems*, Cambridge: Cambridge University Press.

Chomsky, C. (1969) *The Acquisition of Syntax in Children from 5 to 10*, Cambridge, MA: MIT Press.

Chomsky, N. (1957) *Syntactic Structures*, The Hague: Mouton.

Chomsky, N. (1959) 'Review of Skinner (1957)', *Language* 35: 26–58.

Chomsky, N. (1963) 'Formal properties of grammars', in R.D. Luce, R.R. Bush and E. Galanter (eds) *Handbook of Mathematical Psychology*, vol. 2, New York: Wiley.

Chomsky, N. (1965) *Aspects of the Theory of Syntax*, Cambridge, MA: MIT Press.

Chomsky, N. (1967) 'The formal nature of language', in E.H. Lenneberg (ed.) *Biological Foundations of Language*, New York: Wiley.

Chomsky, N. (1972a) *Language and Mind*, enlarged edn, New York: Harcourt Brace Jovanovich.

Chomsky, N. (1972b) *Problems of Knowledge and Freedom*, London: Fontana.
Chomsky, N. (1978) 'On the biological basis of language capacities', in G.A. Miller and E. Lenneberg (eds) *Psychology and Biology of Language and Thought*, New York: Academic Press. Also in Chomsky (1980).
Chomsky, N. (1979) *Language and Responsibility*, Sussex: The Harvester Press.
Chomsky, N. (1980) *Rules and Representations*, Oxford: Blackwell.
Chomsky, N. (1981) *Lectures on Government and Binding*, Dordrecht: Foris.
Chomsky, N. (1982) *Some Concepts and Consequences of the Theory of Government and Binding*, Cambridge, MA: MIT Press.
Chomsky, N. (1986) *Knowledge of Language: Its Nature, Origin and Use*, New York: Praeger.
Chomsky, N. (1988) *Language and Problems of Knowledge*, Cambridge, MA: MIT Press.
Chomsky, N. (1995a) 'Bare phrase structure', in G. Webelhuth (ed.) *Government and Binding Theory and the Minimalist Program*, Oxford: Blackwell.
Chomsky, N. (1995b) *The Minimalist Program*, Cambridge, MA: MIT Press.
Chomsky, N. (2000) *New Horizons in the Study of Language and Mind*, Cambridge: Cambridge University Press.
Chomsky, N. (2002) *On Nature and Language*, eds A. Belletti and L. Rizzi, Cambridge: Cambridge University Press.
Clark, E.V. (1987) 'The principle of contrast: a constraint on language acquisition', in B. MacWhinney (ed.) *Mechanisms of Language Acquisition*, Hillsdale, NJ: Lawrence Erlbaum.
Clark, E.V. (1993) *The Lexicon in Acquisition*, Cambridge: Cambridge University Press.
Clark, H.H. (1996) *Using Language*, Cambridge: Cambridge University Press.
Clark, V.P., Eschholz, P.A. and Rosa, A.F. (eds) (1994) *Language: Introductory Readings*, 5th edn, New York: St Martin's Press.
Clifton, C., Frazier, L. and Connine, C. (1984) 'Lexical expectations in sentence comprehension', *Journal of Verbal Learning and Verbal Behavior* 23: 696–708.
Cohen, A. (1966) 'Errors of speech and their implications for understanding the strategy of language users', reprinted in Fromkin (1973).
Cosmides, L. and Tooby, J. (1995) 'Beyond intuition and instinct blindness: toward an evolutionarily rigorous cognitive science', in J. Mehler and S. Franck (eds) *Cognition on Cognition*, Cambridge, MA: MIT Press.
Cotterill, R. (1998) *Enchanted Looms: Conscious Networks in Brains and Computers*, Cambridge: Cambridge University Press.
Cromer, R.F. (1970) 'Children are nice to understand: surface structure clues for the recovery of a deep structure', *British Journal of Psychology* 61: 397–408.
Cromer, R.F. (1976) 'Developmental strategies for language', in V. Hamilton and M.D. Vernon (eds) *The Development of Cognitive Processes*, London and New York: Academic Press.
Cromer, R.F. (1981) 'Reconceptualizing language acquisition and cognitive development', in R.L. Schiefelbusch and D. Bricker (eds) *Early Language: Acquisition and Intervention*, Baltimore, MD: University Park Press.

Cross, T. (1977) 'Mothers' speech adjustments: the contribution of selected child listener variables', in C.E. Snow and C.A. Ferguson (eds) *Talking to Children: Language Input and Acquisition*, Cambridge: Cambridge University Press.

Cruttenden, A. (1970) 'A phonetic study of babbling', *British Journal of Disorders of Communication* 5: 110–17.

Culicover, P.W. and Jackendoff, R. (2005) *Simpler Syntax*, Oxford: Oxford University Press.

Curtiss, S.R. (1977) *Genie: A Psycholinguistic Study of a Modern-day "Wild Child"*, New York: Academic Press.

Curtiss, S.R. (1981) 'Dissociations between language and cognition: cases and implications', *Journal of Autism and Developmental Disorders* 11: 15–30.

Curtiss, S.R. (1988) 'Abnormal language acquisition and the modularity of language', in F.J. Newmeyer (ed.) *Linguistics: The Cambridge Survey*, vol. 2, Cambridge: Cambridge University Press.

Curtiss, S.R., Fromkin, V., Krashen, S., Rigler, D. and Rigler, M. (1974) 'The linguistic development of Genie', *Language* 50: 528–54.

Cutler, A. (1976) 'Beyond parsing and lexical look-up: an enriched description of auditory sentence comprehension', in R.J. Wales and E. Walker (eds) *New Approaches to Language Mechanisms*, Amsterdam: North Holland.

Cutler, A. (ed.) (1982) *Slips of the Tongue and Speech Production*, Berlin: Mouton.

Cutler, A. (1995) 'Spoken word recognition and production', in J.L. Miller and P.D. Eimas (eds) *Speech, Language and Communication*, San Diego, CA: Academic Press.

Cutler, A. (ed.) (2005) *Twenty-first Century Psycholinguistics: Four Cornerstones*, Mahwah, NJ: Lawrence Erlbaum.

Cutler, A., Klein, W. and Levinson, S. (2005) 'The cornerstones of twenty-first century psycholinguistics', in A. Cutler (ed.) *Twenty-first Century Psycholinguistics: Four Cornerstones*, Mahwah, NJ: Lawrence Erlbaum.

Deacon, T. (1997) *The Symbolic Species: The Co-evolution of Language and the Human Brain*, London: Allen Lane.

Dell, G.S. (1995) 'Speaking and misspeaking', in L.R. Gleitman and M. Liberman (eds) *Language: An Invitation to Cognitive Science*, 2nd edn, vol. 1, Cambridge MA: MIT Press.

Dell, G.S., Juliano, C. and Govindjee, A. (1993) 'Structure and content in language production: a theory of frame constraints in phonological speech errors', *Cognitive Science* 17: 149–95.

Dennis, M. (1983) 'Syntax in brain-injured children', in M. Studdert-Kennedy (ed.) *Psychobiology of Language*, Cambridge, MA: MIT Press.

De Villiers, J.G. and De Villiers, P.A. (1978) *Language Acquisition*, Cambridge, MA: Harvard University Press.

De Villiers, P.A. and De Villiers, J.G. (1979) 'Form and function in the development of sentence negation', *Stanford University Papers and Reports on Child Language Development* 17: 37–64.

de Waal, F.B.M. (1996) *Bonobo: The Forgotten Ape*, San Franciso, CA: University of California Press.

de Waal, F.B.M. (2006) 'Bonobo, sex and society', *Scientific American* 16.2: 14–21.

Donaldson, M. (1978) *Children's Minds*, London: Fontana/Collins.

Dowker, A., Hermelin, B. and Pring, L. (1996) 'A savant poet', *Psychological Medicine* 26: 913–24.

Eimas, P.D. (1985) 'The perception of speech in early infancy', *Scientific American* 252(1) (January): 34–40.

Eimas, P.D., Siqueland, E., Jusczyk, P. and Vigorito, J. (1971) 'Speech perception in infants', *Science* 171: 303–6.

Ellis, A.W. (1980) 'On the Freudian theory of speech errors', in V.A. Fromkin (ed.) *Errors in Linguistic Performance: Slips of the Tongue, Ear, Pen and Hand*, New York: Academic Press.

Ellis, N. and Humphreys, G. (1997) *Connectionist Models in Psychology*, Hove, Sussex: Lawrence Erlbaum.

Elman, J.L., Bates, E.A., Johnson, M.H., Karmiloff-Smith, A., Parisi, D. and Plunkett, K. (1996) *Rethinking Innateness: A Connectionist Perspective on Development*, Cambridge, MA: MIT Press.

Epstein, W. (1961) 'The influence of syntactical structure on learning', *American Journal of Psychology* 7: 80–5.

Ervin, S.M. (1964) 'Imitation and structural change in children's language', in E.H. Lenneberg (ed.) *New Directions in the Study of Language*, Cambridge, MA: MIT Press.

Ervin-Tripp, S. (1971) 'An overview of theories of grammatical development', in D.I. Slobin (ed.) *The Ontogenesis of Grammar*, New York: Academic Press.

Evans, W.E. and Bastian, J. (1969) 'Marine mammal communication: social and ecological factors', in H.T. Andersen (ed.) *The Biology of Marine Mammals*, New York: Academic Press.

Ferguson, C.A. (1978) 'Talking to children: a search for universals', in J.H. Greenberg, C.A. Ferguson and E. Moravcsik (eds) *Universals of Human Language*, vol. 1, Stanford, CA: Stanford University Press.

Ferguson, C.A. and Slobin, D.I. (1973) *Studies in Child Development*, New York: Holt, Rinehart, Winston.

Ferreira, V.S. (1996) 'Is it better to give than to donate? Syntactic flexibility in language production', *Journal of Memory and Language* 35: 724–55.

Field, J. (2004) *Psycholinguistics: The key concepts*, London: Routledge.

Field, J. (2005) *Language and the Mind*, London: Routledge.

Fiez, J.A., Petersen, S.E., Cheney, M.K. and Raichle, M.E. (1992) 'Impaired non-motor learning and error detection associated with cerebellar damage', *Brain* 115: 155–78.

Fillenbaum, S. (1971) 'Psycholinguistics', *Annual Review of Psychology* 22: 251–308.

Firlik, K.S. (2006) *Brain Matters: Adventures of a Brain Surgeon*, London: Weidenfeld & Nicolson.

Fisher, S.E. (2006) 'Tangled webs: tracing the connections between genes and cognition', *Cognition* 101: 270–97.

Fitch, T. (2005) 'Computation and cognition: four distinctions and their implications', in A. Cutler (ed.) *Twenty-first Century Psycholinguistics: Four Cornerstones*, Mahwah, NJ: Lawrence Erlbaum.

Fletcher, P. (1983) 'Verb-form development: lexis or grammar?', in C.I. Phew and C.E. Johnson (eds) *Proceedings of the Second International Congress for the Study of Child Language*, vol. 2, Lanham, MD: University Press of America.

Fletcher, P. (1985) *A Child's Learning of English*, Oxford: Blackwell.

Fletcher, P. and MacWhinney, B. (eds) (1995) *The Handbook of Child Language*, Oxford: Blackwell.

Flores d'Arcais, G.B. (1988) 'Language perception', in F.J. Newmeyer (ed.) *Linguistics: The Cambridge Survey*, vol. 3, Cambridge: Cambridge University Press.

Fodor, J.A. (1966) 'How to learn to talk: some simple ways', in F. Smith and G.A. Miller (eds) *The Genesis of Language*, Cambridge: Cambridge University Press.

Fodor, J.A. and Garrett, M.F. (1966) 'Some reflections on competence and performance', in J. Lyons and R.J. Wales (eds) *Psycholinguistic Papers*, Edinburgh: Edinburgh Univerity Press.

Fodor, J.A. and Garrett, M.F. (1967) 'Some syntactic determinants of sentential complexity', *Perception and Psychophysics* 2: 289–96.

Fodor, J.A., Garrett, M.F. and Bever, T.G. (1968) 'Some syntactic determinants of sentential complexity, II: verb structure', *Perception and Psychophysics* 3: 453–61.

Fodor, J.A., Bever, T.G. and Garrett, M.F. (1974) *The Psychology of Language*, New York: McGraw Hill.

Ford, M., Bresnan, J.W. and Kaplan, R. (1982) 'A competence-based theory of syntactic closure', in J.W. Bresnan (ed.) *The Mental Representation of Grammatical Relations*, Cambridge, MA: MIT Press.

Foss, D. (1970) 'Some effects of ambiguity upon sentence comprehension', *Journal of Verbal Learning and Verbal Behavior* 9: 699–706.

Fourcin, A.J. (1978) 'Acoustic patterns and speech acquisition', in N. Waterson and C. Snow (eds) *The Development of Communication*, Chichester: Wiley.

Fouts, R.S. (1983) 'Chimpanzee language and elephant tails: a theoretical synthesis', in J. de Luce and H. Wilder (eds) *Language in Primates*, New York: Springer-Verlag.

Fouts, R.S. (1997) *Next of Kin*, London: Michael Joseph.

Fouts, R.S., Hirsch, A. and Fouts, D. (1982) 'Cultural transmission of a human language in a chimpanzee mother/infant relationship', in H.E. Fitzgerald, J.A. Mullins and P. Page (eds) *Psychobiological Perspectives: Child Nurturance Series*, vol. 3. New York: Plenum Press.

Fowler, C.A. (1995) 'Speech production', in J.L. Miller and P.D. Eimas (eds) *Speech, Language and Comunication*, San Diego, CA: Academic Press.

Frazier, L. and Rayner, K. (1982) 'Making and correcting errors during sentence comprehension: eye movements in the analysis of structurally ambiguous sentences', *Cognitive Psychology* 14: 178–210.

Frazier, L. and Rayner, K. (1988) 'Parameterizing the language processing system: left- vs. right-branching within and across languages', in J.A. Hawkins (ed.) *Explaining Language Universals*, Oxford: Blackwell.

Frazier, L. and Clifton, C. (1996) *Construal*, Cambridge, MA: MIT Press.

Freud, S. (1901) 'Slips of the tongue', reprinted in V.A. Fromkin (ed.) *Speech Errors as Linguistic Evidence*, The Hague: Mouton.

Fromkin, V.A. (ed.) (1973) *Speech Errors as Linguistic Evidence*, The Hague: Mouton.

Fromkin, V.A. (ed.) (1980) *Errors in Linguistic Performance: Slips of the Tongue, Ear, Pen and Hand*, New York: Academic Press.

Fromkin, V., Rodman, R. and Hyams, N. (2007) *An Introduction to Language*, 8th edn, Boston, MA: Thomson, Wadsworth.

Fry, D.B. (1970) 'Speech reception and perception', in J. Lyons (ed.) *New Horizons in Linguistics*, Harmondsworth: Penguin.

Gallaway, C. and Richards, B.J. (1994) *Input and Interaction in Language Acquisition*, Cambridge: Cambridge University Press.

Gardner, B.T. and Gardner, R.A. (1980) 'Two comparative psychologists look at language acquisition', in K. Nelson (ed.) *Children's Language*, vol. 2, New York: Gardner Press.

Gardner, R.A. and Gardner, B.T. (1969) 'Teaching sign language to a chimpanzee', *Science* 165: 664–72.

Garrett, M.F. (1988) 'Processes in language production', in F.J. Newmeyer (ed.) *Linguistics: The Cambridge Survey*, vol. 3, Cambridge: Cambridge University Press.

Garrett, M.F., Bever, T. and Fodor, J.A. (1966) 'The active use of grammar in speech perception', *Perception and Psychophysics* 1: 30–2.

Gathercole, S.E. and Baddeley, A.D. (1993) *Working Memory and Language*, Hove, Sussex: Lawrence Erlbaum.

Gazzaniga, M.S. (1970) *The Bisected Brain*, New York: Appleton-Century-Crofts.

Gazzaniga, M.S. (1983) 'Right hemisphere language following brain bisection: a 20-year perspective', *American Psychologist* 38: 525–49.

Gentner, D. (2003) 'Why we're so smart', in D. Gentner and S. Goldin-Meadow (eds) *Language in Mind: Advances in the Study of Language and Thought*, Cambridge, MA: MIT Press.

Gentner, D. and Goldin-Meadow, S. (eds) (2003) *Language in Mind: Advances in the Study of Language and Thought*, Cambridge, MA: MIT Press.

Gentner, D., Holyoak, K.J. and Kokinov, B.N. (eds) (2001) *The Analogical Mind: Perspectives from Cognitive Science*, Cambridge, MA: MIT Press.

Gleitman, L.R. (1984) 'Biological predispositions to learn language', in P. Marler and H.S. Terrace (eds) *The Biology of Learning*, Berlin: Springer-Verlag.

Gleitman, L.R. and Wanner, E. (1982) 'Language acquisition: the state of the state of the art', in E. Wanner and L.R. Gleitman (eds) *Language Acquisition: The State of the Art*, Cambridge: Cambridge University Press.

Gleitman, L.R. and Landau, B. (1994) *The Acquisition of the Lexicon*, Cambridge, MA: MIT Press.

Gleitman, L.R. and Gillette, J. (1995) 'The role of syntax in verb learning', in P. Fletcher and B. MacWhinney (eds) *The Handbook of Child Language*, Oxford: Blackwell.

Gleitman, L.R., Gleitman, H. and Shipley, E.F. (1972) 'The emergence of the child as grammarian', *Cognition* 1: 137–64.

Gleitman, L.R., Newport, E.L. and Gleitman, H. (1984) 'The current status of the motherese hypothesis', *Journal of Child Language* 11: 43–79.

Goldberg, A.E. (1995) *Constructions: A Construction Grammar Approach to Argument Structure*, Chicago, IL: University of Chicago Press.

Goldman-Eisler, F. (1964) 'Hesitation, information and levels of speech production', in A.V.S. De Reuck and M.O. O'Connor (eds) *Disorders of Language*, London: Churchill Livingstone.

Goldman-Rakic, P.S. (1982) 'Organization of frontal association cortex in normal and experimentally brain-injured primates', in M.A. Arbib, D. Caplan and J.C. Marshall (eds) *Neural Models of Language Processes*, New York: Academic Press.

Goodglass, H. (1968) 'Studies on the grammar of aphasics', in S. Rosenberg and J.H. Kaplin (eds) *Developments in Applied Psycholinguistics Research*, New York: Macmillan.

Goodluck, H. (1986) 'Language acquisition and linguistic theory', in P. Fletcher and M. Garman (eds) *Language Acquisition: Studies in First Language Development*, 2nd edn, Cambridge: Cambridge University Press.

Gopnik, A., Meltzoff, A. and Kuhl, P. (1999) *How Babies Think*, London: Weidenfeld & Nicolson.

Gopnik, M. (1994) 'Impairments of tense in a familial language disorder', *Journal of Neurolinguistics* 8: 109–33.

Gopnik, M. (ed.) (1997) *The Inheritance and Innateness of Grammars*, Oxford: Oxford University Press.

Gopnik, M. and Crago, M.B. (1991) 'Familial aggregation of a developmental language disorder', *Cognition* 39: 1–50.

Gopnik, M., Dalalakis, J., Fukuda, S.E. and Fukuda, S. (1997) 'The biological basis of language: familial language impairment', in M. Gopnik (ed.) *The Inheritance and Innateness of Grammars*, Oxford: Oxford University Press.

Gough, P.B. (1971) 'Experimental psycholinguistics', in W.O. Dingwall (ed.) *A Survey of Linguistic Science*, Maryland, MD: University of Maryland.

Gould, J.L. and Marler, P. (1987) 'Learning by instinct', *Scientific American* 256(1) (Jan.): 62–73.

Greenfield, P.M. and Savage-Rumbaugh, E.S. (1993) 'Comparing communicative competence in child and chimp: the pragmatics of repetition', *Journal of Child Language* 20: 1–26.

Greenfield, S. (1997) *The Human Brain: A Guided Tour*, London: Weidenfeld.

Griffiths, P. (1986) 'Early vocabulary', in P. Fletcher and M. Garman (eds) *Language Acquisition: Studies in First Language Development*, 2nd edn, Cambridge: Cambridge University Press.

Grosu, A. (1974) 'On the complexity of center-embedding', mimeo.

Gruber, E.H., Beardsley, W. and Caramazza, A. (1978) 'Parallel function strategy in pronoun assignment', *Cognition* 6: 117–33.

Gruber, J.S. (1967) 'Topicalization in child language', *Foundations of Language* 3: 37–65.

Hakes, D.T. (1971) 'Does verb structure affect sentence comprehension?', *Perception and Psychophysics* 10: 229–32.

Halliday, M.A.K. (1975) *Learning How to Mean*, London: Arnold.

Hamburger, H. and Crain, S. (1984) 'Acquisition of cognitive compiling', *Cognition* 17: 85–136.

Handel, S. (1989) *Listening: An Introduction to the Perception of Auditory Events*, Cambridge, MA: MIT Press.

Harley, T.A. (2001) *The Psychology of Language: From Data to Theory*, 2nd edn, Hove, Sussex: Psychology Press.

Harley, T.A. (2006) 'Speech errors: a psycholinguistic approach', in K. Brown (ed.) *The Encyclopaedia of Language and Linguistics* 2nd edn, vol. 11, Oxford: Elsevier.

Harley, T.A. and Bown, H. (1998) 'What causes a tip-of-the-tongue state? Evidence for lexical neighbourhood effects in speech production', *British Journal of Psychology* 89: 151–74.

Harris, M., Barrett, M., Jones, D. and Brookes, S. (1988) 'Linguistic input and early word meaning', *Journal of Child Language* 15: 77–94.

Hauser, M.D. (1996) *The Evolution of Communication*, Cambridge, MA: MIT Press.

Hauser, M.D. (2000) *Wild Minds: What Animals Really Think*, New York: Holt.

Hayes, C. (1951) *The Ape in Our House*, New York: Harper.

Hayes, J.R. (ed.) (1970) *Cognition and the Development of Language*, New York: Wiley.

Heath, S.B. (1983) *Ways with Words*, Cambridge: Cambridge University Press.

Henderson, A., Goldman-Eisler, F. and Skarbek, A. (1965) 'The common value of pausing time in spontaneous speech', *Quarterly Journal of Experimental Psychology* 17: 343–5.

Hirsh-Pasek, K. and Golinkoff, R.M. (1996) *The Origins of Grammar: Evidence from Early Language Comprehension*, Cambridge, MA: MIT Press.

Hockett, C.F. (1963) 'The problem of universals in language', in J.H. Greenberg (ed.) *Universals of Language*, Cambridge, MA: MIT Press.

Hockett, C.F. and Altmann, S. (1968) 'A note on design features', in T. Sebeok (ed.) *Animal Communication: Techniques of Study and Results of Research*, Bloomington, IN: Indiana University Press.

Hugdahl, K. and Davidson, R. (eds) (2004) *The Asymmetrical Brain*, Cambridge, MA: MIT Press.

Jackendoff, R. (1994) *Patterns in the Mind: Language and Human Nature*, New York: Basic Books.

Jackendoff, R. (2002) *Foundations of Language: Brain, Meaning, Grammar, Evolution*, Oxford: Oxford University Press.

Jackson, H.J. (1932) *Selected Writings*, vol. II, London: Hodder & Stoughton.

Jaeger, J.J., Lockwood, A.H., Kemmerer, D.L., Van Valin Jr, R.D., Murphy, B.W. and Khalak, H.G. (1996) 'A positron emission tomographic study of regular and irregular verb morphology in English', *Language* 72: 451–97.

Jakobson, R. (1962) 'Why "mama" and "papa"?', in A. Bar-Adon and W.F. Leopold (eds) *Child Language: A Book of Readings*, Englewood Cliffs, NJ: Prentice Hall.

Johnson-Laird, P.N. (1974) 'Experimental psycholinguistics', *Annual Review of Psychology* 25: 135–60.

Johnston, J.R. and Slobin, D.I. (1979) 'The development of locative expressions in English, Italian, Serbo-Croatian and Turkish', *Journal of Child Language* 6: 529–45.

Jusczyk, P.W. (1997) *The Discovery of Spoken Language*, Cambridge, MA: MIT Press.

Karmiloff-Smith, A. (1979) *A Functional Approach to Child Language: A Study of Determiners and Reference*, Cambridge: Cambridge University Press.

Karmiloff-Smith, A. (1986) 'From meta-processes to conscious access: evidence from children's metalinguistic and repair data', *Cognition* 23: 95–147.

Keele, S.W. (1987) 'Sequencing and timing in skilled perception and action: an overview', in A. Allport *et al.* (eds) *Language Perception and Production*, New York: Academic Press.

Kegl, J. (1994) 'The Nicaraguan sign language project: an overview', *Signpost* 7: 1.

Kegl, J., Senghas, A. and Coppola, M. (1999) 'Creation through contact: sign language emergence and sign language change in Nicaragua', in M. DeGraff (ed.) *Language Creation and Language Change: Creolization, Diachrony and Development*, Cambridge, MA: MIT Press.

Kellogg, W.N. and Kellogg, L.A. (1933) *The Ape and the Child*, New York: McGraw Hill.

Kempen, G. (2000). 'Could grammatical encoding and grammatical decoding be subserved by the same processing module?' *Behavioral and Brain Sciences* 23, 38–9.

Kim, J.J., Marcus, G.F., Pinker, S., Hollander, M. and Coppola, M. (1994) 'Sensitivity of children's inflection to grammatical structure', *Journal of Child Language* 21: 173–209.

Kimball, J. (1973) 'Seven principles of surface structure parsing in natural language', *Cognition* 2: 15–47.

Kimura, D. (1967) 'Functional asymmetry of the brain in dichotic listening', *Cortex* 3: 163–78.

Kimura, D. (1992) 'Sex differences in the brain', *Scientific American* 267(3) (Sept.): 80–7.

Kinoshita, S. (1986) 'Sentence context effect on lexically ambiguous words: evidence for a postaccess inhibition process', *Memory and Cognition* 13: 579–95.

Kinsbourne, M. (1975) 'Minor hemisphere language and cerebral maturation', in E.H. Lenneberg and E. Lenneberg (eds) *Foundations of Language Development*, vols 1–2, New York: Academic Press.

Kinsbourne, M. and Hiscock, M. (1987) 'Language lateralization and disordered language development', in S. Rosenberg (ed.) *Advances in Applied Psycholinguistics*, vol. 1, Cambridge: Cambridge University Press.

Kirchner, W.H. and Towne, W.F. (1994) 'The sensory basis of the honeybee's dance language', *Scientific American* 270(6) (June): 52–9.

Klima, E. and Bellugi, U. (1966) 'Syntactic regularities in the speech of children', in J. Lyons and R.J. Wales (eds) *Psycholinguistics Papers*, Edinburgh: Edinburgh University Press. Revised version in Bar-Adon and Leopold (1971).

Kuczaj II, S.A. (1983) *Crib Speech and Language Play*, New York: Springer-Verlag.

Kuhl, P. and Miller, J.D. (1974) 'Discrimination of speech sounds by the chinchilla:/t/vs/d/in CV syllables', *Journal of the Acoustical Society of America* 56, series 42: abstract.

Kuhl, P. and Miller, J.D. (1975) 'Speech perception by the chinchilla: phonetic boundaries for synthetic VOT stimuli', *Journal of the Acoustical Society of America* 57, series 49: abstract.

Kutas, M. and Van Petten, C.K. (1994) 'Psycholinguistics electrified: event-related brain potential investigations', in M.A. Gernsbacher (ed.) *Handbook of Psycholinguistics*, San Diego, CA: Academic Press.

Lai, C.S.L., Fisher, S.E., Hurst, J.A., Vargha-Khadem, F. and Monaco, A.P. (2001) 'A forkhead-domain gene is mutated in a severe speech and language disorder', *Nature* 413, 519–23.

Landau, B. and Gleitman, L.R. (1985) *Language and Experience: Evidence from the Blind Child*, Cambridge, MA: Harvard University Press.

Lashley, K.S. (1951) 'The problem of serial order in behavior', in L.A. Jefress (ed.) *Cerebral Mechanisms in Behavior*, New York: Wiley. Also in S. Saporta (1961) *Psycholinguistics: A Book of Readings*, New York: Holt, Rinehart & Winston.

Laver, J. (1991) *The Gift of Speech: Papers in the Analysis of Speech and Voice*, Edinburgh: Edinburgh University Press.

Lenneberg, E.H. (1967) *Biological Foundations of Language*, New York: Wiley.

Lester, B.M. and Boukydis, C.F. (1991) 'No language but a cry', in H. Papousek, U. Jürgens and M. Papousek (eds) *Nonverbal Vocal Communication: Comparative and Developmental Approaches*, Cambridge: Cambridge University Press.

Levelt, W.J.M. (1983) 'Monitoring and self-repair in speech', *Cognition* 14: 41–104.

Levelt, W.J.M. (1989) *Speaking: From Intention to Articulation*, Cambridge, MA: MIT Press.

Levelt, W.J.M. (1993) *Lexical Access in Speech Production*, Oxford: Blackwell. Originally published in *Cognition* 42 (1992).

Levelt, W.J.M., Roelofs, A. and Meyer, A.S. (1999) 'A theory of lexical access in speech production', *Behavioral and Brain Sciences* 22: 1–38.

Levinson, S.C. (2003) *Space in Language and Cognition: Explorations in Cognitive Diversity*, Cambridge: Cambridge University Press.

Liberman, A.M., Cooper, F., Shankweiler, D.P. and Studdert-Kennedy, M. (1967) 'Perception of the speech code', *Psychological Review* 74: 431–61.

Lieven, E.V.M. and Pine, J.M. (1995) 'Comparing different views of early grammatical development', *Proceedings of the 27th Annual Child Language Research Forum, Stanford University*, edited by E.V. Clark, 207–16.

Livesley, B. (1972) 'The Alice in Wonderland syndrome', *Teach In* 1: 770–4.

Lloyd, A.L. (1967) *Folk Song in England*, London: Lawrence & Wishart.

Locke, J.L. (1997) 'A theory of neurolinguistic development', *Brain and Language* 58: 265–326.

Lust, B.C. and Foley, C. (eds) (2004) *Child Language: The Essential Readings*, Oxford: Blackwell.

McClelland, J.L. (1988) 'Connectionist models and psychological evidence', *Journal of Memory and Language* 27: 107–23.

McClelland, J.L. and Elman, J.E. (1986) 'The TRACE model of speech perception', *Cognitive Psychology* 18: 1–86.

McClelland, J.L. and Rumelhart, D.E. (eds) (1986) *Parallel Distributed Processing: Explorations in the Microstructure of Cognition*, vol. 2, *Psychological and Biological Models*, Cambridge, MA: MIT Press.

McDaniel, D., McKee, C. and Cairns, H.S. (1996) *Methods for Assessing Children's Syntax*, Cambridge, MA: MIT Press.

McGilvray, J. (ed.) (2005) *The Cambridge Companion to Chomsky*, Cambridge: Cambridge University Press.

MacKain, K., Studdert-Kennedy, M., Spieker, S. and Stern, D. (1983) 'Infant intermodal speech perception is a left-hemisphere function', *Science* 219: 1347–9.

Mackay, D.G. (1987) 'Constraints on theories of sequencing and timing in language perception and production', in A. Allport *et al.* (eds) *Language Perception and Production*, New York: Academic Press.

Mackay, D.G., Allport, A., Prinz, W. and Scherer, E. (1987) 'Relationship and modules within language perception and production: an introduction', in A. Allport *et al.* (eds) *Language Perception and Production*, New York: Academic Press.

Maclay, H. (1973) 'Linguistics and psycholinguistics', in B.J. Kachru, R.B. Lees, Y. Malkiel, A. Pietrangeli and S. Saporta (eds) *Issues in Linguistics*, Chicago, IL: Illinois University Press.

McNeill, D. (1966) 'Developmental psycholinguistics', in F. Smith and G.A. Miller (eds) *The Genesis of Language*, Cambridge, MA: MIT Press.

McNeill, D. (1970) *The Acquisition of Language*, New York: Harper and Row.

McQueen, J.M. (2004) 'Speech perception', in K. Lamberts and R. Goldstone (eds.) *The Handbook of Cognition*, London: Sage.

McQueen, J.M. (2005) 'Spoken-word recognition and production: regular but not inseparable bedfellows', in A. Cutler (ed.) *Twenty-first Century Psycholinguistics: Four Cornerstones*, Mahwah, NJ: Lawrence Erlbaum.

McShane, J. (1979) 'The development of naming', *Language* 17: 879–905.

McShane, J. (1980) *Learning to Talk*, Cambridge: Cambridge University Press.

McShane, J. (1991) *Cognitive Development: An Information Processing Approach*, Oxford: Blackwell.

MacWhinney, B. (1978) *The Acquisition of Morphophonology*, Monographs of the Society for Research in Child Development 43.1–2, Chicago, IL: University of Chicago Press.

MacWhinney, B. (1987) 'The competition model', in B. MacWhinney (ed.) *Mechanisms of Language Acquisition*, Hillsdale, NJ: Lawrence Erlbaum.

MacWhinney, B. and Bates, E. (eds) (1989) *The Cross-linguistic Study of Sentence Processing*, Cambridge: Cambridge University Press.

Maratsos, M. (1982) 'The child's construction of grammatical categories', in E. Wanner and L.R. Gleitman (eds) *Language Acquisition: The State of the Art*, Cambridge: Cambridge University Press.

Marcus, G.F., Pinker, S., Ullman, M., Hollander, M., Rosen, T.J. and Xu, F. (1992) *Overregularization in Language Acquisition*, Monographs of the Society for Research in Child Development 57.4, Chicago, IL: University of Chicago Press.

Marks, L. and Miller, G. (1964) 'The role of semantic and syntactic constraints in the memorization of English sentences', *Journal of Verbal Learning and Verbal Behavior* 3: 1–5.

Marler, P. (1988) 'Birdsong and neurogenesis', *Nature* 334: 106–7.

Marler, P. (1991) 'The instinct to learn', in S. Carey and R. Gelman (eds) *The Epigenesis of Mind: Essays on Biology and Cognition*, Hillsdale, NJ: Lawrence Erlbaum.

Marshall, J.C. (1970) 'The biology of communication in man and animals', in J. Lyons (ed.) *New Horizons in Linguistics*, Harmondsworth: Penguin.

Marshall, J.C. (1987) 'Review of Savage-Rumbaugh' (1986), *Nature* 325: 310.

Marslen-Wilson, W.D. (ed.) (1989) *Lexical Representation and Process*, Cambridge, MA: MIT Press.

Marslen-Wilson, W.D. (1993) 'Issues of process and representation in lexical access', in G.T.M. Altmann and R. Shillcock (eds) *Cognitive Models of Speech Processing*, Hove, Sussex: Lawrence Erlbaum.

Marslen-Wilson, W.D. and Tyler, L.K. (1980) 'The temporal structure of spoken language understanding', *Cognition* 8: 1–71.

Matthei, E.H. (1981) 'Children's interpretation of sentences containing reciprocals', in S.L. Tavakolian (ed.) *Language Acquisition and Linguistic Theory*, Cambridge, MA: MIT Press.

Matthei, E.H. and Roeper, T. (1983) *Understanding and Producing Speech*, London: Fontana.

Mazurkewich, I. and White, L. (1984) 'The acquisition of the dative alternation: unlearning overgeneralizations', *Cognition* 16: 261–83.

Mehler, J. and Carey, P. (1968) 'The interaction of veracity and syntax in the processing of sentences', *Perception and Psychophysics* 3: 109–11.

Mehler, J., Jusczyk, P., Lambertz, G., Halsted, N., Bertoncini, J. and Amiel-Tison, C. (1988) 'A precursor of language acquisition in young infants', *Cognition* 29: 143–78.

Miles, H.L. (1983) 'Apes and language: the search for communicative competence', in J. de Luce and H. Wilder (eds) *Language in Primates*, New York: Springer-Verlag.

Miller, G.A. (1962) 'Some psychological studies of grammar', *American Psychologist* 1: 748–62.

Miller, G.A. (1991) *The Science of Words*, New York: Scientific American Library.

Miller, G.A. and Chomsky, N. (1963) 'Finitary models of language users', in R.D. Luce and E. Galamter (eds) *Handbook of Mathematical Psychology*, vol. 2, New York: Wiley.

Miller, G.A. and McKean, K. (1964) 'A chronometric study of some relations between sentences', *Quarterly Journal of Experimental Psychology* 16: 297–308. Also in Oldfield and Marshall (1968).

Miller, J.L. and Eimas, P.D. (eds) (1995) *Speech, Language and Communication*, San Diego, CA: Academic Press.

Miller, W. and Ervin, S. (1964) 'The development of grammar in child language', in U. Bellugi and R. Brown (eds) *The Acquisition of Language*, Monographs of the Society for Research in Child Development 29.1, Chicago, IL: University of Chicago Press.

Milner, B., Branch, C. and Rasmussen, T. (1964) 'Observations on cerebral dominance', in A.V.S. De Reuck and M.O. O'Connor (eds) (1964) *Disorders of Language*, London: Churchill Livingstone. Also in Oldfield and Marshall (1968).

Morse, P.A. (1976) 'Speech perception in the human infant and rhesus monkey', in S. Harnad, H. Steklis and J. Lancaster (eds) *Origins and Evolution of Language and Speech*, Annals of the New York Academy of Sciences, vol. 280, New York: New York Academy of Sciences.

Motley, M.T. (1985) 'Slips of the tongue', *Scientific American* 253(3) (Sept.): 114–19.

Müller, Ralph-A. (1996) 'Innateness, autonomy, universality? Neuro-biological approaches to language', *Behavioral and Brain Sciences* 19: 611–75.

Nelson, K. (1973) *Structure and strategy in learning to talk*, Monograph of the Society for Research in Child Development 38: 1–2.

Newport, E.L. (1991) 'Contrasting conceptions of the critical period for language', in S. Carey and R. Gelman (eds) *The Epigenesis of Mind: Essays on Biology and Cognition*, Hillsdale, NJ: Lawrence Erlbaum.

Newport, E.L., Gleitman, H. and Gleitman, L.R. (1977) 'Mother I'd rather do it myself: the contribution of selected child listener variables', in C.E. Snow and C.A. Ferguson (eds) *Talking to Children: Language Input and Acquisition*, Cambridge: Cambridge University Press.

Nooteboom, S.G. (1969) 'The tongue slips into patterns', reprinted in V.A. Fromkin (ed.) *Speech Errors as Linguistic Evidence*, The Hague: Mouton.

Norris, D. (1994) 'Shortlist: a connectionist model of continuous speech recognition', *Cognition* 52: 189–234.

Norris, D. (2005). 'How do computational models help us develop better theories?', in A. Cutler (ed.) *Twenty-first Century Psycholinguistics: Four Cornerstones*, Mahwah, NJ: Lawrence Erlbaum.

Nottebohm, F. (1975) 'A zoologist's view of some language phenomena with particular emphasis on vocal learning', in E.H. Lenneberg and E. Lenneberg (eds) *Foundations of Language Development*, vols 1–2, New York: Academic Press.

Nottebohm, F. (1984) 'Vocal learning and its possible relation to replaceable synapses and neurons', in D. Caplan, A.R. Lecours and A. Smith (eds) *Biological Perspectives on Language*, Cambridge, MA: MIT Press.

Nygaard, L.C. and Pisoni, D.B. (1995) 'Speech perception: new directions in research and theory', in J.L. Miller and P.D. Eimas (eds) *Speech, Language and Communication*, San Diego, CA: Academic Press.

Obler, L.K. and Gjerlow, K. (1999) *Language and the Brain*, Cambridge: Cambridge University Press.

O'Grady, W. (1997) *Syntactic Development*, Chicago, IL: University of Chicago Press.

O'Grady, W. (2005) *How Children Learn Language*, Cambridge: Cambridge University Press.

Oldfield, R.C. and Marshall, J.C. (1968) *Language: Selected Readings*, Harmondsworth: Penguin.

Osherson, D.N. and Wasow, T. (1976) 'Task specificity and species-specificity in the study of language: a methodological note', *Cognition* 4: 203–14.

Peirce, C.S. (1932) *Collected Papers of Charles Sanders Peirce*, eds by C. Hartshorne and P. Weiss, vol. 2, Cambridge, MA: Harvard University Press.

Penfield, W. and Roberts, L. (1959) *Speech and Brain Mechanisms*, Princeton, NJ: Princeton University Press.

Pepperberg, I.M. (2000) *The Alex Studies: Cognitive and Communicative Abilities of Grey Parrots*, Cambridge, MA: Harvard University Press.

Peters, A.M. (1977) 'Language learning strategies: does the whole equal the sum of the parts?', *Language* 53: 560–73.

Peters, A.M. (1983) *The Units of Language Acquisition*, Cambridge: Cambridge University Press.

Peters, A.M. and Menn, L. (1993) 'False starts and filler syllables: ways to learn grammatical morphemes', *Language* 69: 742–77.

Petitto, L.A. (2005) 'How the brain begets language', in J. McGilvray (ed.) *The Cambridge Companion to Chomsky*, Cambridge: University Press.

Petitto, L.A. and Seidenberg, M.S. (1979) 'On the evidence for linguistic abilities in signing apes', *Brain and Language* 8: 162–83.

Pinker, S. (1984) *Language Learnability and Language Development*, Cambridge, MA: Harvard University Press.

Pinker, S. (1987) 'The bootstrapping problem in language acquisition', in B. MacWhinney (ed.) *Mechanisms of Language Acquisition*, Hillsdale, NJ: Lawrence Erlbaum.

Pinker, S. (1989) *Learnability and Cognition: The Acquisition of Argument Structure*, Cambridge, MA: MIT Press.

Pinker, S. (1994) *The Language Instinct: The New Science of Language and Mind*, London: Allen Lane.

Pinker, S. and Prince, A. (1988) 'On language and connectionism: analysis of a parallel distributed processing model of language acquisition', *Cognition* 28: 73–193.

Plunkett, K. (1995) 'Connectionist approaches to language acquisition', in P. Fletcher and B. MacWhinney (eds) *The Handbook of Child Language*, Oxford: Blackwell.

Posner, M.I. and Raichle, M.E. (1994) *Images of Mind*, New York: W.H. Freeman & Co (Scientific American Library).

Pulvermüller, F. (2002) *The Neuroscience of Language: On Brain Circuits of Words and Serial Order*. Cambridge: Cambridge University Press.

Raichle, M.E. (1994) 'Visualizing the mind', *Scientific American* 270(4) (April): 36–43.

Ramachandran, V.S. and Oberman, L.M. (2006) 'Broken mirrors: A theory of autism', *Scientific American* 295(5) (Nov.): 38–45.

Ridley, M. (2003) *Nature via Nurture: Genes, Experience and what makes us Human*, London: Harper.

Rizzolatti, G. and Arbib, M. (1998) 'Language within our grasp', *Trends in Neurosciences* 21: 188.

Rizzolatti, G., Fogassi, L. and Gallese, G. (2006) 'Mirrors in the mind', *Scientific American* 295(5) (Nov.): 30–7.

Roelofs, A. (1992) 'A spreading-activation theory of lemma retrieval in speaking', *Cognition* 42: 107–42.

Roelofs, A. (1997) 'The WEAVER model of word-form encoding in speech production', *Cognition* 64, 249–84.

Roelofs, A. (2005) 'From Popper to Lakatos: A case for cumulative computational modeling', in A. Cutler (ed.) *Twenty-first Century Psycholinguistics: Four Cornerstones*, Mahwah, NJ: Lawrence Erlbaum.

Roeper, T. and Williams, E. (eds) (1987) *Parameter Setting*, Dordrecht: Reidel.

Rondal, J. (1994) 'Exceptional cases of language development in mental retardation: the relative autonomy of language as a cognitive system', in H. Tager-Flusberg (ed.) *Constraints on Language Acquisition: Studies of Atypical Children*, Hillsdale, NJ: Lawrence Erlbaum.

Rosenfield, D. (1978) 'Some neurological techniques for accessing localization of function', in E. Walker (ed.) *Explorations in the Biology of Language*, Sussex: The Harvester Press.

Rumbaugh, D.M. (1977) *Language Learning by a Chimpanzee: The LANA Project*, New York: Academic Press.

Rumbaugh, D.M. and Washburn, D.A. (2004) *Intelligence of Apes and Other Rational Beings*, New Haven, CT: Yale University Press.

Rumelhart, D.E. and McClelland, J.L. (eds) (1986) *Parallel Distributed Processing: Explorations in the Microstructure of Cognition*, vol. 1, Foundations, Cambridge, MA: MIT Press.

Rymer, R. (1993) *Genie: Escape from a Silent Childhood*, London: Michael Joseph.

Sampson, G. (1975) *The Form of Language*, London: Weidenfeld & Nicolson.

Sampson, G. (1980) *Making Sense*, Oxford: Oxford University Press.

Savage-Rumbaugh, E.S. (1986) *Ape Language: From Conditioned Response to Symbol*, Oxford: Oxford University Press.

Savage-Rumbaugh, E.S. and Lewin, R. (1994) *Kanzi: The Ape at the Brink of the Human Mind*, New York: Doubleday.

Savage-Rumbaugh, E.S., Murphy, J., Sevcik, R.A., Brakke, K.E., Williams, S.L. and Rumbaugh, D.M. (1993) *Language comprehension in ape and child* (with commentary by Elizabeth Bates and a reply by E. Sue Savage-Rumbaugh), Monographs of the Society for Research in Child Development 58.3–4, Chicago, IL: University of Chicago Press.

Savage-Rumbaugh, E.S., Shanker, S.G. and Taylor, T.J. (1998) *Apes, Language and the Human Mind*, Oxford: Oxford University Press.

Saxton, M. (2000) 'Negative evidence and negative feedback', *First Language* 20, 221–52.

Schaller, S. (1995) *A Man Without Words*, Berkeley, CA: University of California Press.

Schlesinger, I.M. (1967) 'A note on the relationship between psychological and linguistic theories', *Foundations of Language*, 3: 397–402.

Scovel, T. (1988) *A Time to Speak: A Psycholinguistic Examination of the Critical Period for Language Acquisition*, Rowley, MA: Newbury House.

Seidenberg, M.S. (1995) 'Visual word recognition: an overview', in J.L. Miller and P.D. Eimas (eds) *Speech, Language and Communication*, San Diego, CA: Academic Press.

Seidenberg, M.S., Tanenhaus, M.K., Leiman, J.M. and Bienkowski, M. (1982) 'Automatic access of the meaning of ambiguous words in context: some limitations of knowledge-based processing', *Cognitive Psychology* 14: 481– 537.

Senghas, A. (1994) 'Nicaragua's lessons for language acquisition', *Signpost* 7(1): 32–9.

Senghas, A. and Coppola, M. (2001) 'Children creating language: how Nicaraguan sign language acquired a spatial grammar', *Psychological Science* 12 (4), 323–8.

Seyfarth, R.M., Cheney, D.L. and Marler, P. (1980a) 'Monkey responses to three different alarm calls: evidence for predator classification and semantic communication', *Science* 210: 801–3.

Seyfarth, R.M., Cheney, D.L. and Marler, P. (1980b) 'Vervet monkey alarm calls: semantic communication in a free-ranging primate', *Animal Behavior* 28: 1070–94.

Shanker, S.G., Savage-Rumbaugh, S. and Taylor, T.J. (1999). 'Kanzi: A new beginning', *Animal Learning and Behavior* 27 (1) 24–5.

Shapiro, L.P., Zurif, E. and Grimshaw, J. (1987) 'Sentence processing and the mental representation of verbs', *Cognition* 27: 219–46.

Shattuck-Hufnagel, S. (1979) 'Speech errors as evidence for a serial-ordering mechanism in sentence production', in W.E. Cooper and E.C.T. Walker (eds) *Sentence Processing*, New York: Lawrence Erlbaum.

Shatz, M. (1982) 'On mechanisms of language acquisition: can features of the communicative environment account for development?', in E. Wanner and L.R. Gleitman (eds) *Language Acquisition: The State of the Art*, Cambridge: Cambridge University Press.

Shenk, D. (2001/2002) *The Forgetting. Understanding Alzheimer's: A Biography of a Disease*, New York and London: HarperCollins.

Shirai, Y. and Andersen, R.W. (1995) 'The acquisition of tense-aspect morphology: a prototype account', *Language* 71: 743–62.

Sinclair-de-Zwart, H. (1969) 'Developmental psycholinguistics', in D. Elkind and J. Flavell (eds) *Studies in Cognitive Development*, Oxford: Oxford University Press.

Skinner, B.F. (1957) *Verbal Behavior*, New York: Appleton-Century-Crofts.

Slobin, D.I. (1966a) 'The acquisition of Russian as a native language', in F. Smith and G.A. Miller (eds) *The Genesis of Language*, Cambridge, MA: MIT Press.

Slobin, D.I. (1966b) 'Grammatical transformations and sentence comprehension in childhood and adulthood', *Journal of Verbal Learning and Verbal Behavior* 5: 219–27.

Slobin, D.I. (1971a) 'On the learning of morphological rules', in D.I. Slobin (ed.) *The Ontogenesis of Grammar*, New York: Academic Press.

Slobin, D.I. (1971b) *Psycholinguistics*, Glenview, IL: Scott Foresmann.

Slobin, D.I. (1973) 'Cognitive prerequisites for the development of grammar', in C.A. Ferguson and D.I. Slobin (eds) *Studies of Child Language Development*, New York: Holt, Rinehart and Winston.

Slobin, D.I. (1975) 'On the nature of talk to children', in E.H. Lenneberg and E. Lenneberg (eds) *Foundations of Language Development*, vols 1–2, New York: Academic Press.

Slobin, D.I. (1982) 'Universal and particular in the acquisition of language', in E. Wanner and L.R. Gleitman (eds) *Language Acquisition: The State of the Art*, Cambridge: Cambridge University Press.

Slobin, D.I. (ed.) (1986a) *The Crosslinguistic Study of Language Acquisition*, vols 1–2, Hillsdale, NJ: Lawrence Erlbaum.

Slobin, D.I. (1986b) 'Why study acquisition crosslinguistically?', in D.I. Slobin (ed.) *The Crosslinguistic Study of Language Acquisition*, vols 1–2, Hillsdale, NJ: Lawrence Erlbaum.

Slobin, D.I. (1986c) 'Crosslinguistic evidence for the language-making capacity', in D.I. Slobin (ed.) *The Crosslinguistic Study of Language Acquisition*, vols 1–2, Hillsdale, NJ: Lawrence Erlbaum.

Slobin, D.I. (ed.) (1992) *The Crosslinguistic Study of Language Acquisition*, vol. 3, Hillsdale, NJ: Lawrence Erlbaum.

Slobin, D.I. (ed.) (1997a) *The Crosslinguistic Study of Language Acquisition*, vol 4, Hillsdale, NJ: Lawrence Erlbaum.

Slobin, D.I. (ed.) (1997b) *The Crosslinguistic Study of Language Acquisition*, vol. 4–5, Hillsdale, NJ: Lawrence Erlbaum.

Slobin, D.I. and Welsh, C.A. (1973) 'Elicited imitation as a research tool in developmental psycholinguistics', in C.A. Ferguson and D.I. Slobin (eds) *Studies of Child Language Development*, New York: Holt, Rinehart & Winston.

Smith, N.V. (1973) *The Acquisition of Phonology*, Cambridge: Cambridge University Press.

Smith, N. and Tsimpli, I.-M. (1995) *The Mind of a Savant: Language Learning and Modularity*, Oxford: Blackwell.

Snow, C.E. and Ferguson, C.A. (eds) (1977) *Talking to Children: Language Input and Acquisition*, Cambridge: Cambridge University Press.

Springer, S.P. and Deutsch, G. (1998) *Left Brain, Right Brain*, 5th edn, New York: W.H. Freeman.

Stahlke, H.F.W. (1980) 'On asking the question: can apes learn language?' in K. Nelson (ed.) *Children's Language*, vol. 2, New York: Gardner Press.

Stamenov, M. (2002) 'Some features that make mirror neurons and human language faculty unique', in Stamenov, M. and Gallese, V. (eds) *Mirror Neurons and the Evolution of Brain and Language*, Amsterdam: John Benjamins.

Stoel-Gammon, C. and Cooper, A. (1984) 'Patterns of early lexical and phonological development', *Journal of Child Language* 11: 247–71.

Stowe, L.A., Haverkort, M. and Zwarts, F. (2005) 'Rethinking the neurological basis of language', *Lingua* 115: 997–1042.

Stromswolo, K. (2001) 'The heritability of language: a review and meta-analysis of twin, adoption and linkage studies', *Language* 77, 647–723.

Struhsaker, T.T. (1967) 'Auditory communication among vervet monkeys (Cercopithecus aethiops)', in S.A. Altmann (ed.) *Social Communication Among Primates*, Chicago, IL: Chicago University Press.

Swinney, D. (1979) 'Lexical access during sentence comprehension: (re)-consideration of context effects', *Journal of Verbal Learning and Verbal Behavior* 18: 645–59.

Tanenhaus, M.K. (1988) 'Psycholinguistics: an overview', in F.J. Newmeyer (ed.) *Linguistics: The Cambridge Survey*, vol. 3, Cambridge: Cambridge University Press.

Tanenhaus, M.K. and Trueswell, J.C. (1995) 'Sentence comprehension', in J.L. Miller and P.D. Eimas (eds) *Speech, Language and Communication*, San Diego, CA: Academic Press.

Tanenhaus, M.K., Leiman, K.H. and Seidenberg, M.S. (1979) 'Evidence for multiple stages in the processing of ambiguous words in syntactic contexts', *Journal of Verbal Learning and Verbal Behavior* 18: 427–41.

Tanenhaus, M.K., Carlson, G.N. and Seidenberg, M.S. (1985) 'Do listeners compute linguistic representations?', in D.R. Dowty et al. (eds) *Natural Language Parsing: Psychological, Computational and Theoretical Perspectives*, Cambridge: Cambridge University Press.

Tanenhaus, M.K., Boland, J.E., Mauner, G.A. and Carlson, G.N. (1993) 'More on combinatory lexical information: thematic structure in parsing and interpretation', in G.T.M. Altmann and R. Shillcock (eds) *Cognitive Models of Speech Processing*, Hove, Sussex: Lawrence Erlbaum.

Taylor, J.R. (2002) *Cognitive Grammar*, Oxford: Oxford University Press.

Terrace, H.S. (1979a) *Nim*, New York: Knopf.

Terrace, H.S. (1983) 'Apes who "talk": language or projection of language by their teachers?', in J. de Luce and H. Wilder (eds) *Language in Primates*, New York: Springer-Verlag.

Thorpe, W.H. (1961) *Bird Song: The Biology of Vocal Communication and Expression in Birds*, Cambridge: Cambridge University Press.

Thorpe, W.H. (1963) *Learning and Instinct in Animals*, 2nd edn, London: Methuen.

Thorpe, W.H. (1972) 'Vocal communication in birds', in R.A. Hinde (ed.) *Non-verbal Communication*, Cambridge: Cambridge University Press.

Tomasello, M. (1992) *First Verbs: A Case Study of Early Grammatical Development*, Cambridge: Cambridge University Press.

Tomasello, M. (2003) *Constructing a Language: A Usage-based Theory of Language Acquisition*, Cambridge, MA: Harvard University Press.

Tomasello, M. and Brooks, P. (1998) 'Young children's earliest transitive and intransitive constructions', *Cognitive Linguistics* 9, 379–95.

Tomasello, M., Carpenter, M., Call, J., Behne, T. and Moll, H. (2005) 'Understanding and sharing intentions: the origins of cultural cognition', *Behavioral and Brain Sciences* 28, 675–735.

Townsend, D.J. and Bever, T.G. (2001) *Sentence Comprehension: The Integration of Habits and Rules*, Cambridge, MA: MIT Press.

Treffert, D.A. (1989/1990) *Extraordinary People*. London: Black Swan.

Ungerer, F. and Schmid, H.-J. (1996) *An Introduction to Cognitive Linguistics*, London: Longman.

Vargha-Khadem, F. and Polkey, C.E. (1992) 'A review of cognitive outcome after hemidecortication in humans', in F.D. Rose and D.A. Johnson (eds) *Recovery from Brain Damage*, New York: Plenum Press.

Vargha-Khadem, F., O'Gorman, A.M. and Watters, G.V. (1985) 'Aphasia and handedness in relation to hemisphere side, age at injury and severity of cerebral lesion during childhood', *Brain* 8: 677–96.

Vihman, M.M. (1996) *Phonological Development: The Origins of Language in the Child*, Oxford: Blackwell.

Vihman, M.M., Macken, M.A., Miller, R., Simmons, H. and Miller, J. (1985) 'From babbling to speech: a re-assessment of the continuity issue', *Language* 61: 397–445.

von Frisch, K. (1950) *Bees: Their Vision, Chemical Sense and Language*, Ithaca, NY: Cornell University Press.

von Frisch, K. (1954) *The Dancing Bees*, London: Methuen.

von Frisch, K. (1967) *The Dance and Orientation of Bees*, trans. L.E. Chadwick, Cambridge, MA: Harvard University Press.

Vygotsky, L.S. (1962) *Thought and Language*, Cambridge, MA: MIT Press.

Wallman, J. (1992) *Aping Language*, Cambridge: Cambridge University Press.

Wason, P.C. (1965) 'The contexts of plausible denial', *Journal of Verbal Learning and Verbal Behavior* 4: 7–11. Also in Oldfield and Marshall (1968).

Watt, W.C. (1970) 'On two hypotheses concerning psycholinguistics', in J.R. Hayes (ed.) *Cognition and the Development of Language*, New York: Wiley.

Weir, R.H. (1962) *Language in the Crib*, The Hague: Mouton.

Weir, R.H. (1966) 'Some questions on the child's learning of phonology', in F. Smith and G.A. Miller (eds) *The Genesis of Language*, Cambridge, MA: MIT Press.

Wells, G. (1974) 'Learning to code experience through language', *Journal of Child Language* 1: 243–69.

Wells, G. (1979) 'Learning and using the auxiliary verb in English', in V. Lee (ed.) (1979) *Language Development*, London: Croom Helm and The Open University Press.

Wells, G. (1986) *The Meaning Makers: Children Learning Language and Using Language to Learn*, London: Hodder and Stoughton.

Wetherell, M., Taylor, S. and Yates, S.J. (2001) *Discourse as Data: A Guide for Analysis*, London: Sage.

Wilson, B. and Peters, A.M. (1988) 'What are you cookin' on a hot?', *Language* 64: 249–73.

Yamada, J. (1988) 'The independence of language: evidence from a retarded hyperlinguistic individual', in L.M. Hyman and C.N. Li (eds) *Language, Speech and Mind*, New York: Routledge.

Yamada, J.L. (1990) *Laura: A Case for the Modularity of Language*, Cambridge, MA: MIT Press.

Yngve, V. (1961/1972) 'The depth hypothesis'. Reprinted in F.W. Householder (1972) *Syntactic Theory 1: Structuralist*, Harmondsworth: Penguin.

Zangwill, O.L. (1973) 'The neurology of language', in N. Minnis (ed.) (1973) *Linguistics at Large*, St Albans: Paladin.

Zock, M. (1997) 'Sentence generation by pattern matching: the problem of syntactic choice', in *Recent Advances in Natural Language Processing*, Amsterdam: John Benjamins.

INDEX

www.routledge.com/linguistics

Routledge English Language Introductions
Psycholinguistics: A resource book for students

Psycholinguistics
A resource book for students

John Field

Routledge English Language Introductions cover core areas of language study and are one-stop resources for students.

Assuming no prior knowledge, books in the series offer an accessible overview of the subject, with activities, study questions, commentaries and key readings – all in the same volume. The innovative and flexible 'two-dimensional' structure is built around four sections – introduction, development, exploration and extension – which offer self-contained stages for study. Each topic can also be read across these sections, enabling the reader to build gradually on the knowledge gained.

Psycholinguistics:

- is a comprehensive introduction to psycholinguistic theory
- covers the core areas of psycholinguistics: language as a human attribute, language and the brain, vocabulary storage and use, language and memory, the four skills (writing, reading, listening, speaking), comprehension, language impairment and deprivation
- draws on a range of real texts, data and examples, including a Radio Four interview, an essay written by a deaf writer, and the transcript of a therapy session addressing stuttering
- provides classic readings by the key names in the discipline, including Jean Aitchison, Terrence Deacon, Robert Logie, Willem Levelt and Dorothy Bishop.

Written by an experienced teacher, this accessible textbook is an essential resource for all students of English language, linguistics and psychology.

Pb: 978-0-415-27600-9
Hb: 978-0-415-27599-6

For more information and to order a copy visit
www.routledge.com/9780415276009

Available from all good bookshops